Frank Worrall is Britain's No. 1 sports biographer and writes exclusively for John Blake Publishing. He is the author of eighteen books on sport, including the bestselling *Jamie Vardy: The Boy From Nowhere*, *Roy Keane: Red Man Walking*, *Rooney: Wayne's World*, *Celtic United: Glasgow and Manchester*, *Lewis Hamilton: Triple World Champion – The Biography* and *Rory McIlroy – The Biography*. Rock star Rod Stewart once hailed *Celtic United* as 'the last good book I read'. Frank's website, frankworrall.com, has details of all his books, and he can be found at @frankworrall on Twitter.

HARRY
KANE

HARRY
KANE
ENGLAND'S HERO

FRANK WORRALL

JOHN BLAKE

Published by John Blake Publishing,
2.25 The Plaza,
535 Kings Road,
Chelsea Harbour,
London SW10 0SZ

www.johnblakebooks.com

www.facebook.com/johnblakebooks 🖪
twitter.com/jblakebooks 🗗

First published in paperback in 2017
This revised and updated edition published in 2018

ISBN: 978 1 78946 044 5

British Library Cataloguing-in-Publication Data:

A catalogue record for this book is available from the British Library.

Design by www.envydesign.co.uk

Printed and bound in Great Britain by Clays Ltd, Elcograf S.p.A

1 3 5 7 9 10 8 6 4 2

Papers used by John Blake Publishing are natural, recyclable products made from
wood grown in sustainable forests. The manufacturing processes conform to the
environmental regulations of the country of origin.

Every attempt has been made to contact the relevant copyright-holders,
but some were unobtainable. We would be grateful if the appropriate people
could contact us.

John Blake Publishing is an imprint of Bonnier Publishing
www.bonnierpublishing.com

This book is dedicated to Natalie McEwan,
a great girl and a loyal Spurs fan.

CONTENTS

ACKNOWLEDGEMENTS

SPECIAL THANKS: Toby Buchan, James Hodgkinson, Sarah Fortune and all at John Blake Publishing, and Dominic Turnbull of *The Sun on Sunday*.

THANKS: Steven Gordon, Dan Jeoffroy, Steven McEwan, Jo Porter, Jon Moorhead, Will Hagerty, Dave Morgan, Andy Clayton, Danny Bottono, Ben Felsenburg, Alex Butler, Roy Stone, Colin Forshaw, Ian Rondeau, Tom Henderson Smith, Graham Nicholson, Shaf Karim, James Edwards and Drs Rupert Morrall, Stephen Evans, Will Webb and Will Faux.

Not forgetting: Angela, Frankie, Jude, Barbara, Frank, Bob and Stephen, Gill, Lucy, Alex, Suzanne, Michael and William.

CHAPTER ONE

BEGINNINGS

SUNDAY, 18 SEPTEMBER 2016

There's a crisis brewing in North London – and, more specifically, in N17. Just four minutes remain in the Premier League clash at White Hart Lane when a sudden deathly hush descends upon the stadium, broken only by the chants of defiant Sunderland fans. 'You're not singing any more,' they yell, as if chalking up some sort of relevant victory over their rivals despite their own team's wretched showing over the previous eighty-six minutes. There is no reply from the Spurs fans, just that ominous hush, accompanied by faces distorted with dread. Their concern, quite correctly, is with events on the pitch right now, not with trying to get one over on the group of away fans parked noisily on the other side of the ground.

It's a fear that is easy to understand – one rooted in future weeks of potential loss and disappointment. For the one man their team is built around, the one man who can be relied upon to give his everything and score the goals that can take them to the promised land of Premier League and Champions League glory, lies prostrate before them. And now he is being helped on to a stretcher and carried off, applause ringing in his ears but anxiety filling the guts of these loyal supporters who grimly witness his exit.

For that is the importance Harry Kane now has to their good times, their hopes and their dreams. The local boy done good who can claim to be the most feared striker in the Premier League and whose reputation is fast spreading globally. The local boy who was the subject of £60 million transfer whispers at Manchester United just a couple of months earlier. The local boy who dismissed such talk as 'rubbish': 'Why would I want to leave this club, MY club?' he had said, laughing, shaking his head as if the very idea was madness. Which it was: Harry Kane was Tottenham through and through. He IS Tottenham through and through: a star striker who's happy to be owned by the fans at the club he adores. And proud to be their main man now and for years to come.

Just as they are proud to have him around and to know that he is clearly loyal to them and their football club. 'Harry Kane, he's one of our own,' they chant regularly. Even now they chant it, trying to lift their main man's spirits as he sits on the stretcher, looking as if he needs a lift, his face glum and despondent, his hand clutching the painful ankle that led him to collapse and end up in the physios' care.

'That's a bloody bad blow,' lifelong fan Steven McEwan groans as Harry disappears down the tunnel. 'How are we gonna cope without him? Who's gonna score the goals? Let's hope Harry won't be out too bloody long.'

Tottenham are third in the table – and Kane had put them there with a parting gift before his injury. With the goal that put Sunderland to the sword on the hour mark and left Spurs one place above bitter local rivals Arsenal and four points off Manchester City and the Premier League summit.

SUNDAY, 6 NOVEMBER 2016

The fans' fears had proved to have substance. Harry's ankle ligaments' injury keeps him on the sidelines for eight weeks but he finally returns for the big Premier League clash with Arsenal on this first Sunday in November. And, naturally enough, he scores on his return as the teams grind out a draw. His return had been greeted with delirious delight by Spurs fans. Little wonder: prior to kick-off Tottenham were without a win in six games in all competitions and had scored just three times. Plus, two of those goals had come from the penalty spot and they had dropped to fifth in the table. So Harry's physical return and goal proves very welcome indeed. OK, his strike is also from the spot but his coolness in taking and hammering the penalty home is typically admirable, and typically successful. A sign of his mental strength, too.

And the whole episode, from injury to return, from the team's decline during his absence and revival after it, serves only to highlight the player's importance. From being a reserve who was regularly farmed out on loan and viewed as third-choice striker until the previous season, Harry Kane had certainly come a long way. He was every manager's dream pro – an Englishman who did not drink, did not smoke and stayed out of nightclubs. He was a settled, measured guy who preferred spending free time with his long-term girlfriend Kate Goodland, whom he'd known since childhood, and who was expecting their first baby. Not for Harry Kane the shameful front-page headlines of sleaze and bad behaviour that went hand in hand with some big-name players. He would rather take his two Labrador dogs, Brady and Wilson, out for a walk with Kate than jeopardise his health and career with hangers-on in various bars or nightclubs, or seek out more sordid places for entertainment.

He had even named his dogs after American football quarterbacks Tom Brady and Russell Wilson and, if Kate was out, his idea of relaxation was to watch a big NFL game on the box, or to head out for a round of golf with old friends.

Harry Kane was the prototype of how a modern-era English footballer should live. He had grafted hard to make it to the top of his trade and was damned if he would risk it all after all the effort he had put in to get there. Yes, his is a true Roy of the Rovers tale, of a local boy who had hit the big time, having started from relatively humble beginnings.

EARLY LIFE

It was Wednesday, 28 July 1993, and London wasn't having the best of summers, with just three days without rain that month, but the sun shone the day dad Pat Kane, mum Kim and elder son Charlie welcomed Harry Edward into their family in Walthamstow, East London. Their house was just five miles from White Hart Lane and the family were all fervent

Spurs fans. When Kim took the boy home from hospital, she would dance around the living room with him in her arms, singing the words to the UB40 No.1 hit of the time, '(I Can't Help) Falling in Love with You'. Prior to his birth she had told friends she was sure the baby would be another boy and that he would be a lively, sports-loving youngster as he grew up, if his constant kicking during her pregnancy was anything to go by.

And she would be proved absolutely spot on. Harry was a very active boy who loved all sport, but football was his favourite. He played from the moment he could kick a ball around the garden and the park with his dad, who also loved the game. When it got dark he and his pals played in the road under the street lights, such was his love of soccer. Harry's kickabouts would move on to a more competitive plane at primary and secondary school and youth level, when the Kanes moved down the road to Chingford, the place where David Beckham was born, just four miles from Walthamstow. Harry was a talented player, too, even at such a young age, always strong and determined, and hard to shift off the ball, even though he wasn't then as physically tough as David. Attending the same secondary school as Beckham helped his development – the fact that one England legend had been at Chingford Foundation School bode well for potential future ones like Harry. Beckham's grounding showed that the school took its football seriously, and that it was keen to nurture young sporting talent.

He was supported at all times during his development by his mum and dad. Pat would drive the boy all over the place for matches and would take him to see Spurs at the Lane when he was old enough. But Harry believes his talent may have come from his mum's sporting roots. He said, 'I think the sporting genes come from my mum's side of the family although the topic is a hot debate in the Kane household. Dad probably won't like me saying that, but I think my granddad Eric on my mum's side was quite a good footballer, and played at a decent level.'

But he also acknowledges that there was talent too on dad Pat's side. Pat was born in Galway, Ireland, and was a football fanatic who loved a game with his mates and watching matches with his dad and Harry's paternal granddad, Michael. It was Michael who brought the Kane dynasty to England after emigrating from Ireland as a young man. Michael died in May 2013 and Harry went to Ireland for the funeral. Harry will always have a love for Ireland as well as England, given his family roots and his liking for the more peaceful lifestyle it offers in comparison to the hustle and bustle of London.

When he was eight Harry joined the youth set-up at Arsenal and stayed for a year. It was a move that would, of course, be a controversial talking point years later. Some Gunners fans would continually snipe at their Spurs counterparts with the claim that Harry was not really 'one of their own'. That he had, in fact, been a secret Arsenal fan. In January 2015 a picture emerged of Harry in an Arsenal shirt when he played for the club in a youth tournament in 2001. Gunners' fans subsequently taunted their rivals with the line 'Harry Kane once played for Arsenal.'

A month later, before a Spurs/Arsenal game, they pointed to another picture of Harry, aged eight, in an Arsenal shirt celebrating the Gunners' title win that year. It was mischief of the highest order and Harry felt it necessary to defend himself against the jibes. He said, 'I wanted to wear a Tottenham kit but I don't think that would've gone down too well. I was eight years old. I was at Arsenal for a year and obviously I was a kid, I just wanted to play football.'

He also had the last laugh in that he scored in the match against Arsenal, firing Spurs to a memorable victory, the same day as the picture appeared in February 2015. 'Of course it was nice to score after that picture,' he said, smiling afterwards. 'I'm Tottenham through and through and this shows that. It was an emotional day and one I was very pleased with. Most of my family were Spurs fans and I grew up fifteen minutes from the ground, so I was always going to be a Spurs fan.'

Harry's dream came true at the age of eleven when he finally joined Tottenham on youth terms. He had attended games as a fan with dad Pat and was bowled over to now meet the players he idolised – and he would in later life learn that other top-class performers at the club had, like him, grown up nearby and supported the club in their youth. That Tottenham were truly a club who had a place for local talent and nurtured those who had it to become stars of the domestic and international arenas. He said, 'It's good to have that connection. I wasn't the sort who had posters on my wall but I liked to collect stickers. I had sticker books and magazines. Teddy Sheringham was my hero. I was able to meet him a few years ago and got to know him a bit. Like me, he grew up around the area and he was a Tottenham fan.'

Harry was, of course, still at school as he played first for Arsenal youth and then Spurs. And he was just as driven to win everything at Chingford Foundation as he was at Tottenham. 'Harry was always dedicated and driven to succeed,' said Mark Leadon, Harry's former PE teacher. 'When he played for the school, he gave it everything. He scored a lot of goals and we had a very successful team and he was outstanding. He was always technically gifted and a real team player. He didn't expect to be treated differently. He wasn't one to keep the ball if a pass was on. He was never like that. Going through school, he was never egotistic. He was a normal pupil.'

Kane was an all-rounder who loved all sports – indeed his favourite pastime nowadays, as we have mentioned, is watching American Football, and playing video games of the sport. He has even intimated he would like to become an NFL pro when he retires from football! He said, 'It depends on how my football career goes but, when I am finished, I would love to go to the NFL and be a kicker. Even if I got to play just one game it is something I would like to do. It's a long way off yet. But it is definitely something I have thought about.' At school, he was also a very good cricketer, who batted and bowled for the first team.

But it was football that Harry loved the most – and the sport in which he traded his dreams. As well as school, he also found an anchor for his growing footballing ambitions with a local youth club set-up in the East End: Ridgeway Rovers.

It was at Ridgeway that his talent was allowed to blossom and where he found solace when things weren't going quite to plan at Arsenal and Tottenham. Remarkably, Spurs would follow Arsenal in initially letting him go, after a failed trial. He would also fail to make the grade at Watford's academy in a two-month spell. How they and Arsenal are regretting their decision nowadays, as Harry continues to establish himself as England's top striker. As Gunners' boss Arsène Wenger would admit, 'I found it quite funny, you know, and you are always a bit angry as well because I asked: "Why did he go?" But at that age, boys can move here and there.'

Not that Ridgeway were unhappy to see the youngster return time and again, often down in the dumps, after his stints at their three big-time neighbours. As Ridgeway club chairman Ian Marshall points out, they were always happy to welcome him back with open arms when the going got tough. They liked his never-give-up attitude and, more importantly, they totally believed in him – that he was good enough to make a name for himself in the professional game. Marshall said, 'I think Harry was picked up at the age of eight or nine but he was forever coming back. He went to Arsenal and they let him go, he had a trial at Spurs and they didn't sign him, then went to Watford where he scored a few goals before eventually signing for Spurs. The rest is history but he was with us in between. Most of the kids are well aware that he played here. One of them tweeted the other day that "Harry Kane was one of our own".'

Another fated link is that Beckham also played for Ridgeway and benefitted from the school 'wrapping an arm around him'.

There's more of the Beckham/Kane 'similar production line to England glory' in a later chapter.

But Tottenham was where Harry was determined to return. And he vowed that when his next chance came at the Lane, he would not let it go. He would give his everything and he would not fail; he could not fail. It was his destiny to play for Spurs, the club he supported, the club he loved; he was convinced of that.

Eventually, that opportunity to return to the club did occur. Harry had another stab at success when the youth set-up agreed to let him show he was up to it. It would not be an immediate breakthrough. Harry was initially viewed as not physically strong enough and not fast enough. But the coaches could see he had natural talent and technique and that he was probably their most determined individual. He would never give in or accept he was beaten and they loved that about him – whether it was in training or in matches. It would be a similar story when he moved up the age groups and, even to make it in the seniors, he would have to prove himself out on loan to four clubs.

While Beckham would have a relatively easy, cushioned ride to the top of the game, Kane would constantly have to batter down doors and show he was good enough. Nothing came easily to him but he would admit that experience was of benefit later in his career as the battles ensured he toughened up mentally, emotionally and physically. By the time he was twenty-one, he would be ready for the Premier League after a ten-year apprenticeship of hard knocks.

His 'second coming' as a youngster at Tottenham saw him

playing in midfield, initially in a holding role and then in a central attacking position. Gradually, he was bulking up and working at increasing his speed, although he would never be the fastest player, even when he played for the first team and England. As with Teddy Sheringham, the first yard would always be in his head; he was instinctive and clever and had the inbuilt vision to see how a game was developing and where he should be heading. His Chingford Foundation PE Teacher Mark Leadon said he even noticed that Harry was a step ahead of his fellow youngsters with his vision when at school. He said, 'Aged eleven Harry was technically very gifted, with a great first touch, and a very clever player; he always knew where to go, right from an early stage.' And Alex Inglethorpe, the Spurs Under-18 coach when Harry joined at thirteen, also noted that inherent natural ability of the boy to read the game. He would add, 'Harry had a lovely technique – an ability to pass and receive and shoot.' Tottenham's former Under-21 coach and short-term manager, Tim Sherwood, is just as quick to praise Kane for his efforts to learn quickly, saying, 'He was a coach's dream to look after, because you only had to tell him once and it was in there and he would try to apply it on the field.'

Harry made his mark with the Under-16 team at White Hart Lane, playing a part in two junior tournaments in Mexico and Switzerland in the 2008–09 season, and scoring three goals. In July 2009, on his sixteenth birthday, he took a big step forward in his burgeoning career by signing a scholarship contract with Tottenham. And a year later, as he started to make a big impression with the academy coaches, he was rewarded with his first professional contract. He was still not the most powerful of players so they played him in the hole, behind the main striker, the role in which his hero Sheringham would excel. On the academy website at the time they outlined his skills in this way, saying: 'Playing just behind a central striker, Harry made a huge impact during his first full season in the Academy, establishing himself as one of the most highly-rated youngsters at the club.'

The boy then went on to impress with the Under-21s and, in particular, the section's head coach, Sherwood. In fact, he was so impressive Sherwood decided it would be best if he leave the club! But it would only be a temporary parting of the ways. Tim felt Harry would benefit from a loan spell to beef him up and provide him with a physical edge – so he sent him off on loan to Leyton Orient, and the rough and tumble world of the lower leagues. It would turn out to be an inspired move by the man Harry credits with much of his progress from the age of seventeen.

Harry Kane was happy with the loan move and keen to head off and board the Orient express, another staging post towards his dream destination of the Tottenham first team and, ultimately, the England national team.

CHAPTER TWO

THE LOAN RANGER

L eyton Orient, Millwall, Norwich and Leicester. Maybe not the world's most glamorous teams, like the Real Madrids, Barcelonas or even Manchester Uniteds, but these are the destinations where Harry Kane headed to develop his craft as a footballer worthy of national and international prestige. They were the places where he had breathing space to develop his special talent away from the spotlight and intense analysis of the backroom team and fans at White Hart Lane. The moves gave him the necessary space to proceed at his own pace – and offered an atmosphere in which he learnt to toughen up and deal with anything defenders threw at him. As two of the loan spells plunged him into the lower leagues, it was also an opportunity for Harry to become confident that he could deal with ANY rough and tumble, as lower league defenders do not stand on ceremony. No, the loans meant Harry had to give as good as he got, or he would fail the auditions and questions could be asked back at his parent club.

All in all, the four loan spells could be seen as the making of Harry Kane the footballer, Harry Kane the striker who is temperamentally sound and measured, and Harry Kane the man, who appreciates just how lucky he is to be a well-paid footballer who has every privilege and luxury and never forgets where he came from and the debt he owes to the Spurs fans who now help pay his wages.

He was already a lad who always listened to advice and had a great deal of humility and self-knowledge. Now, the loans would impress upon him that he must never take his situation or his position for granted. Working in the lower leagues was a good lesson in just how fortunate he was as a person and a footballer, and only served to cement his belief that talent alone was not enough; hard work was also key to bringing results and maintaining them. The lower league loans taught Harry to keep working even when others might think they 'had made it'. He would never fall into that trap after the grounding the loans provided. They had indeed been damned hard work at times but had given him the gifts of deep gratitude and drilled even deeper into his belief that you had to keep working however high up you got; that the journey never ended if you wanted to be the best.

Certainly his work ethic and efforts in his loan moves were well respected by his fellow pros at those clubs, and even by managers of other clubs in following years. Burnley boss Sean Dyche, for instance, made it clear he had also wanted Harry on loan when he took over at Turf Moor in 2012 and that those earlier loans had indeed been beneficial to Kane's later career. Speaking to the press before a Burnley game against Spurs three years later, Dyche said, 'He's a player that most people would have had a look at when he wasn't in the side at Tottenham. It's a good reflection of how the loan system can work, and it doesn't have to be the glory loan – the one where it works every time. He's had his ups and downs on loan but that can be a massive part of a young player's development, experiencing the fact that it doesn't always work hand in glove. It's not always perfect, you don't play every week, you have to challenge yourself to keep going and keep grinding and be professional every day to be ready to play when you're called upon.

'He was out at Millwall and it was possibly a step too early when he went out to Norwich to play there, and then Leicester a few bits and bobs off the bench. All of that for a young man who seems to me to have a very good temperament, and a very good desire to be a footballer, shows if you stick at it long enough you get your rewards. It has to be the ups and downs of football to bring the reality.'

And when it was reported in March 2016 that world football's governing body FIFA was planning to end the emergency loan system that had been so popular in England, many spoke out, saying it would mean players like Kane would struggle to make a name for themselves and have a chance to develop, as Harry did, at their own pace if they could not go out on loan as easily. The plan would mean no more emergency loans were allowed outside the traditional summer and winter transfer windows.

Ipswich manager Mick McCarthy led the voices of dismay, at the same time citing Harry's example, that such a helpful way to aid youngsters could be on the way out. McCarthy told *BBC Look East*, 'Where are they going to play? You're only allowed three overage players in the Under-21s. If you've got a squad of twenty-four or twenty-five and some need to have some football, somebody beneath us could loan one of our players – what's wrong in doing that?

'Harry Kane wouldn't be the England striker he is without him going to Millwall, Leicester and Norwich. Without having those experiences going out, they don't get to be the players they are today.'

Talking of England, it is telling that in one picture from his loan at Leicester in 2013, Kane is seen on the subs' bench with Jamie Vardy and Danny Drinkwater. David Nugent and Chris Wood started the match up front instead of Kane and Vardy. And although Harry would come on as a sub, Jamie did not even make it off the bench. Fast-forward three years and all three of those subs that day would be in the England set-up. Which just goes to show that a player on loan can develop in tandem, and remarkably well, with those who are also pushing for regular starting spots at the loan clubs the loanee arrives at. The Premier League's two top scorers in the 2015–16 campaign could not make the first eleven, along with a powerful midfielder.

When Harry was made aware of the picture at an England training session that also included Drinkwater, he commented to the *Daily Mirror*, 'Me and Danny Drinkwater were having a joke and he showed me a picture of us three sitting there on the bench as we played at Watford. It is crazy. Football is a funny game and it can change quickly. It shows what hard work and dedication can do. We have come a long way but it does not stop here as we have a lot of hard work to do to keep progressing.'

Once again, note Harry's references to hard work and dedication. Those are characteristics close to his heart and part of the explanation behind how he exploded on to the scene seemingly from nowhere when he finally made the Spurs first team. Of course, it was hardly that: he had been out on loan and grafted ferociously behind the scenes when he returned to the Lane. He had been determined to get his big chance – and when it finally came, no way was he going to blow it.

Yet there is one man who does not believe the loans benefitted Harry. That man is Tim Sherwood, who would become Tottenham's short-term boss and then take the reins at Aston Villa. He did not thrive in those posts but was a revelation when he was in charge of the Spurs kids at the Lane – and, to give him his full credit, WAS the man who gave Harry a regular run in the first team when he was in charge at Tottenham.

But when talking about Harry's loan moves, he insists they were not totally beneficial, as he was not getting enough starts and that the managers of the loan clubs were hardly rhapsodising about Harry's efforts when he did play. Sherwood told the *Express* in April 2016, 'I spoke to the managers our players were working for when they went out on loan. But I always maintain that I never listened too much to the reports of the other manager. I never used those to judge a player too far. Other people could judge him a certain way, I didn't. Because if you judged Harry Kane on his loans, then he would probably be a League One player now. But that just shows the character of the kid. He took those knocks by going on loan and being told he was not good enough – basically, that is what they were saying by not playing him. They were saying he was not up to standard.

'[Then] there was a crossroads with Harry where we told him, "No more loans – you get sold or you get into the team". Luckily, a few months later I got the manager's job and the rest is history.'

It is not a common view, but it is a view Sherwood is entitled to. It does suggest that if it wasn't for Tim, then Harry would probably never have got a proper chance at the Lane, and that Tim saw things in him that others did not. That is also possible, but others at the loan clubs believed Harry was a star in the making, as did fans at those very same clubs. And I am convinced Harry does not regret making the loan moves, for reasons outlined earlier in this chapter.

Given that disparity of view, it is appropriate that we now put it to the test by taking a more in-depth look at each of the moves and assess how Harry performed at each club, how he felt and how the clubs and fans felt towards him during his loan spells and by the time he had moved on.

His loan spell record reads like this: five goals in eighteen appearances for Leyton Orient; none for Norwich in five appearances; nine for Millwall in twenty-seven appearances and two for Leicester in fifteen games. That is a total of sixteen goals in sixty-five games. OK, it is hardly an earth-shattering record, but it remains respectable for a young lad – an average of a goal every four appearances, and don't forget those games weren't all ninety-minute showings, not by a long way. For a boy away from his comfort zone, still learning his trade and the art of marksmanship, they are, I would contend, quietly confident statistics. A sign of a player developing amid a tough environment that tested both his character to fit into new arenas and his ability to deliver the goods without the reassurances and encouragement of the Spurs academy team, including Sherwood.

Harry had been thrown in at the deep end away from the Lane – and on several occasions, too – and was playing with and against seasoned pros who knew a trick or two. He wasn't quite the proverbial lamb to slaughter but he certainly had to learn – and learn quickly – if he were to survive, let alone thrive in these alien arenas. It wasn't like playing with fellow kids in the academy at Spurs; it was much more competitive and fierce with guys a lot older and a lot more streetwise in terms of football and, on occasions, its darker arts.

Harry learned quickly how to deal with big defenders who would hit him hard and who wanted him to know they were there. They would not pussyfoot around with a new kid on the block and they made their presence felt swiftly, and sometimes painfully, in matches. It was a tough grounding but one which would stand Kane in good stead when he returned to the Lane and finally made the Spurs first team. By then, he was no innocent abroad – he knew what to expect from defenders long in the tooth, how not to get sucked in by their nudges and illegal challenges, and, most importantly, how to beat them with a swerve of the body or a deft leap over any violent attempt to halt his progress.

First stopping-off point on the road for Harry was Leyton Orient, where he arrived the day after the New Year in 2011. He signed a deal to stay with the club until the end of the season and later told pals he enjoyed his time at Brisbane Road. Harry was seventeen when he made his debut for the Os, coming on as a sub for Scott McGleish with fifteen minutes to go at Rochdale. McGleish would later tell *BBC Sport* how much he admired Kane for stepping down into League One to progress. He said he was impressed with how Harry did not act as though he was entitled, just because he had come from such a big club as Tottenham. He just got on with the job, knuckling down in training and working hard to prove himself when he was called upon for first-team outings.

It might have only been a seventeen-minute cameo but Kane used them to impress, bustling and battling with the home defence and proving a dangerous attacking presence. Dale fan Steve Hayes was there that day and said, 'It was a typical winter day in Rochdale – dull and wet and grey! There had been a piece in the papers that Orient might bring on this kid from Tottenham and I thought he did well when he came on as a sub, with not a lot of time to show what he could do. I'd never have thought he would be a big star who one day would become England's centre-forward, or that he would win the Golden Boot. But then you wouldn't, would you, after such a short space of time to judge him in? Obviously he had talent, and looked as if he had good technical ability but he was only really at the start of the journey. Still, it's something to tell the family – that once I saw an England international playing at Spotland, and Rochdale held them to a 1–1 draw! I'm dead pleased Kane made it – he's a good lad, seems right down-to-earth and grounded.'

It was a real bog of a pitch and an awful night. As Dale boss Keith Hill pointed out, the match should not have taken place, adding: 'I don't think it was the right decision for the game to go ahead and it should have been called off, probably at half-time, it was a farce. That as a spectator going to a football match it wasn't worth watching, I won't watch it again on the DVD, it was awful.'

The night was a nightmare weather-wise but Harry would certainly never forget his pro debut on that soggy, awful pitch in a rain-drenched town in the north-west of England. He would admit, 'I remember like it was yesterday. The pitch was really wet and boggy and they'd thought about calling it off. I went on and charged about everywhere. I don't think even the manager was expecting that from me. They thought I was on loan from Spurs and I'd be waiting to get on the ball and do a bit. I was determined to show what I could do and here was my chance. Here I was, starting my career at Rochdale. I've always seen every game I've played as the chance to get where I want to go. Through all my loan moves, that's always been the case.'

He later admitted he enjoyed his spell at Orient, and that the Millwall loan was also worthwhile – the other two, at Norwich and Leicester, were maybe not as good as he didn't get enough game time – as he outlined to the *Daily Mail*, 'I've enjoyed them all and taken something from them. I feel like

I've been able to take something from them and become a better player.'

In his first home game for Orient, Harry, wearing the number 29 shirt, did what came naturally… hitting the back of the net. 'To score in that game as a seventeen-year-old was something I'll never forget,' Harry said. 'It was just brilliant.' He was on target as Orient thrashed Sheffield Wednesday 4–0, grabbing the second goal. This is how the *Sheffield Star* witnessed Harry's arrival on the footballing scene with that goal: 'Six minutes after the opener, Harry Kane, a 17-year-old centre-forward on loan from Spurs and making his full debut, ran in behind the defence unhindered to score, with Jones and sub Mark Beevers closest as he burst into space to meet a free-kick.' The description just about summed up where Harry was in his career – an unknown kid on loan from Spurs, but one who still had the nous to crack a battle-hardened lower league backline.

Harry now enjoyed a run of games with the League One outfit and a few weeks later was on target again, this time grabbing a brace as Orient hit four again, with Bristol Rovers the victims of a 4–1 lashing at Brisbane Road. The double was all the more remarkable as Harry had only appeared as a sub but as the local rag, the *Hackney Gazette,* pointed out, 'Young substitute Harry Kane grabbed two second-half goals to seal a victory against Bristol Rovers, as the home side stretched their unbeaten run to 10 games.' Kane scored his first with a finely drilled shot, and his second a close-range header. O's assistant boss Kevin Nugent praised his young striker for the impact he had had from the bench, saying he had taken his chances well and put himself in contention for more starting roles.

Harry was hoping he would get a start, especially if it could be in the next match – the FA Cup clash with Tottenham's arch rivals, Arsenal! He admitted, 'The tie is extra special for me being a Spurs player. Maybe if I score the winner, I could become a Tottenham legend without even playing for them yet!'

It was not to be – but Harry did not let that get him down. He continued to buckle down in training and do his damnedest to show boss Russell Slade he should be in the side. He was rewarded with a nod from Slade to come off the bench as a nineteenth minute sub at Huddersfield and repaid that faith by netting on seventy-three minutes. His headed goal put the visitors right back in the game after they had gone 2–0 down. It would inspire them to what had seemed an unlikely 2–2 draw.

Unfortunately for Harry he would also be dismissed for a second yellow card just four minutes after his goal. He was unhappy at the decision – it seemed a harsh one after he accidentally fouled Anthony Pilkington. Slade agreed, while also pointing out he was pleased with Harry's goal and the point his team achieved, going on to say, 'It was a horrendous start from us and we didn't settle or threaten and looked to be heading for a toothless defeat. They failed to finish us off and I felt if we stayed in the game we could have got something. I had a look at the sending off situation and it was very harsh on Harry Kane as it didn't look like he touched him.'

O's skipper McGleish felt that the goal was something of a turning point for Kane in that his bravery and determination to score it set him aside from other loanees who had arrived from the Premier League. McGleish said, 'The first thing I thought when he walked through the door at our training ground was, "Here we go, another typical Tottenham player". I had seen them all before. Very good, pleasing on the eye, but not much in the way of blistering pace and a little bit of a lightweight. Harry had something of the Glenn Hoddle about him – but he still had so far to go. I watched him in training and he was an incredible finisher. But it was how he stood up to matches that was really going to matter. The turning point came at Huddersfield a few weeks after his debut. He had come on as a substitute and late in the game scored a good goal – a really brave header where he had to risk getting hurt. That was what we had not seen in training – a bit of bravery. Mind you, four minutes later he was sent off for a second yellow card – nothing malicious, but perhaps the blood was pumping. That is all part of growing up. And Harry really wanted to progress. He listened. He wanted to do better.'

And Harry would later concede that playing in such games DID toughen him up and encourage him to become more physical in his game, saying, 'Any seventeen-year-old going to play League football is going to have to learn fast how to toughen themselves up. You have to if you want to make a career for yourself. It was certainly what I had to do and it has helped me in my career so far.'

A fortnight later Harry was on target once again, this time helping Orient to a win rather than a draw. He also started for the club and lasted until seven minutes from time when he was replaced by McGleish in the 2–0 victory at Walsall. Harry headed the visitors in front just before the break and Jon Téhoué's goal eleven minutes after the interval secured the win and maintained the club's unbeaten league run, taking it to twelve games. They were in the play-off zones and on target for a crack at promotion to the Championship, so Harry was earning his money and proving to be a lucky charm.

Kane would play a part in another ten league games for Orient until the end of the season but would draw a blank in front of goal. Cruelly, the team would finish just one place outside of the play-off zone and miss out on promotion. But Kane had worked hard and left with fond memories and with the fans truly appreciating his efforts and goals. They would long remember that England's future number 9 had once played in front of them for their club.

Harry would now return to White Hart Lane and aim to get into the Spurs team. First, he would take a well-earned summer sunshine break with his girlfriend and rest his body after a tough learning session at the hands of League One's hard-men. He had come through it unscathed and proud of his efforts at Brisbane Road. The loan spell had toughened him up and added another dimension to his game: he knew full well now that he would have to beef up his physique so that he could cope with the attention of the most difficult of defenders.

He then returned to pre-season training with Tottenham and surprised some of the squad with just how difficult he was too push off the ball. Harry had great hopes that this could be a breakthrough season at the club he loved but he would once again find himself out on loan the following January. His stint at Orient had been recognised of sorts – he played six games for Spurs before leaving in the January of 2012 for Millwall, but all those Spurs matches were in the Europa League, which was not at the top of the club's list of priorities. Sure, it would be great if they won it, or reached the latter stages, but it was one of Tottenham's lesser ambitions given the concentration on league success, and making the promised land of the Champions League. The FA Cup also took precedence, so the Europa fitted in on a level with the League Cup, or maybe a notch less. That would change by 2016–17, as by then winning the Europa League would guarantee you a place in the following season's Champions League group stage. But that was not the case in 2011.

Still, Harry was grateful for any first-team opportunities and he did score a goal in those six appearances in Europe's second-tier tournament, hitting the back of the net against Shamrock Rovers in the middle of December, 2011.

Within a month, though, he was plying his trade away from the Lane for the second time in a year. While January 2011 had seen him head off to East London, he now took up residence south of the Thames, at Millwall. Lions boss Kenny Jackett had taken note of Harry's impressive stint at Orient and enquired about his availability. Tottenham talked with Harry and both parties agreed a further loan might help his development as his route to regular first-team football at the Lane was not yet guaranteed. At the end of December, 2011, it was confirmed that Harry and teammate Ryan Mason would move to the New Den on a six-month loan from 1 January, on youth loans. Harry was eighteen and midfielder Ryan was twenty.

Jackett was delighted with the double coup. He told the

Millwall official website, 'Both are attacking players and I think our goalscoring options, which do need to improve, will be helped by the acquisition of these two players. Harry is a goalscorer and Ryan is a very creative player with experience of playing in the Championship.' Both moved without having made their league debuts for Spurs, but both were told that their time would come. Ryan had already made fifteen appearances on loan at Doncaster that season and had played once for Tottenham, also in Europe.

Both would become popular signings with the Millwall fans, despite being from a club they abhorred. The two worked hard and Harry, in particular, was well liked as his seven goals in twenty-two games played a big part in keeping Millwall from being relegated from the Championship. Likewise, Harry would later admit he had fond memories of that loan spell, telling the *London Evening Standard* in 2015, 'I'll never forget it. The relief on everyone's faces – the players, the fans. It showed me how much the game could mean. People were playing for their livelihoods and had they been relegated, it would have been a big downer for the club. You have to do your job otherwise you won't be in the game long so to be thrown into that at 18 was really good. That experience three years ago is one of the things that has made me who I am today. It was a big stepping stone to where I am now.'

Such was his impression and work at the New Den that he won the club's Young Player of the Year award. The award was decided by boss Jackett, and he admitted that both club and fans would be sad to see Harry leave at the end of his loan spell. He said it had 'been hard to look past Harry' for the gong and added, 'He has fitted in very well at Millwall despite only being here half a season. He's fitted in with the players and the crowd and developed as well. I felt he came here as a boy and is a man now – and plays like a man on the pitch. It's been a good relationship and he deserves the award.'

Former Lions skipper Alan Dunne would tell of how impressed he was with Kane's attitude and talent, saying, 'One day in training he scored the best goal I have ever seen. It came from the goalkeeper's throw. He flicked the ball over his marker and hit a stunning volley from the narrowest of angles. It was like Marco van Basten. I thought, "Wow, who is this quiet kid?"'

Dunne would later tell Sky Sports, 'He was a really quiet lad, a shy lad who didn't say much. But when he went out on the football pitch he showed glimpses of magic I'd never seen before from anyone at Millwall.'

But Harry's debut for the Lions would end in misery as they lost 1–0 at Bristol City. The loss left them fourth from bottom and fearing the drop – yet by the end of Kane's loan spell they had survived. A 6–0 home loss to Birmingham a fortnight later had set the alarm bells ringing but three days later Harry grabbed his first goals to settle nerves a little. True, the 5–0 win over Dagenham and Redbridge was in the FA Cup, not the league, but it suggested better times may lie ahead if Harry could maintain his goals run. The five goals ended an eight-game run without a goal as Kane bagged two and Darius Henderson hit a hat-trick. The BBC summed up Harry's contribution in this way: 'Kane – who was superb throughout – completed the rout when he headed in a cross from the left from close range. The Tottenham youngster, who was not born when Spurs last won the FA Cup in 1991, was at the heart of everything and could yet prove a useful asset for Harry Redknapp [the then Spurs boss].'

Lions assistant boss Joe Gallen admitted they were delighted at the way Harry had settled and how his partnership with Henderson had worked so well, adding, 'We've been saying we needed a win and to do that we needed some goals, so to score five was a good confidence boost, especially for the forwards. All round it's been a good evening for us, but now we've got to do it in the league. We'll see in the next few weeks whether these two guys can score the goals we need.'

At the end of February, Harry scored again in the 3–1 win at Burnley. The win moved Millwall seven points clear of the drop zone as Harry grabbed the third goal. The club's official website summed up Kane's contribution, stating, 'Harry Kane bagged his first League goal for The Lions with a third 21 minutes from the end to wrap up three points. Henry turned provider on 69 minutes with the final, perfectly weighted pass slipped through to Kane. The teenage striker composed himself before despatching a low shot into the bottom right corner to spark chants of "We want four" from the 250 or so travelling fans.'

A few days later and Harry was in the starting line-up when the Lions travelled to Peterborough for another vital game in their battle to avoid the drop – and he was on target again. Millwall cruised to a 3–0 win, putting more space between them and relegation. Harry completed the scoring with a quite brilliant shot from some thirty yards out, showing he could score more than close-range shots and headers. His full bag of tricks was beginning to assemble as the more competitive games he played, the better he got. Clearly, there was something in this loan business. Unlike some players, he had gone from his parent club and given his all to the loan club. It was paying off with dividends as the goals rolled in and the fans stood to applaud him for his efforts.

This was truly an honest boy: one who would never simply take the money and think the big time was his entitlement. No, with Harry Kane you knew what you were getting. Full commitment and dedication to the cause wherever he was playing. In this case, his aim was twofold: to do his best to save Millwall from relegation and to improve his own game and develop as a goalscorer. He was succeeding on both counts.

Lions assistant boss Gallen praised Harry after the game for his increasing maturity when under pressure, and his ability to score from any situation. He added that it had been the club's 'best performance of the season' and that if they kept playing like that their relegation worries would fade, 'We could have had more,' he said. 'We fully deserved to win so well and I'm pleased for the lads and the supporters. We know our home form isn't right at the moment, but our away performances are spot on.'

Harry was also buzzing in the dressing room. He had reached double figures with his brilliant effort and told reporters he felt the goal was his best so far, also saying, 'I've scored ten senior goals now and that's the best. I've had a few chances in recent weeks, hit the woodwork, seen goalkeepers make great saves, so it was great to get on the scoresheet again. The most important thing was the result and it was a great three points for us. That's two goals in the Championship now and I'll keep going to get as many as I can. It's a fantastic experience for me.'

The great thing was that during the loan spells, he was allowed to improve his game by the clubs encouraging him to be versatile. While he mainly played up front, there were times when he dropped back into an attacking midfield role – and even played on the wing, too. This gave him a greater understanding of the game and showed him the importance of becoming a complete, rounded player. He may have started off as something of a gangly lad, but the loans showed him that he needed to beef up if he was to be the best. The versatility and more powerful physique would make him a better all-round attacking player in the long-run.

As he would admit some years later to *The Sun*, 'I've always fancied myself as a finisher and obviously the more you practise and the older I got, getting a bit more power behind the shots, it just kind of naturally turned into it. I think a bit of it is obviously getting older, your muscles develop more, you get a bit more power, but I worked hard on it as well. I put a lot of work in the gym on my power, and my lower body side of it, because I felt like I needed to get a bit more pace in my game.

'When I was younger I used to play any position – I played a few games at centre-back, some as a holding midfielder, some as a midfield 10, and I also played as a striker and on the wing. I think I'm a versatile player who could probably play anywhere but I've always liked scoring goals – as long as I'm scoring goals I'll be staying up front.'

Millwall were definitely appreciative of his goalscoring that season as he continued to chip into the relegation battle collection pot. A month after the 3–0 win at the Posh, the Lions were at it again, this time beating Doncaster away by the same margin. And, yet again, Harry was on target: he seemed to be their lucky talisman as they notched up these vital big wins away from the New Den. Donny were also in the relegation mix and the nationals led the way in unison acclaiming Harry as a wrecking ball, with variations of the headline, 'Dean Saunders Kaned'. The former footballer was on the edge as a manager at Donny, and Harry's goal and all-round contribution hardly made life any easier that weekend. As *The Star* pointed out, 'Dean Saunders' Donny desperately needed the victory. But they coughed up soft goals for Andy Keogh and Harry Kane for the visitors inside 12 minutes and Darius Henderson added a third after the break. With just seven minutes gone James Henry coasted past left-back Tommy Spurr and clipped over a cross for an unmarked Keogh to nod in from six yards. And just five minutes later Millwall doubled their advantage when Donny keeper Carl Ikeme made a mess of on-loan Spurs man Kane's hopeful 35-yarder.'

Kane earned more pats on the back for his goal and performance from boss Kenny Jackett, whose decision to bring him in on loan to save their season was fast looking like a masterstroke. Jackett added, 'I'm very pleased with both the result and the performance. We are doing particularly well in our away games and this was another example.'

It was all going well for Harry but, as Kenny was continually saying, it would be even better if he and his temporary teammates could find more consistent levels of good form at home. So it was timely, and so very welcome for the club, when Harry scored in their next two home games, goals which also brought wins. Indeed, he also hit the back of the net in the away match sandwiched in between, making it three goals in three games. Not bad going for a kid who had only arrived on loan three months earlier.

The first of the three came at the start of April, 2012, and visitors Hull City were the victims as they crashed 2–0. Amazingly, it was also Millwall's first home win of 2012. Kane opened the scoring with a first-half header and the club dedicated the win to legend Barry Kitchener, who had died a week previously at the age of sixty-four. It was an emotional day as they remembered their former centre-half, marking it with a win that was so badly needed. It also marked the club's thousandth home league win – a landmark they had been trying to notch since Boxing Day, such had been the barren run of poor results in front of their own fans.

Just three days later and the boys were facing another crunch league game, away at Portsmouth. Pompey were never easy to beat on their own turf, but the Lions kept their nerve and earned a 1–0 victory courtesy of Kane's second goal, the middle one, of the three in succession. The goal was vital – it moved Millwall closer to safety, but left Pompey on the brink of relegation to League One. The phrase 'a six-pointer' is often used in terms of key games at the top or bottom of a division; a cliché maybe, but if ever there was such a game, this was it. You could tell at the final whistle as the Lions rejoiced as if they had won the league, and Pompey's players trooped dejectedly off the pitch.

Harry's killer strike came a few minutes before the interval and meant the team had won three of their last five matches, putting them eight points clear of the drop zone while leaving Pompey nine adrift. At eighteen, he had all but ensured that the Lions would be in the Championship next season and assistant boss Gallen admitted the Lions owed a debt to the lad, saying, 'He has a very good all-round game. He's developing nicely and he will score a lot in the future.'

That prophesy would come true – but even Gallen would probably admit he never anticipated Harry Kane would become SUCH a lethal striker. One who would become the saviour of both club AND country in years to come. The player's development from a loan spell hopeful to international hero remains nothing short of remarkable: a real *Boy's Own*, *Roy of the Rovers* story.

The third of Harry's three-in-three came the following Saturday when Millwall beat Leicester 2–1 at the New Den. There had been an expectation that the Foxes might wreck Millwall's relegation-beating run as they were fighting to make the play-offs, and possible promotion to the Premier League. But this third win on the trot instead damaged their hopes – and at the same time secured Millwall's Championship status for another season. Harry Kane had achieved what the management had asked of him when he joined back in January: he had helped the club retain their membership of English football's second tier.

Harry scored on twenty-three minutes when the Foxes failed

to clear a free kick. He was on hand to strike the ball home and then played a big part in the goal that would secure the win, as hapless Paul Konchesky fouled him in the box. Andy Keogh made no mistake, converting from the penalty spot. My friends at *The Sun* made it clear how much of an influence Kane had had on helping Millwall stay up, claiming that boss Jackett keeping Harry for another season was a major priority, adding that: 'Millwall boss Kenny Jackett can only hope that Spurs extend the loan of Harry Kane. The 18-year-old striker has now scored in each of his last three games for the Lions and his 23rd-minute opener against play-off hopefuls Leicester set up a third straight win. It also guaranteed Millwall their place in the Championship next season.'

Jackett himself was under no illusions how important his decision to bring in Kane had been on his team's fortunes, telling reporters, 'The partnership of Kane and Andy Keogh has made the difference. Early in the season that was the sort of game we might have lost by the odd goal but the two of them create a threat all of the time. But with Kane, we can only wait as he is still a Spurs player. It was very important to preserve our Championship status. Thankfully we found form, results and a way of winning. We tried to have a settled side and, as I say, the Keogh and Kane partnership has worked for us up front, but this was a real hard-working performance again and we deserved to win.'

The Lions' official website also celebrated survival – and applauded the impact of Kane in achieving that after the match, 'Millwall's very own brand of Special K served up a goal double to secure Championship football at The Den for another season. Goals in either half from Harry Kane and an Andy Keogh penalty put The Lions 2–0 ahead, and although Foxes sub Danny Drinkwater reduced the arrears nine minutes from time, Kenny Jackett's side held on for a victory that sparked wild celebrations at the final whistle.'

Harry's work was done at the New Den now that the club had avoided the drop. But the season wasn't quite over. He played in the three final league games over the next fortnight and helped Millwall consolidate further their position in the table as they finished unbeaten in all three. They won 1–0 at Coventry, 3–0 at Ipswich and drew 2–2 at home with Blackpool on the final day of the campaign. Harry bade farewell in typical style, signing off with a goal when they hosted the Seasiders. His late equaliser preserved their unbeaten end to the season and he was applauded off by the Millwall fans who knew he had contributed in a major way for them and their club. He might have been from north of the river but he would always be sure of a warm welcome if he returned as a player or to watch a game. Harry drilled the ball home in the bottom left-hand corner to earn a deserved point against the promotion-chasers.

Kane admitted he had had 'a great time' at the club and was 'absolutely certain' he had made the right decision to join them on loan. It had been an excellent, competitive learning curve and he had shown he could score goals against the toughest, roughest of defenders. He left with his head high and these words from Kenny Jackett ringing in his ears: 'We've watched Harry develop as the season has gone on and his progress has been superb. We matched Blackpool today and our finish to the season has been outstanding.' His loan spell at the New Den would go down as his most successful of four periods away from Tottenham because his efforts and goals had actually made history for a club by ensuring they were not relegated. It was a major achievement for a boy of eighteen and a sign of his maturity, determination and talent that he would give so much to a club that was not his natural home.

The final two loan destinations were not nearly as successful for Harry – mainly because he was not given as much of a chance at Norwich and Leicester and so did not figure as much, or have the opportunity to show just how his game had developed. The loan spell at Norwich was limited, due to him picking up an injury and when he moved to Leicester he was behind Jamie Vardy, David Nugent and Chris Wood for an automatic starting role. Harry had spent the 2012–13 pre-season with Tottenham and even made his Premier League debut, when he came off the bench, during a match against Newcastle United. He then joined the Canaries on loan for the full season but his injury meant he had to go back to Tottenham for treatment on a broken bone in his foot.

He was then farmed out to Leicester from February 2013 for what would be his final spell away from White Hart Lane.

Harry played just five times for Norwich – three in the league, one in the Capital One Cup and one in the FA Cup. He failed to find the net in any of those games and his final showing for the club was on 26 January 2013, in the FA Cup loss at home to Luton. His only real consolation was that he started that game.

Certainly, no one could have predicted his spell at Carrow

Road would end in failure. Boss Chris Hughton had extremely high hopes when the boy arrived, believing he could add some spice to his attacking options. He told *canaries.co.uk*, 'I'm delighted to bring in someone of the quality of Harry. He is a very talented young player and has bags of potential. He enjoys scoring goals as he has shown coming through the ranks at Spurs and during some good loan spells as well.'

The club's official website also reckoned he was a good gamble, outlining his rapid progress to their fans like this: 'A talented Walthamstow-born forward, Kane has had successful loan spells with Leyton Orient and Millwall over the past two seasons, and made his Spurs debut in a UEFA Europa League play-off game against Hearts in August, 2011. The 19-year-old won many admirers during his loan with Orient, finding the net five times in 18 appearances during the second half of the 2010–11 campaign. He then continued to flourish for Millwall last season, joining the Lions in January 2012 and scoring a further 10 times in 27 games as he struck up a fruitful partnership with Andy Keogh, helping to secure the side's Championship status and winning the club's Young Player of the Year award in the process.'

So it was disappointing for both player and club when things did not go to plan because of those injury setbacks.

When he returned early to the Lane, there were suggestions that he might go back to Millwall for another loan spell. Indeed Lions chief executive Andy Ambler was well up for that idea, telling *Lions Live*, 'Of course we would love Harry to come back. The rumour is that he is going back to Spurs from Norwich. We've already enquired about Kane and we were doing so throughout the course of January. But Kane could be in Spurs' squad if they don't sign a striker, in which case he won't come out. But if Harry is available come next week, and he wants to play, I think we're in a good position to go and get him. But Spurs might have other ideas. They may want to send him to somewhere like Cardiff, who they think have a better chance of getting to the Premier League. There's all sorts of things to take into account.'

In the event, it would be neither Millwall nor Cardiff that would be his next destination. Instead Harry would head up the M1 to Leicester, again with great hopes of making a major impact on a club that was scrapping to make the Premier League from the Championship. Foxes manager Nigel Pearson told BBC Radio Leicester, 'Hopefully he will bring goals and a fresh impetus. It keeps the competition really keen. He's a player we know quite a lot about and I am delighted. He can play as wide striker or as a central striker. He is a decent size as well and gives us another option in forward positions. If you are going to bring players in on loan they have to have a hunger for success and I am confident we have another player coming into our ranks who will bring a lot of positive qualities to the squad.'

The good news for Harry was that before Spurs sent him off to Leicester they insisted he sign a new contract which would see him committed to the Lane until the summer of 2017. The Foxes fans were happy that Kane would be arriving – on the message boards they seemed unanimous in believing that Harry would replace David Nugent up front, as the veteran striker appeared weary in recent matches and, they reckoned, a chance to recharge his batteries with a well-earned rest would do his game a power of good. And Tottenham fans were pleased as well that Harry would eventually return to the Lane – they recognised these loan deals would sharpen him up and toughen him up and looked forward to the day when he returned for good to lead the Spurs attack. As one fan, Ricardo, put it, 'Great news, great striker, our future number 9.'

Harry would score on his debut for Leicester but it would be a tough time at the club as they pushed for promotion from the Championship to the Premier League. He would make a total of thirteen appearances and score twice. That first goal came on his home debut when the Foxes thrashed Blackburn 3–0 at the King Power Stadium towards the end of February, 2013. Harry nodded home the Foxes' second goal just before the interval and played a good match in place of Nugent, who had not been rested but was injured. It would be somewhat ironic that when Harry left the field on eighty-three minutes he was replaced by Jamie Vardy. Both men were finding it hard to get consistent games at their clubs, yet their progress would be mirrored during the next two to three years as both made massive strides and became rivals for a starting place with England, let alone Leicester.

Boss Pearson admitted to being 'very pleased' with Kane's overall performance and 'encouraged' by the nineteen-year-old's eye for goal, and added, 'The result was always going to be more important but to get a very comprehensive win is pleasing. We looked very dangerous, very fluent and, when we had to defend in the second half, we showed good levels of discipline.'

But it would be another two months before Kane hit the back of the net again for City, due to limited opportunities to prove himself for the full ninety minutes. He came on just before the hour mark as a substitute and grabbed Leicester's goal in the 2–1 home reverse to fellow promotion challengers, Watford. The visitors had stormed into a 2–0 lead before Harry headed home and gave Leicester hope. But it was not to be and Watford headed back down south with the crucial three points. Harry was glad to have broken his two-month goals duck but disappointed he had not been able to help his loan club to a better result against such close promotion rivals.

Ironically, it would be against Watford that Harry would suffer the most disappointment in one single game of all his loan spells. Leicester and Watford would meet in the Championship play-off semi-finals in May, 2013. The Foxes triumphed in the first game at the King Power by 1–0, with Harry playing his part as a sixty-third-minute sub, but it was Nugent who scored the vital goal as the teams prepared to clash again at Vicarage Road three days later. Harry was optimistic that the Foxes could hold out and that he would help them to the play-offs final at Wembley. But they crashed 3–1 at Watford and Harry would later admit how low he felt after the game, telling *Sport* magazine, 'When I was on loan at Leicester, we were playing against Watford in the playoff game. Anthony Knockaert had a penalty to take us to Wembley. He missed it, and they went up the other end and scored from the rebound. It was crazy, because it had happened in a Brentford game the week before. So for it to happen twice in a week…'

That would be the end of Kane's travels. He would pack

his bags and leave Leicester, returning home for good to first love, Tottenham. Although disappointed at how it had panned out at the King Power – and for his teammates who were in tears after the playoff defeat – he knew the spells away from his home club had overall been of benefit. He knew that he had developed as a man and as a footballer. Now he was ready to show the fans at the Lane what he was made of – and they would be surprised at just how far he had come since those loans. But before moving on to his first full season at Spurs, let's take a look at how Harry's loans are comparable to David Beckham, another lad local to the East End, and one who could just as easily have starred for Tottenham. And how a loan spell also helped him to become the most famous footballer in the world – and how Harry trod a similar path and could easily follow him as an icon for club and country.

CHAPTER THREE

BECK TO THE FUTURE

It is pertinent that Harry always maintains that his loan spells were a boon for his career rather than a negative. He would often point out that another East London lad went on loan from a massive club to a smaller one – and that it did not do him any harm, either. Yes, Harry was referring to England and Man United legend, David Beckham – who could just as easily have played for Spurs, like Harry.

A couple of years back Becks commented on Harry's progress, saying he had done brilliantly so far and had everything required to make it to the very top of the game. That prompted Harry to say, 'It's amazing to hear those sort of compliments from a real legend of the game. It means I'm doing something right, which is good.' And Harry's mum Kim would admit, 'David Beckham was an inspiration for him.'

The dynamic duo first met when Harry visited Beckham's

football academy, aged eleven, in 2005, in Greenwich, South London. David was just launching the venture and Harry is pictured with him, with a skinhead haircut and proud as David poses with his arm around him. There is also a picture on file of Beckham picking out Harry – and shaking his hand. Harry was a star pupil who showed off his skills with the ball and impressed Beckham no end.

He had visited the academy with other pupils from Chingford Foundation School where he was a pupil – the same school Beckham himself once attended. Mementoes of the famous duo adorn the school's walls. There is a signed and framed Beckham 23 shirt, from his time at Real Madrid, and a Harry Kane 17 shirt, also signed and framed, from his England Under-21 days. Mark Leadon, assistant head teacher at the school and PE head when Harry attended, said it was seeing what Beckham had achieved after attending the same school that convinced him he could also aim for the stars. Mark told *The Sun*, 'Harry came in to give an assembly and said Beckham was a role model. He said he aspired to be like him, because he'd seen it could be done. Harry donated a signed Under-21 shirt to the school and that's an inspiration to current players.'

Harry and Becks also started out playing for the same youth team – Ridgeway Rovers. The club itself are keen to point out how proud they are when Harry pops in to see how the kids are doing – and just as delighted to have had Becks as part of their great history. Their website states, 'Ridgeway Rovers was formed in 1979 and was made famous by being the first club David Beckham played for. David played for the Under-10s team and scored over 100 goals. He then progressed to become what he is today. Ridgeway is a top youth/junior development club. They are also a household name in the North East London area. Ridgeway's main aims are to develop players' potential and provide a top level of coaching in a friendly safe environment. The club has teams throughout different age groups, which are trained and managed by coaches who are FA qualified.'

Both Harry and David remain grateful to the Rovers and try to give something back whenever the opportunity arises. The club is brilliantly run and provides a conveyor belt of talent, even though finances are tight. Sharing in its history is one of the most common bonds Kane and his inspiration, Beckham, have.

David Robert Joseph Beckham was born five miles from Harry in Leytonstone on 2 May 1975, to working-class parents Ted, a gas engineer, and Sandra, a hairdresser. They would later move to Chingford, where Harry would grow up, thus cementing further the link between the two players.

Ted, a footie fanatic, would become the biggest influence on Beckham's drive towards professional football as he helped develop his skills – just as Harry's dad Pat backed his boy to make it. Ted himself was a useful amateur player and he would drill into his son the need to keep working at his own game. He was a forceful taskmaster: a hard but inspiring Svengali to the young Beckham. David would say of him: 'My dad would tell me if I'd done well, but if I'd done badly he'd definitely tell me I'd done badly. He certainly never told me I was the best. What I was told was to work hard at it, and that's what I did.'

That attitude is also similar to Kane and his desire to succeed, doing whatever hard work was needed. Ted would have David out on the local football pitch for hours, concentrating on improving his game, building up his skills and his stamina. David was also a strong cross-country runner – regularly finishing first in his age group in the Essex cross-country championships – and this would help him develop physically.

But while Harry would be taken under the wing of Tottenham, David would end up with Manchester United, after they moved smartly to secure his services. United sent their London scout Malcolm Fidgeon to watch him playing for Waltham Forest Under-12s and he was invited for a trial at Old Trafford. For the next three years he would continue to make progress in the Essex Sunday League – alternating it with trips up to United for more trial games and to watch training. United wanted him to be part of their set-up from an early age and were delighted to secure his signature on a two-year schoolboy deal on his thirteenth birthday.

When he reached sixteen, Becks was faced with his first major footballing decision. Unlike Harry, he opted against his local team Spurs, instead going to United. He left home and signed on as a trainee at Old Trafford on 8 July 1991.

Now would come another link with Harry's development. Just as Kane's youth coaches worried about his physical development – on account of him being 'gangly', 'not as physically developed as others' and 'not being as quick' – so David's fretted about his frame. David and dad Ted knew he had the skill to make it big, and he put in the hours of training and stamina building to allay fears that he was too lightweight.

Eric Harrison, who coached and cajoled Beckham and

the boys who would become known as 'Fergie's Fledglings' admitted everyone was relieved when the boy suddenly shot up in size. He said: 'I told David when he was sixteen that, if he continued his progress, he would definitely play in our first team. I was a little worried because, physically, he was behind everybody else, didn't have the strength. Then he shot up six inches overnight, at sixteen going on seventeen. He had worries himself if he would make it.'

And, like fellow local lad Kane, he would continue to push for optimum fitness throughout his career. In 2000, Steve McClaren, then United's assistant to Alex Ferguson, would comment on just how much effort Beckham put into his fitness training when he revealed: 'I remember a year ago, giving him a rest of a week, ten days, when we were rotating the squad just after Christmas. The day he returned to training was the fitness test day. He had had ten days of doing practically nothing, as he admitted, which was what we wanted. He came and did the "bleep" test [a commonly used fitness gauge in which players run over a set distance, wait for the bleep, then run back with the distance between bleeps becoming gradually shorter] and we had to tell him to stop because he was the only one left standing and he would have kept running and running.'

Beckham took another step to his destiny when he signed as a professional on 23 January 1993, and made his first full appearance in September 1994 against Port Vale, in the League Cup. It would be the first of his 311 games for United, in which he scored seventy-four goals and won eleven medals. He grabbed his first goal for United the following December in the 4–0 Champions League win over Turkish side Galatasaray.

Harry had a similar softly-softly development to the first team at Spurs, with those loans and a gentle introduction when he returned to the Lane for good. In early 1995 Beckham would also hit the loan trail, just as Harry had, although he would only play at one club. Ferguson told Beckham he was 'a late developer' and needed hardening up, and sent the golden boy on loan to Preston North End.

I asked a senior United insider about this and was told: 'That angle was just to keep the Press off the case, it actually seems Ferguson had already marked Beckham's card as a bit of a wide Cockney boy, and wanted to pull him down a peg or two. Beckham was nearly in tears, believing his dream was over before it had properly got off the ground.'

He even told his dad Ted: 'Dad, the boss wants me to go out on loan to Preston... I don't know whether they hate me, I think they want to get rid of me. He [Ferguson] said it would do me good and make me stronger. He said I could go there just for games and keep training with United in the week.'

But United honestly believed it would benefit him – just as the Spurs academy reckoned loan moves would help Harry.

To his credit, Beckham, again like Harry, made the most of his loan. He decided to live and train in Preston to show his new lower-league teammates he was no big-time Charlie – just as Harry had dug in and battled at Orient and Millwall. He scored on his debut against Doncaster and manager Gary Peters made it clear he wanted the boy to stay. Ferguson, realising the boy had made rapid progress, quickly did an about-turn, ordering Beckham back to Old Trafford after he had completed just five games.

But Peters, like Harry's bosses at Orient and Millwall, had only praise for the boy. He said: 'He did really well for us and I was sorry to see him go. He was a great pro from the first day and quickly won over the trust and affection of the other lads. We could have gone great guns if we had kept him in our side for a full season, but Alex pulled the plug just as he was settling in.'

Just as Harry had appreciated working and learning with honest pros at Orient and Millwall, so Becks learned from his seniors at Preston, including one particular stalwart, tough tackling centre-back, David Moyes, who, of course, would go on to manage Manchester United. When Becks made his League debut as a Preston player in 1995, he played alongside Moyes. In his book, *My Side*, Becks said: 'David Moyes was the top man. He was a centre-half and the kind who would throw himself into any tackle possible, even some that weren't. He'd be shouting, geeing people up and was passionate about winning games.

'He was club captain and talked to me and got me involved right from the off. It's not just hindsight, you could tell then that David was going to be a manager. He knew straight away what I was about, that I'd be quiet, keep myself to myself and just talk when I needed to. He put himself out to bring me into the group, to look after me, and I really appreciated that.'

And the North End fans appreciated Beckham's loan efforts. Later, of course, they would be able to say they had seen the biggest name in world football play for them – even if Beckham would never lay claim to being of the same quality as Sir Tom Finney, the genius with whom Preston will eternally be associated. Similarly, Orient fans could talk of the days they watched England's number one centre-forward make his living at their club!

David would score his first Premier League goal for United in the first match of the 1995/96 season, the 3–1 loss at Villa Park that had prompted Alan Hansen's infamous 'Kids don't win titles' jibe. At the time, Fergie liked the way his Cockney boy lived his life (although that wouldn't last, of course). David was the leading light of the new breed of English footballer who didn't drink, didn't do drugs, was clean-living and lived for his football. And, of course, Harry lives the same teetotal, disciplined and measured lifestyle.

Harry will admit Beckham is his role model for how a pro should train and work hard. And how he should live his life by avoiding alcohol and temptation, instead opting for family and stability. Of course, some pundits argue that Harry and David differ in that Harry is not money-mad while David is. They claim everything Becks does is aimed at bolstering his bank balance and the so-called 'Brand Beckham'; that he changed after marrying Victoria; that he became obsessed with fame and fortune after noting how she lived as a pop star. But friends and associates say Becks is a warm, engaging character – full of generous spirit, compassion and a general lack of selfishness. A decent guy who was adamant he wanted to be judged by his footballing efforts alone, and who laughed off the idea that he was using the game as a vehicle to enhance his bank balance and Brand Beckham. In private, I am told, he is endearing, easy to talk to, easy to listen to and a man who is polite and kind.

There are no edges to him; he has never been on the massive ego trip many have accused him of or ever chased the solo aim of being the best-known sportsman on the planet.

That he in fact did become the most famous footballer in the world says a lot about him. Of course, there was some truth in the belief that his marriage to Victoria and their subsequent constant appearances in the news and fashion sections of the papers and magazines contributed to their worldwide fame. But David never set out purely to court that fame or to achieve that aim.

He is a much more down-to-earth, easy-going guy than the tabloids will have you believe. Indeed, he has a compassionate spirit and a good heart that would have you mark him down as a man of solid grounding and strong beliefs, both moral and religious – although the tabloids would no doubt disagree, given the February 2017 furore over leaked emails that suggested David was hell bent on being given a knighthood.

Much like Harry Kane, in fact. Harry has constantly maintained his admiration for how David lives his life in a goldfish bowl every day – yet still manages to be a family man at heart. His sons and daughter and wife are the mainstays of his existence. Just as family and his long-term girlfriend Kate are the mainstays of Harry's. Family is the rock upon which Harry and David have both been able to build strong foundations.

David stayed on a straight and narrow path that led to more rewards both on the pitch and off. It meant that as he approached the twilight of his career he was viewed universally as a likeable, decent man – and his ambassadorial efforts during the 2012 London Olympics cemented that perception.

Then came something truly exceptional, something which Harry Kane openly applauds and admires Beckham for, at the club which would provide the footballing finale for his career. At the end of January 2013, it was announced that Becks would be joining Paris Saint-Germain. He had received some top offers to return to the Premier League – I am told Tottenham and West Ham were among the bidders – but endeared himself to Man United fans by admitting he could not have returned to face the club he loved.

Instead, he opted for another new challenge – to work for the Qatari owners of Paris Saint-Germain and his old AC Milan boss Carlo Ancelotti, who by now was at the helm of the famous old club in the French capital. He signed a five-month contract and explained, 'I'm very lucky. I'm thirty-seven and I got a lot of offers, more now than I've probably had in my career. I'm very honoured by that.

'Every club I've played for throughout the world I've been successful with. I was successful with Manchester United and always said I'd never want to play for another English club. I had a lot of history with Manchester United. It's the team I support and the team I dreamt of playing for.'

But as if his appearance in Paris wasn't enough of a surprise, Beckham now made a move that left even the most hardened cynics among the world's press corps gathered there stunned. It was a move that, for me, best sums up the man and his integrity and flies in the face of those claims of greed and selfishness: Becks disclosed that he would play without a salary at PSG – instead donating what he would have earned to help disadvantaged children.

David explained the altruistic decision in this way: 'I won't receive any salary. My salary will go to a local children's charity in Paris. It's something exciting and something I'm not sure has been done before.' He did not know the exact amount the charity would receive but conceded it would be a lot of money. 'I'm very excited about it,' he added. 'To be able to give a huge sum to a children's charity in Paris. It's very special.'

Even then, there were some cynics who rubbished his decision, claiming it was simply a move to generate good publicity for the footballer; that the anticipated £2 million windfall was but 'peanuts' to a man of Beckham's wealth. There were also snipes that Beckham would still leave Paris a much richer man because of the money he would bank from commercial deals and merchandising income.

And some financial analysts criticised the move as a ploy to avoid paying taxes while he stayed in Paris. The latter argument was surely nonsensical: if he had paid his taxes, he would have still been left with some money in his pocket, wouldn't he? As it was, he had none by giving it all away…

OK, so he did indeed garner excellent worldwide publicity for the move – and he did pocket money from other sources as a result of his successful stint in Paris. But, the fact is this: David Beckham still volunteered an estimated £2 million of his wages to help those who most needed help. Whichever way you look at it, David Beckham carried out a philanthropic act of some depth and weight. And I know that Harry is just as keen to help those less fortunate than himself. He is always the first player, whether it be with Spurs or England, to volunteer when it comes to visiting charity appeals or helping out at good causes, especially children's charities. In April 2016, for instance, he headed to the Noah's Ark Hospice which provides support for children and young people with life-limiting or life-threatening conditions and their families in central and north London. Harry had a kickabout with three of the children and helped out with some gardening.

A year earlier he had supported the Honeypot Children's Charity, which helps vulnerable kids, visiting a family and learning of the difficulties they face when children have to be the main carer for a parent and, sometimes, a sibling. Harry has also backed the 'Shoot For Love' charity, which donates much-needed cash for children with cancer. He is still young but has made it clear he will always make himself available for worthy charities that are close to his heart. Not on a scale of Beckham's £2 million windfall yet, but still as vital and selfless in his own way.

Kind and big-hearted, Harry would also love to emulate his fellow Chingford lad's career highs. Becks made 115 appearances for England – a one-time record for an outfield player – and regularly captained the side during Sven-Göran Eriksson's tenure. And, in a glittering career that spanned two decades, he also notched up trophies and records galore by the time he retired at the age of thirty-eight. He is the only British player to win titles in four different countries – England, with Manchester United; Spain, with Real Madrid; America with Los Angeles Galaxy and France with Paris Saint-Germain. And his trophy cabinet is fit to burst – among his medals are six Premier League titles, one European Cup and two FA Cups with United, plus those other three league winners' medals in those other countries and a Spanish Cup winner's medal to boot.

Little wonder that Harry always points to Beckham as his inspirational, number one example of how a footballer should live his life and play the game. With fierce determination and graft, and letting his game do the talking when many wondered if he had lost it when Brand Beckham reared its head. And trying to live a decent life with family and stability as the base that would propel a man forwards in his professional life. Kane and Beckham – two local lads who had done not just 'good', but wonderful beyond any expectations. From Ridgeway Rovers and Chingford Foundation School to the top teams in England and worldwide fame. True East End glory boys – and real decent guys, too, even if some critics will argue that Becks has lost some of his sheen after those leaked 'knighthood' emails.

CHAPTER FOUR

EARNING HIS SPURS

Harry may have signed his first professional contract with Tottenham in July 2010, but it was not until April 2014 – almost four years later – that he could really feel he had become a permanent part of the club's set-up. The good news was that he had been an early starter, not a Johnny-come-lately to the big time, like say, Leicester's Jamie Vardy. By April 2014, he was only twenty and time was on his side. Plus he had been hardened, improved physically and mentally and learned valuable football and life lessons by those four loan spells away from White Hart Lane.

Harry had never once complained of his lot. He had got his head down and worked hard at the various loan clubs, always determined and believing he would eventually return to his big love, Tottenham, and would be given his chance to thrive. It was this optimistic nature and will to succeed whatever it took – and however long it took – that would enable him to break through into the first team and become a regular, and that would endear him to fans at the Lane, who called him 'one of their own'. The true story of 'the local boy done bloody good'.

Between those four loan spells Harry would make some appearances for Tottenham and show encouraging signs of the skills he could bring to his home club when the management decided he had worked away long enough. When they decided loans would no longer benefit his development.

Harry made his senior debut aged eighteen for Spurs after completing his first loan spell at Orient. On 25 August 2011, he started in Tottenham's second leg Europa League qualification tie at home to Hearts. The team had won the first leg 5–0 in Edinburgh and so the second game was all but a formality, highlighted by the line-up showing six academy graduates. It was not the greatest of debuts: the match ended 0–0 and Harry fluffed his chance of opening his goal account by missing a penalty, which he had won. Then again, the youngster had the guts to step up to the plate for the spot kick but his shot was well saved by Hearts keeper Jamie MacDonald, who redeemed himself after fouling Kane for the penalty award. At full-time, Spurs boss Harry Redknapp, always a brilliant motivator and man manager, put his arm around Kane's shoulder and told him not to let the miss bother him. There would be plenty of occasions when he WOULD score from the spot, the boss reassured him and told reporters he was pleased with all his youngsters and that some of them had a very bright future ahead of them, adding that, 'They all did well – and this will only improve them. This is a big stage for them, a massive step up, but it can only do them good.'

Kane was being well managed at the club, carefully nurtured and cared for with the long-term in mind. Everyone behind the scenes was convinced he had what it took, the only question was how long before he was ready. That was the thinking behind the loans and these occasional appearances. There was no point rushing him in and seeing the whole project collapse before it had been started, as was the case with many a youngster at clubs in England. No, Tottenham were prepared to go gently and sensitively with the boy, encouraging him and supporting him, all the time assessing his development and judging when he would be finally ready to take that huge step up to being a first-team regular.

Just as Alex Ferguson had sent David Beckham out on loan, so Redknapp rolled the same dice with Harry Kane. In both cases, there was never a doubt about ability and potential, and there was never a plan to loan them with a view to transfer. No, these boys were at the heart of their clubs' future projects – to propel the stars of their youth team into eventual stars of their first teams. I was told Harry enjoyed his debut and running out before the Spurs fans, who gave him and the other five youngsters a rousing welcome, but that he was annoyed with himself for missing the penalty. He wouldn't let it prey on his mind but he would be twice as determined to hit the target next time such an opportunity arose.

Harry made another five appearances for Tottenham that season – all of them coming in Europa League matches – before he was farmed out for a second loan spell, at Millwall in

January 2012. That loan would arguably prove to be his finest, as he helped the Lions beat the drop from the Championship with his goals and input. His second Spurs game came on 15 September 2011, against top Greek outfit PAOK Thessaloniki. Unfortunately, his efforts would not bring the first Spurs goal he yearned for, but a yellow card for a foul! Having said that, he was denied a blatant first-half penalty for a clear trip in the box by the hosts. Redknapp had once again made mass changes, bringing in the kids, for this first Europa League proper match that he had dubbed 'a nuisance' as it interfered with his Premier League plans.

But that annoyance was music to the ears of the kids – including young Harry – as it gave them another opportunity to show their worth. Harry ran forcefully at the Greek defence on several occasions, earning nods of approval from Redknapp and his assistants on the bench, but was unable to break them down. Yet it was another first-team game under his belt and showed, once again, that he certainly had the temperament, character and ability to play on the big stage. He could only improve with more games and more experience.

For now, those matches would come in European competition, albeit in a tournament that his boss felt was hardly anything to shout about – saying that it only caused problems and complicated his assault on the Premier League. First team regulars may have taken his words to heart – and felt that even if they messed up in the Europa League it would be OK. Maybe the boss would even be happy if they were eliminated…

But the academy kids had no such thoughts: their only

aim was to impress on these rare outings and Harry Kane was as keen as anyone to do just that. He played his part in the next four matches – a 3–1 home win over Shamrock Rovers, a 1–0 loss at Rubin, a 2–1 home defeat by PAOK and a 4–0 win in Ireland against Shamrock. It all added up to a campaign that had its shares of both highs and lows. For Harry, the biggest high would come in that final group game in Ireland – as he notched his first senior goal for Tottenham. The win was bittersweet for Harry, as it proved to not be enough to save Spurs from exiting the competition, although his boss did not share those sentiments. Kane arrived as a late substitute for Jermain Defoe and grabbed his goal smartly, with a close-range effort in added time. It meant he signed off his first clutch of games for the club with a signal of intent. That, given a regular run of games, he could ease his way to scoring on a regular basis.

Another youngster, Andros Townsend, was chosen to speak before the waiting media and he explained how the European experience had benefitted him, Harry and the other lads in the Spurs team. He said, 'We did well. For the first twenty minutes we were slow but after we got the first goal we pushed on. We can't blame PAOK for not getting the result – the problem was the last two games where we lost against PAOK and Rubin. It's our own fault. It's been massive for us youngsters to get game time, not in reserve matches but in the Europa League against hostile crowds like PAOK and Rubin.'

Harry, in turn, told pals that he had thrived on being part of Spurs' European campaign and that it had made him hungry to be involved more often. That ambition would have to wait as he was now sent out on loan to Millwall for the last six months of the season. He moved to the New Den with fellow youngster Ryan Mason, and helped the club survive in the Championship.

Then it was back to White Hart Lane for 2012–13 pre-season training and matches. Harry started the friendly clash at Southend United and really gave new boss André Villas-Boas something to think about as he grabbed a brilliant hat-trick in a 6-0 rout. Southend's official website summed up the demolition act, saying, 'Freddy Eastwood responded shooting wide from distance for United before Kane completed his hat-trick in the 78th minute. This time the former Millwall loanee squeezed an effort under Bentley who had made a couple of strong saves previously to keep the score down. That just left Jonathan Obika to add a sixth in the 82nd minute as he got the wrong side of defender Mark Phillips to head in from close range to wrap up a disappointed end to Southend's pre-season against an impressive looking Tottenham reserve team.'

Southend may have viewed the visitors as 'reserves' but the boys who played that day were aiming much higher. Harry, in particular, was confident he would make the grade and eight days later he won a big vote of confidence when Spurs' Portuguese manager brought him on as a substitute for his Premier League bow. Harry's big moment arrived at Newcastle in the eighty-fifth minute. OK, it was only a brief cameo – but the boy had finally arrived as far as his Tottenham dream and career was concerned. He now had his debut in the bag and knew he could plough on with the aim of playing for more minutes and showing what he could do when the occasions arose. He was still a long way off being a first-team regular, but Villas-Boas's faith had shown him that he was on the right track. That if he kept plugging away and working hard – even on loan – his efforts were being noted. He was under consideration and in the first team manager's thoughts.

Spurs lost the match 2–1 at St James' Park and some commentators claimed the fact Harry was brought on reflected on the lack of top-notch talented strikers at the club. Sure, he was young and inexperienced but let's not go with that notion that he only appeared because there was no one else at the club capable of opening up defence. He appeared on merit and Spurs did have world-beater Gareth Bale and goal-getter Jermain Defoe in the team, along with tricky winger Aaron Lennon that day. Villas-Boas said Harry had done well in his brief appearance and admitted the club were taking a 'softly-softly' approach with the boy's development.

He said there had been positive signs that the club were going in the right direction despite the disappointing defeat, going on to say, 'There were good positive signs that we came to Newcastle, a difficult ground to play and against a team that did so well last season and we showed that we are the better team. But they came out with the three points and we wanted to obviously avoid that but I have to praise my team for what they did.' Yet despite Villas-Boas's encouragement, it was decided that Harry would benefit more from another loan move, rather than appearing occasionally as a substitute. Regular appearances would help his game and his confidence. To my mind, that was the right thinking. And Harry had no qualms about exiting temporarily to another club. He had proved at Orient and Millwall that he was a player on the up and now would, it was hoped, develop at a higher level, this time in the Premier League itself at Norwich City. It did not work out quite like that as injury hit his chances. He returned to the Lane at the end of the year and then was sent out on another loan when 2013 began – this time heading to the King Power Stadium in Leicester. Once again, the loan did not really work out as he found himself down the pecking order for a starting role, along with, remarkably, Jamie Vardy. Both men would eventually break through with their clubs and go on to play for England. With the benefit of hindsight, it is extremely surprising that they both played at the same club for half a season in 2013 – and both struggled to get games, let alone become automatic starters.

As Sir Alex Ferguson would once comment, 'Football eh? Bloody hell!' It is one of the idiosyncrasies of the beautiful game that a player can be seen as a flop one season and then turn into an apparent world-beater the next. Both Harry and Jamie would prove they WERE good enough for the top once they got the chance to permanently impress rather than being stuck on the sidelines. At least Harry knew time was on his side and that Tottenham had a definite plan for him. They had told him they were sending him out on loan so he could gain experience and toughen up – and he is the first to admit that such a policy was forward looking and that he did indeed benefit from his spells at Orient and Millwall. OK, the loans at Norwich and Leicester were not as successful but being a determined boy he did his best to take positives from all four moves.

In Vardy's case, time was against him. He was a latecomer to the big time, joining Leicester at the age of twenty-five in 2012. For him, every match started on the bench was a worry as the clock was ticking on his chances to prove he COULD be a success away from minnows football. At the same time, he was ambitious and as blinkered as Kane in his belief he could deliver the goods when given the chance – and the Foxes had splashed £1 million on him to take him from Fleetwood Town FC. That might not sound much in these days of £89 million transfers, but it was the biggest ever fee for a non-league player, which meant Leicester had great faith in Vardy's ability to adapt and thrive.

Like Harry, Vardy is no 'big-time Charlie' who has no time for the fans. Both men appreciate the debt they owe to those on the terraces who pay their wages and that is why Harry and Jamie are fans' favourites at their respective clubs. They both give everything to the cause and make sure they sign autographs and spend time with their team's supporters when opportunities arise. You will never see Harry or Jamie deliberately avoiding signing autographs – in fact, both go out of their way to do so.

When Cliff Ginetta, chairman of Leicester City Supporters Club, talks with undisguised affection for Vardy, it could be Spurs fans talking about Harry. Here's what he says: 'He's working class and he's our hero. He's a throwback to the footballers of old who used to climb up the ladder to make it in the top league. He's one of us. He's not like the other prima donna footballers. Vardy plays through the pain barrier for the club, even if he's got two broken bones in his wrist.'

And the fact that Fleetwood Town FC almost went into a period of official mourning when Vardy was sold highlighted the loyalty and love the player had given and received – again very similar to Harry's relationship with Tottenham and the fans at the Lane. Fleetwood chairman Andy Pilley was almost in tears when he admitted that he had finally had to let Vardy go, at the same time applauding the player for his loyalty to the selling club. Pilley went on to say, 'We had £1 million bids in January and he had only been with us three months. But I desperately didn't want him to go because if he went we would lose a huge chance of promotion to the Football League. We managed to persuade him to stay for three more months… I was delighted because he could have spat his dummy out and been a pain to us after we didn't let him go in the January but he rolled his sleeves up and got the goals to get us promoted.'

Not only did Jamie's goals win Fleetwood promotion to the Football League, they also helped them lift the title. And his reward was to finally play in the League, but it would not be in the bottom tier with the Cod Army. His exploits had earned him a £1 million move to Leicester City and a stab at Championship-level football, with the prospect of the Premier League now just an enticing one division away.

Harry had had to go away from Spurs on loan to eventually come back and become the fans' hero at the Lane. Vardy had to go the long way round to Leicester, where he too would become the terrace idol. And Vardy's first words to the press and his new fans merely survived to emphasise how close to Harry he was in terms of outlook on football, and how he felt lucky to have the chance to achieve his dreams with a big club, saying, 'The standard of the players is going to be a lot better. But I've played in the FA Cup a few times this year and managed to do well against the league clubs and hopefully I can carry that on. Competition for places can only benefit you. If you know you've got that much competition then you're just going to have to work that extra bit harder so you can catch the gaffer's eye. If you're not playing with any confidence then you're not going to play well at all. You've always got to have that inner confidence and that comes with the goals.'

So when the pair joined up for England duty in 2016 they would look back with wry smiles at that time they were thrown together for half a season in 2013, when they were both struggling to get a game at Leicester and sitting on the subs' bench together. Harry learned the importance of patience and awaiting your chance to shine at Norwich and Leicester, but was bursting to show what he could do when he finally returned to Spurs in the summer of 2013, and was told by the management that his loan spells had come to an end.

He played his last loan game on Sunday, 12 May 2013, coming on as a sub for Leicester in their 3–1 Championship play-off defeat at Watford. It had ended in tears for Leicester who had failed in their bid to return to the Premier League and Harry was sad that he had been unable to fire them back to the top. Then again, he had never really been given the chance to do so. But for Harry Kane the journey to the summit of English football was now afoot. This time he would return to the Lane and be afforded opportunities to show how he had developed and that the club's long search for a striker of the highest class was over. They did not need to spend millions on another expensive import who might flop – for the answer to their goal problems was right under their very nose. The era of Kane, the home-grown hero of the Lane, was nearly upon us.

CHAPTER FIVE

SHERWOOD'S BOY

After his loan at Leicester ended, Harry returned to the Lane wondering what was next. He had done all Tottenham had asked of him in going away to gain experience and toughen up and was keen to finally be given his chance to break through at Spurs. Of course, he would have gone away for another loan if absolutely necessary but he wanted to stay – and stay for good. He need not have worried as he headed away for a summer holiday. The big clue to his future had been provided in February 2013 when Tottenham tied him down until the summer of 2017 with a new contract. Would they really have put down such a solid marker of their belief in him – with a four-year deal guarantee – if they did not see his future with them? Exactly.

However, Tim Sherwood, who would take over from André Villas-Boas as Spurs boss at the end of 2013, said it was not that simple. He later claimed that after the Leicester loan the club decided Harry needed to stay and prove himself – or be sold. He said, 'There was a crossroads with Harry where we told him, "No more loans – you get sold or you get into the team". Luckily, a few months later I got the manager's job and the rest is history.'

I am not certain that it was so black and white. Why would the club issue such an ultimatum on a lad who was only twenty? Why would they put him under so much pressure just months after they had given him a new four-year contract? Maybe Tim is keen to take full credit for Harry's rise – as his words 'luckily a few months later I got the manager's job' suggest. And there is no doubt that he SHOULD get major credit for promoting Harry and other youngsters after Villas-Boas seemed more inclined to go with established names. But I believe Harry would have made it anyway, whoever took over from Villas-Boas. Cream always rises to the top and any manager worth their salt would have noticed the unstoppable talent of the young striker knocking on the first team door.

Even Nigel Pearson, the Leicester manager who had only given Harry a sniff of a starting role during the loan, told reporters in December 2014 that the player had immense potential, and that only circumstances at the time prevented him from playing more, continuing, 'Harry came in at a difficult time for us and I think for him. We were in a terrible run then just as we are now. So it wasn't always easy for him, but he handled himself exceptionally well.

'Of course, he's a couple of years older now, with more experience – and as a very likeable and level-headed young man, as he was then, he's proved to be an outstanding talent. He's doing very well for himself and for his club at the moment. I'd like to think he'd look back on his time here as valuable, whether in terms of the appearances he made or of being able to deal with setbacks in football. In hindsight you learn as much from the difficult times as you do from the positive. Harry was very popular and the staff rated him highly.'

Villas-Boas had also undoubtedly been aware of the boy's potential but used him sparingly during his final six months at the club. Harry made just six appearances from August 2013 until the end of the year, scoring one goal. Was Villas-Boas's decision made for the interests of the player, by adopting a 'softly softly' approach, or was it a sign of his over-cautious nature and his doubts about propelling youngsters into the first team? Before his first game in command, in August 2012, the Portuguese had told the press he was impressed with Harry and that he could be a part of the first team squad straight away, adding that, 'Kane is a young striker who we believe in and who we trust for the future. We think he can be a part of our plans. I can give you an example. Last year we had two strikers in Chelsea [where he was previously manager] of great dimension. Tottenham had three strikers of great dimension, Adebayor, Defoe and Pavlyuchenko. Normally there is one that doesn't get enough time that he feels he should be credited with. That's not because you don't rotate enough, but because when you play a system with one striker, it is very difficult to get the third one to play enough. Normally, on my teams, I like to promote the third one as a young striker who is competing for that place a bit more aggressively.' Yet a year plus two months later he was contemplating sending Harry out on loan again – just two months after Sherwood had suggested his loan spells were over. In October, 2013, Tim said, 'At the moment what I've been speaking to Harry about is that we are studying the possibility of him going out on loan as well – but we are happy for him to try to compete for his place, and so is he.

'We have lots of options up front and he understands that, but he is happy to continue to push for his place. He has been given that opportunity because he has been excellent in training, so we believe a lot in his future. We can't have a loan situation that does not work for him, like the ones that we have had before. That's why we have been very cautious with his next step, and we have not been in a rush in that situation. Why haven't the loans worked before? Because he didn't play.'

It was extremely confusing for the player. On the one hand, he had been told there would be no more loans and that he was doing great at Spurs. On the other, the manager was contemplating sending him out on loan again. Harking back to Tim Sherwood's comments, it was fortunate for Harry that he DID take over as boss in December 2013, as Villas-Boas appeared to change his mind on his future every few months.

During that bleak spell under Villas-Boas, Harry made just two starts for Tottenham – against Aston Villa at the end of September, and Hull a month later. Two ninety-minute opportunities to prove he was the answer to the club's striker problems. Harry's first game under Villas-Boas was in the Europa League clash at Dinamo Tbilisi, coming on as a sub for Roberto Soldado as Spurs sauntered to a 5–0 win. Soldado had been brought in by Villas-Boas to lead the attack from Valencia a few days before the season started. And as he cost £26 million, he was clearly going to be one of the Portuguese's first names on the team sheet. Harry would face one hell of a battle to displace the Spaniard after he had cost so much money. This was his big problem; his huge hurdle as he tried to carve out a name for himself at Tottenham. How did he become a regular starter when Villas-Boas clearly favoured older, big-bucks buys? Villas-Boas was hardly likely to drop a man upon whom he had staked his reputation upon for a kid, was he? This explained the lack of opportunities as summer turned into autumn and autumn became winter.

It would be tough from the very start for Harry as Soldado scored the winning goal on his debut in the opening game of the season, albeit from a penalty, as Spurs beat Crystal Palace 1–0. Villas-Boas was almost purring with delight at the display from his man, telling a post-match press conference that he believed Soldado, twenty-eight, could score at least twenty goals in his debut season at the Lane, adding, 'Of course, I think so. His career speaks for itself. To see him so confidently step up and put it to the same side as against Espanyol [in a pre-season friendly] was important for us. It's good to see him creating some chances out there. Most of these players arrived at a later stage – particularly Paulinho and Soldado, who had only two or three weeks with us. We can only sit and develop towards the future. Bearing in mind that for all them the Premier League is a different proposition to the leagues that they have played in terms of intensity and passion for the game, I think they did extremely well.'

With his manager having such faith in Soldado, and such a personal reputation investment, Harry would clearly have to be patient and hope for the best. His first senior goal for the club finally arrived when they played Hull City at home in the League Cup (also known as the Carling Cup) fourth round on Wednesday, 30 October 2013. Harry started up front, partnering Jermain Defoe and the pair put in a display that augured well for a potential link-up. It was 1–1 after ninety minutes and Hull took the lead in the first period of extra time when Paul McShane nodded home. On 108 minutes Harry grabbed the vital equaliser, shooting precisely into the bottom of the net. That goal took the game to penalties, a showdown which Spurs would win 8–7 as Kane netted confidently with their fifth penalty.

He was celebrating at the end of a testing encounter, knowing he had done well but not enough to displace Soldado as the club's first choice number 9. Villas-Boas praised the fans for their raucous support but did not have any public words of commendation for Kane. It struck me at the time that he was probably not going to be the man who propelled Harry to the top of the tree. He was a manager who believed first and foremost in players who had already been there and got the price tag to prove it rather than one of the people who instinctively felt youth could be trusted to win the day. In that respect, he was like his former mentor José Mourinho rather than, say, Sir Alex Ferguson, or the man who would eventually become Tottenham chief, Mauricio Pochettino.

Kane would play just one more game for Villas-Boas, the 2–1 win over FC Sheriff in the Europa League a week later.

Coming on as a seventieth minute sub for Gylfi Sigurðson, he did not have enough time to stamp his influence on the game. Instead, the headlines would go to fellow striker Defoe, who entered the record books by scoring his twenty-third European goal for the club, one more than the great Martin Chivers. Defoe made history by slotting home a penalty after Érik Lamela was tripped in the box. Lamela himself had netted the opener for Spurs.

The win meant Tottenham had reached the knockout stage of the competition early. Of course, Harry was 'chuffed' that the team had got out of the group but he was wondering what Villas-Boas's plans for himself were. The manager had already mooted the idea of another loan but Harry wanted to stay and prove himself. That was not at all easy with only odd minutes here and there. He really needed something unexpected to break the deadlock; something that would convince Villas-Boas to give him a proper chance. He knew he had time on his side and he was a patient, measured guy. But he also was ambitious – and ambitious to make it with the club he loved.

Ten days before Christmas 2013, the catalyst that would propel him forward came out of the blue. On 15 December, Liverpool thrashed Spurs 5–0 at White Hart Lane. It was the club's biggest home loss in sixteen years. Tottenham did not have a single shot on goal and to rub it in Liverpool were without talisman and skipper Steven Gerrard. Add to that the 6–0 defeat at Manchester City the previous month and mutiny was in the air among fans. The boos rang out around White Hart Lane and Spurs found themselves seventh in the table, eight points behind Arsenal. Harry had played no part in the Liverpool debacle, and the fingers of blame were pointing specifically on the manager. To give him his due, Villas-Boas did not attempt to deflect the blame on to anyone but himself.

After the match he told *BBC Sport*, 'It's my responsibility because I put them in the shape and the formation and we hope we are able to put our challenge in the Premier League back on track. The reality is we are not that far off. This is a top-four squad but in our Premier League form we are not there. It's not the points tally that's the problem, it's the expression of the results. It's the second expressive scoreline that we've suffered in the season. All of us had high expectations for this season, we still have them. Again, I repeat we are not far off.'

It was his responsibility and he would pay the price a day later when Spurs sacked him. A brief club statement said, 'The club can announce that agreement has been reached with head coach André Villas-Boas for the termination of his services. The decision was by mutual consent and in the interests of all parties.' First he was sacked by Chelsea, now he was out at Tottenham. Two big jobs in London football; two big flops. The 'mutual consent' line was a camouflage; everyone in the game knew he had been dismissed after a series of poor results. His consolation was a fat pay cheque to leave the club – the game is one of the few industries in which failure is regularly richly rewarded with million-pound plus pay-offs.

For Harry, the consolation would not be in monetary terms, immediately at least, but in that he would now be managed by a man who truly believed in him. And a man who had no qualms about putting him in the side ahead of Villas-Boas's expensive fellow flop, Soldado, when the time was right. Just a week after Villas-Boas's departure Spurs confirmed that Sherwood would take charge of the first team, on a contract to the end of the 2014/15 season. Spurs chairman, Daniel Levy, said, 'We were extremely reluctant to make a change mid-season, but felt we had to do so in the club's best interests. We have a great squad and we owe them a Head Coach who will bring out the best in them and allow them to flourish and enjoy a strong, exciting finish to the season. We are in the fortunate position of having within our club a talented coach in Tim Sherwood. We believe Tim has both the knowledge and the drive to take the squad forward.'

Sherwood had made clear he wanted the job after he stepped in as interim boss and led Spurs to victory over Southampton. But he did not want a stopgap role. 'What would be ideal for me would be to have a chat with the chairman and see what's best for the football club moving forward,' he said. 'I need to know what they're thinking. I don't want this job for five minutes. It's a massive club with history and tradition. But whatever happens needs to be right for me, too.'

Never one to hold his tongue, Sherwood will always be forthright and opinionated. The feeling around Fleet Street was that he may well have been viewed as a stopgap, with an eighteen-month deal to sweeten him if he was sacked, or just in case he did turn things around dramatically. The big question surrounded whether he could step up to the plate with big-name stars after working with academy kids. It would be a different world completely, with rampant egos galore and much more challenging briefs and players.

Harry was pleased Tim had got the job – finally, it appeared he might be given a chance to show his worth with a manager who knew all about him and believed that if you were good enough you were old enough, however young you might be. Yet it would be the first week in April, 2014, before Sherwood gave Harry his big breakthrough – three months, surprisingly. In the interim, he stuck with Soldado and Emmanuel Adebayor, with Harry coming on as a sub regularly. It was as though Sherwood had lost his nerve, but let's not forget he was effectively still 'auditioning' for the job and felt that the more experienced players could guide him through the minefield, at least until the end of the season.

But by the first week of April he decided to throw caution to the wind and to trust his instincts with kids like Harry. And after he was relieved of his duties at the end of the 2013/14 season it was revealed by chairman Levy that there WAS a break clause in the eighteen-month deal, so he had little to lose. It is understood that his forthrightness did not go down well with the chairman – and that criticisms of the board over his handling of his situation and fans' unhappiness at certain results all contributed to his dismissal. Levy explained in a club statement, 'We appointed Tim mid-season as someone who knew both the players and the club. We agreed an eighteen-month contract with a break clause at the end of the season and we have now exercised that option. Since appointing Tim as assistant first team coach in 2008 and then as technical co-ordinator in 2010 and head of football development in 2012, we have been supportive of him during football management changes throughout that period.'

It was a blow to Harry. Sherwood had eventually promoted

him to the role of first-team regular from April and his position would now be decided by another manager, who might or might not appreciate his worth. Certainly he had worked hard to stay in the team once Sherwood had promoted him at the start of April, 2014. His first Premier League start came at White Hart Lane with Sunderland the visitors on 7 April. The match ended 5–1 in Tottenham's favour and Kane played his part by scoring on the hour. It would be the first of many Premier League goals for him and came after the break. Harry did not allow pre-match speculation on Sherwood's future at the club to distract him, slotting the ball home just before the hour mark. A few minutes later Harry showed the bravery that would become part of his game by colliding with an opponent for a 50/50 ball. He had to leave the pitch to have a bandage round his head but returned soon after. Nothing was going to interfere with his debut start in the league after he had waited so long, and so patiently, for it. A goal, a sore head and a 5–1 win to boot: not at all bad for the debutant boy who had justified Sherwood's decision to go with him up front.

After the match Harry celebrated with his girlfriend and family and Sherwood told him he had 'done good' and that he would be in contention to start the next match. In April 2016, Tim would elaborate on Harry's progress at the time – and explain why he had decided he could hold him back no longer. He told the *Express*, 'He was just ready. There was nothing I wanted more than for Roberto Soldado to succeed. But every day in training Harry was outscoring him. Then before the Sunderland game, I casually mentioned to him that he would be starting as we walked off the training pitch at the end of Friday's session. I think he said something like, "Yeah, about time!" That told me he was ready.'

Sherwood knew Harry could survive in the big-time but admits the player still had to convince some fans during the Sunderland game that he was good enough to play in the Premier League, explaining, 'This is how strong the kid is. When Harry did not score in the first twenty-five minutes or so, they were singing Soldado's name for him to come on the pitch. It wasn't, "He's one of our own" back then. We were 1–0 down and he had to win them over. Some kids might have gone under, but I knew he was strong enough. In fact, it was perfect for him, because I knew he could handle it... he's a tough cookie.'

Kane kept his place for the next match, the Premier League away clash at West Brom and hit the back of the net for the second game in a row. It ended 3–3 but the real story was that Harry helped Spurs grab a point after they were 3–0 down. He grabbed their second goal, heading home from an Aaron Lennon cross and Christian Eriksen hit the third. Twice Harry had gone close before grabbing his goal. Tottenham were playing great in attack under Sherwood – and his decision to start Harry was clearly being vindicated – but their defending under him bordered on the farcical. He admitted as much after the match, saying, 'It was crazy. We might as well put 1–0 up on the scoreboard before we start. At 3–0, I thought we were going to win the game. We totally dominated. They never had a shot on goal in the second half. Hugo Lloris was getting frostbite out there. I thought our supporters got us back in the game. They never left us, they are knowledgeable and knew we were battering West Brom. Expectations to be challenging for Champions League are too great. I am proud to be the manager of this great football club and long may it continue.' Sherwood was whistling in the wind – the team were not performing as a unit and his public utterances hardly endeared him to the board.

But he was doing some good – and long-term at that – for Tottenham by persevering with Kane. Harry was benefitting from his faith as the regular outings boosted his confidence and belief. Could he score for the third Premier League game in a row? He could. After starting for the third successive match, this time at home to local rivals Fulham, he once again headed home a Lennon cross, on forty-eight minutes. Harry was replaced by Soldado on seventy-nine minutes but he had made his point – three goals in three games was irrefutable proof that he could cut it. He was 'buzzing' after the game and it was only a pity that Sherwood could not have publicly applauded him. But the Spurs boss had enough on his plate coping with discontent from the dressing room and the fans over his comments about certain senior players and their talent.

It was left to the Spurs fans to take to the message boards to salute their new hero, Harry Kane. One said, 'Harry's on three in a row. I hope Soldado's watching.' Another added, 'Harry Kane at twenty is quality.' While another said, 'Harry Kane's emergence shows that Sherwood is on the right track. The boy is a natural goalscorer – but Villas-Boas never gave him a proper chance. Kane is the future and the now.'

Harry would start the final three league games of Tottenham's season – and the final three with Sherwood in command –

but would not find the net again that campaign. Two weeks after the season had ended the club announced their new head coach would be Mauricio Pochettino, the Argentine who was in charge at Southampton. He was renowned as a coach who loved attacking football and who liked to give youth a chance. Spurs chairman Levy was certainly of the opinion that the long search for a man who could take the club forward 'in the right way' had finally come to an end. He said, 'In Mauricio I believe we have a head coach who, with his high energy, attacking football, will embrace the style of play we associate with our club. He has a proven ability to develop each player as an individual, whilst building great team spirit and a winning mentality. We have a talented squad that Mauricio is excited to be coaching next season.'

Pochettino said he was excited because there were talented players at the club, saying, 'This is a club with tremendous history and prestige and I am honoured to have been given this opportunity to be its head coach. There is an abundance of top-class talent at the club and I am looking forward to starting work with the squad. Tottenham Hotspur has a huge following across the world and I have great admiration for the passion the fans show for this team. We are determined to give the supporters the kind of attacking football and success that we are all looking to achieve.'

He added that he believed in starting with a clean slate so that everyone got a fair chance to impress but that he would also have no hesitation in bringing on young players. If they were good enough, they were old enough and he had showed at Southampton that he believed in youth.

It all sounded good but what would be the reality for Harry Kane? Would Pochettino continue to start him and trust in him – or would he want to assess whether Soldado and Adebayor deserved the nod? Would Harry be the Argentine's third choice striker or had he done enough under Sherwood to show his true worth to the new boss? He, and we, were about to find out.

CHAPTER SIX

HURRICANE FORCE

With the arrival of a new boss, Harry Kane came to pre-season training keen to impress Mauricio Pochettino, but anxious about whether the Argentine would give him a chance – or whether he would play safe and go for Soldado and Adebayor at his expense. Harry had the feeling he was making a breakthrough when Sherwood took over during the previous campaign, but now wondered if he would be back to square one – virtually out of the picture – or square two, a back-up option to the two senior strikers. It was a worry; I was told by reliable sources that Harry had doubts, but that, being positive, he believed he WOULD convince Pochettino to play him. And, he had told friends, there was also the fact that the new boss was renowned for giving young players a chance – as he had done at Southampton, the club he had just left.

So it wasn't all gloom but it wasn't all joy either... more

a belief within Harry that his chance would come if he kept his head down and did what he always did, whatever his situation, that is: train hard, work hard and keep your body and mind in tip-top shape so that you were ready if and when the opportunity arose to start in the first team. Pochettino had made it clear when he arrived for the new season that, as far as he was concerned, everyone started with the slate wiped clean. Everyone would be given their chance to shine, no matter how well or badly they had fared under Villas-Boas and Sherwood. Of course, every manager will come into a new club with that rather weary claim – but few keep to it for more than a couple of weeks.

Yet Pochettino was the exception to the rule. He DID give players who might have been expected to be out on their backsides a fair crack of the whip. For Harry, that meant an early spell of frustration. He had broken through under Sherwood and become a starter but now he would be back on the bench, coming on as a sub for Adebayor or Soldado as the new boss checked out the form and talent of the older pros. The first league match of the season was on Saturday, 16 August 2014, but it was not until Sunday, 9 November, almost three months, that Kane made his first Premier League start under Pochettino. Sure, he came off the bench on numerous occasions and did start in Europa League ties – but he had done that under Villas-Boas. It seemed unfair that the boy was back in the shadows as far as the big league was concerned but Pochettino would later admit that he HAD been keeping a close eye on his young striker's progress and that he HAD been planning to throw him in as a starter when he believed the time was right.

Statistically, it is easy to see why the boss had been contemplating just how long he could hold back his young charge. Harry had come on as a sub six times in the league and started six games in the Europa League and one in the Carling Cup before his 9 November league start. Yet in those fourteen games, he had managed to score a remarkable TEN goals. That was deadly marksmanship and was putting an intolerable pressure on Soldado and Adebayor to deliver at a similar strike pace – which they simply could not match. So it was little wonder that, after three months of due diligence, Pochettino decided that he could no longer keep Harry on the bench, or keep as an option for less important matches. He had given both of his senior match players a good chance to prove themselves but the old-timers had been spectacularly upstaged by the young kid on the block.

The era of Harry Kane, one of Tottenham's own, was imminent and it was well deserved after the efforts Harry had put in and the patience he had shown in the background. It had, of course, also been his love of the club that had kept him determined to be a success. He had had four loan spells but now wanted to make it back at White Hart Lane. The apprenticeship was over: it was time to unleash him on top defences in the Premier League. Harry Kane was ready for the big time and he would not blow his chance in this ground-making and groundbreaking season: no, he would grab it with both hands as his feet did the talking with goals galore.

Tottenham had been searching high and low and for an eternity to find the man who could grab them goals on a regular basis, and the answer had been right there before them on their very own doorstep. It was their good fortune, and good management of young players like Harry in their academy by Sherwood and his team, that had ended up with such a result. Harry Kane was made in Tottenham and made by Tottenham: he literally was one of their own and the club would benefit as he became a prolific marksman when set free.

Those fourteen games at the start of that season under Pochettino had been the final examination, with Kane passing with honours. No one could doubt his ability after he hit those ten goals in such a short spell, especially as he had often needed to make an immediate impact, given the number of sub appearances. There had not been time to settle into the game or get the feel of it; such luxuries are often denied the sub who comes on late in a match. Harry had to hit the ground running and make an impact or face being left on the bench, or being dropped from the squad. It was a testing challenge and very much to his credit that he managed it so well and showed the new boss what he was capable of in limited time frames. He had passed every test the club had posed him, from loans to sub appearances to fighting against older pros for a spot, and had failed none. It was only fair that he now lifted the prize – being a regular starter for the club he loved and the fans who lifted and backed him in every game he played.

The tests at the start of the 2014/15 season had begun with those appearances as a sub and in the Europa League. By the end of August, Kane had two goals to his credit, both in Europe and both against the same outfit – AEL Limassol of Cyprus. Harry scored in the 2–1 away win and the 3–0 home victory. By the end of the following month he had also netted in the Capital One Cup (otherwise known as the League Cup) as Spurs beat Nottingham Forest 3–1 at the Lane. A week after that he had scored again, this time back in Europe in the 1–1 home draw with Beşiktaş of Turkey.

But his crowning glory in this tricky spell of the season came at the end of October 2014, as Harry netted a hat-trick as the hapless Greek outfit Asteras were thrashed 5–1 in north London. Harry had started the match up front alongside Adebayor but finished it alone after the big Togolese striker was withdrawn. It was his first professional hat-trick and a major plus as he battled to earn a regular first team role. As if that triple-goal show wasn't enough of a memory to take from the game, Harry also had to play in goal at the end of it after number 1 Hugo Lloris was sent off. Harry then suffered the ignominy of letting in a goal, from the first shot with which he was challenged. It was some game and some contrast of fortunes – from hat-trick hero to goalkeeping zero!

He scored with two shots and a header but allowed a free kick to slip underneath him and into the goal when he took over from the Frenchman in goal. After the final whistle Harry walked off with the match ball for his hat-trick exploits – and the goalkeeping gloves for his not-so wonderful exploits between the sticks. 'What a crazy night that was,' Harry said as he headed down to the dressing room. And he couldn't help but smile and shake his head as he told reporters, 'It was a great result for us, a great win, and obviously I'm happy to get the hat-trick. I thought it was good to get the second and third, extra goals when the team are dead on their feet and when we want to start killing off teams. It was a great night until I went in goal. In fairness I think I'll leave that to the keepers from now on!'

He then elaborated upon his first pro hat-trick and how he hoped performances like this would earn him more run-outs for Tottenham and, hopefully, England. Kane told reporters, 'It was great to get my first professional hat-trick and for Spurs as well. As regards to stepping in goal it was one to forget with letting in that goal but it was a fun night. I got the goal early on and felt there were more goals there. Every striker has to get themselves in the right place at the right time and I was able to do that today with the rebound and the header from Federico Fazio's cross. My aim is to get into the senior England squad but I've got to just keep concentrating on my club football and do well every time I get the chance. Andros Townsend got his chance, was playing well and got his reward. It's great to see him get that trust and hopefully if I keep doing what I'm doing that might happen in the future. Under-21 international football is important and we've done well and are looking forward to next year's championships. As a striker you want to get your goals on any stage.

'I fancied myself in goal. I think I'm all right in goal but obviously not. Hugo obviously makes it look easier than it is. I don't think anyone else wanted to go in but I think someone will have to step up next time. I was hoping the free kick would hit the wall and I probably should have kicked it away. I felt bad for the defenders who played well all night and Hugo, who was brilliant, but it happened and it's something I'll have to live with for the rest of my life. I got hold of the match ball at the end – safe hands on that one!'

Pochettino was surprisingly downbeat at his post-match press conference, bemoaning the fact that Lloris had suffered a red card. He said, 'I'm happy for the result, 5–1. I'm disappointed with the last five minutes. We need to manage the game better. It was unlucky because it was a red card but I am not happy. Our defensive line was very high and we gave them the opportunity to play in behind. We were not ready and focused. We gave them the opportunity to play one-on-one with our keeper.'

But behind the scenes, I was told, it was a different story, especially over his evaluation of Kane's performance and potential. He was not in the least concerned about the goalkeeping value of his youngster; he was simply delighted that the boy had hit a hat-trick that had propelled the team to the top of their group, and that it confirmed that he had a boy of massive potential on the books. One who might well give Adebayor and Soldado a run for their money.

Spurs' army of loyal fans were certainly coming around to that way of thinking. They liked Soldado, Adebayor not so much, but Kane was making a strong case for recognition – and increased playing time. As one fan said, 'Kane's got to be given a chance in the league. Adebayor and Soldado have managed three goals between them in all competitions this season, and those have come against QPR, Forest and AEL Limassol. He may not be able to hold the ball up like Adebayor does, but his runs and his general link-up play would more than make up for that in my view.' While another argued, 'He has got to start some games now. He is more versatile than Adebayor in overall forward play and more clinical than Soldado in putting chances away.' And a third added, 'Agreed on Kane. Obviously the line-up last night suggests Soldado will start, but I wonder whether those goals will provide a change of thought. Could, and probably should, go two up against Newcastle anyway, we ran the two games against them last season, created a load of chances and somehow ended up losing that home game. If Sherwood has a legacy, beyond Kane and Bentaleb, it's that there are some games where you don't need to flood the midfield.'

The clamour was growing and it surely couldn't be long now before Harry was promoted from bench duty to a regular starting role, could it? It wouldn't be – just over two weeks, to be exact. Time was fast running out for Adebayor and Soldado.

Yet after scoring that hat-trick, Kane was relegated back to the bench for the next game – inevitably a Premier League match – against Newcastle at home. Adebayor started and Soldado was on the bench, although the one replaced the other seven minutes from time. Harry came on approaching the seventy-minute mark, taking over from Capoue. Adebayor had put Spurs ahead, but by the time Kane arrived on the scene, they were 2–1 down. Afterwards boss Pochettino admitted that his team had not been strong enough mentally, that they lacked the resolve to finish the job after going ahead.

He said, 'We need to improve a lot. It's not tactical or physical it's our mentality. It's a big hit for us. We need to be stronger and to have more focus. Today in the second half, straight from the kick-off we conceded a goal. It's crazy. Seven or six seconds before they scored all was happiness and there was good energy in the stadium. Our supporters were happy and believed that we would get a good result. But in this moment, I think it was difficult to manage in our head. Our heads had gone and we started to take rash decisions on the pitch. It was difficult because twelve or fourteen minutes later, we conceded another goal. At 2–1, it was difficult.'

Pochettino was clearly examining all aspects of the team and coming to conclusions about the players he had inherited. This was particularly so in attack, as he was a coach who loved his teams to go forward and entertain. He had promoted young players at Southampton and they had not let him down – and so what if he now did the same at Tottenham? Surely, the outcome would be similar? The Argentine was now giving serious consideration as to whether Harry Kane should be starting up front. He had seen the boy had pace, enthusiasm and, most important of all, a knack of being in the right place at the right time. He had fire in his belly and would give everything to send the fans home happy. He was Tottenham through and through whereas Adebayor and Soldado did not have the same allegiance, the same bond with the fans and the same link with the badge.

Kane was raring to go; Pochettino had seen that in training, he had seen it in the boy's displays from the bench and when he had started – and delivered so emphatically – in Europe. Now Harry would face the final audition. Pochettino started him in the next match, a Carling Cup clash at the Lane against Brighton. And he scored. Then he dropped him to the bench for the game after that, the Premier League visit to Aston Villa, and he scored when he came on for Adebayor after fifty-eight minutes. Finally, he brought him back into the team for the return against Asteras in Greece. Needless to say, Kane scored again.

Those three matches coming straight after the disappointing home loss to Newcastle convinced Pochettino that the time for dithering was over. The time for relying on the tested but not-so-trusted alternatives was over. The time for him to give Harry Kane his head was beginning. Sunday, 9 November 2014 would mark the true start of Kane's glittering career at White Hart Lane: no longer would he be a sub or a smaller tournament stand-in. From now on, he would be the first name on the team sheet. He was the future, the rock around which Pochettino would now build a team to compete for the league title and, ultimately he planned, the Champions League.

Plus the fans were growing mutinous over Pochettino's continued reliance on Adebayor. The *Daily Mail*'s Neil Ashton summed up the unrest on the terraces after the Togo international's efforts at Aston Villa, when Kane came on to replace him, scored and gave Spurs new hope: 'At White Hart Lane on Sunday, Mauricio Pochettino has to make the biggest decision of his short career as head coach of Tottenham: Emmanuel Adebayor cannot play. The striker's lack of commitment at Villa Park last Sunday, when he was dragged off after 58 minutes, was not just an affront to his team-mates, it was an insult to the sport itself. For Pochettino to make his mark at Spurs, to show the players that he really is the boss, Adebayor cannot be in that team to face Stoke City. It would be a brave man to argue that it was anything other than the presence of Kane, sprinting everywhere and hustling Villa defenders, that brought Spurs back into this game.'

It was a viewpoint echoed around Fleet Street as well as among many Tottenham fans. Kane had to replace Adebayor; one would die for the club, the other sometimes did not appear even to be bothered enough to run up a sweat for the badge.

Pochettino didn't need the Press or the fans to convince him what needed doing; he could see it with his own eyes. And here was a manager who was far from in thrall to the achievements a player may have notched up previously. He was only interested in the now, and Kane was clearly the now and the future. Adebayor was the past and it was a long time since he had been at the very top of his game. From that lazy display at Villa Park onwards, he was on his way out of Tottenham. Pochettino wanted to create a hunger and a desire to win and be the best, and to that end he believed youth was the best policy.

So it was that on 9 November, Harry stepped up from the shadows for the final time and finally set up creating his own legend as a Tottenham player. He started the game and would now start every big game when he was fit. This was the beginning of his fast track curve to being a Spurs AND England regular. He would be the first name on Pochettino's team sheet every week and one of the first on the national team's too.

But his new life would not get off to a blinder as Spurs crashed at home in Harry's first game as a starter, with a 2–1 home defeat against Stoke, a game both he and Pochettino expected to win. Soldado was banished to the bench and Adebayor did not even make the bench. Harry had a header saved but could not save his team, who struggled to find their rhythm against a side of battlers. Spurs also had Kyle Naughton sent off late on to compound their misery. Pochettino had told Harry prior to the game that he was now giving him a run in the team and that, if he produced the goods, he would stay there. Harry played OK, running and competing and causing the Stoke backline jitters with his power but it was to be one of those afternoons as Spurs slumped to a third defeat in their last four league matches. It had not been the coronation Harry would have hoped for, but it made him even more determined to score the goals that would lift the club out of the doldrums and, hopefully, into the top four.

After that loss they were twelfth in the table – this was not the script anyone at the Lane had signed up for with the arrival of a bright young manager. But although there was a sense of disappointment around the place, there was no panic or despondency. As Pochettino said afterwards, 'There is no pressure. We need to improve a lot and improve quickly. When we conceded we started to make rash decisions and felt uncomfortable on the pitch. We made some mistakes and we need to change mentally.'

There he was again with that word 'mentally'. The boss had mentioned previously that he wanted his players to toughen up mentally and now he was telling them they HAD to – or else. Harry told pals that things would improve and that, given the service he needed which was generally missing against Stoke, he WOULD score the goals that would propel them up the table. It was just a case of the team gelling with some new components and understanding exactly what the new manager wanted and how they should achieve it. No, it was far from doom and gloom that November – if anything, the Stoke defeat only served to make the players even more determined to turn things around and show that they were worthy of the shirt.

Harry was as good as his word, scoring in the very next game, the Premier League outing at Hull City. Partnering Soldado up front, Kane inspired Tottenham to a 2–1 victory. And this was a match that suggested the team had toughened up mentally, as they came from behind to win. Ex-Spurs player Jake Livermore put the Tigers ahead but Kane's tenth goal of the season levelled it and Christian Eriksen's late goal snatched victory. Harry had rifled home a rebound after an Eriksen free kick hit the post. He showed in that moment that his concentration was spot on as he seized the opportunity as Hull's defence dithered.

It would be the start of a three-match unbeaten run which justified Pochettino's faith in Kane as his main man. Ironically, in the next game – a Europa League tie against Partizan Belgrade – Harry now found himself back on the bench with Soldado starting. It was the completion of a reversal of fortunes: Harry had previously started in Europe as it was deemed a secondary tournament while Roberto and Adebayor traditionally sat out the games. Now the wheel had turned full circle with Harry viewed as the number one striker and Soldado getting the nod for the European games.

No matter. Tottenham won 1–0 and approached their

Premier League home encounter with Everton in much better spirits. That ended with another win, this time 2–1, and everything was suddenly looking much brighter at the club.

But Harry and Co. were brought right back down to earth as they crashed 3–0 at Stamford Bridge in the Premier League clash at the start of December. And to make matters worse, Harry wasted a couple of good chances in the first half – hitting the bar with one shot and sending the ball wide of the post with another. The loss put Spurs back down to tenth in the table but, to their credit, they never stopped battling and at the end of play the scoreline certainly flattered Chelsea. Pochettino admitted as much when speaking to reporters, saying, 'We're very disappointed because we created some chances to score and after we conceded in Chelsea's first action, the game changed. After two or three minutes we made a mistake and they scored again. But I want to congratulate my players because they were brave in the second half. Today you could see that we have a very young squad who need games.' He wasn't just making excuses – the squad was young and they were basically outmuscled and outfoxed by the likes of old-timers like Didier Drogba and Nemanja Matic.

Spurs fans weren't stupid: they liked it that Pochettino was going to rely on youth and keep faith with Harry Kane, Érik Lamela and Ryan Mason. A mix of home-grown talent and the cream from abroad – and Pochettino had made it clear he planned to promote more kids and bring in the best youngsters around. The possession stats showed just how well and composed the team had been even though, on paper, they had taken something of a lashing. Spurs bossed it 60 per cent to 40 per cent – against Chelsea who were six points clear at the top, and at Stamford Bridge, too.

So there was much to be optimistic about and from now on the team – and Harry – could only get better. And they would. They now went on an eight-match unbeaten run and Harry scored six goals in those eight games, justifying his place in the team. That successful run began with no fireworks. In fact, it was something of a grind as Spurs spluttered to a 0–0 draw at home by Crystal Palace. But they then accelerated to four consecutive wins after that, with Harry netting in each of those games.

But the result that really catapulted Harry into the headlines came in the first game of the new year of 2015. On New Year's Day, he grabbed a brilliant brace and won a penalty as Tottenham gained such sweet revenge against the Chelsea team, who had thrashed them 3–0 less than a month earlier. The 5–3 triumph at the Lane got the new year off to a sensational start for Kane and his teammates as they proved they were now hitting form and, on their day, were a match for anyone – including the team who would go on to lift the Premier League crown that season.

Harry's goals came with a piledriver and a rather more simple tap-in and he won the penalty which Andros Townsend converted after bamboozling Gary Cahill and forcing the defender to concede the spot kick with a blatant foul. Harry's double meant he had scored seventeen goals in all competitions so far in the campaign – a feat bettered only by Man City's Sergio Agüero, who had scored nineteen. But let's not forget Kane did not start for his club until November and had to pick at crumbs as a sub for nearly three months, while Aguero was the first name on the City team sheet. It was some achievement for the lad who had to prove himself at Tottenham and who was in his first full season in the Premier League. Already, he was snapping at the heels of Agüero and showing he could score goals at this level and handle the pressure and physicality of the Premier League. All the loan moves and sweating it out as a reserve had finally paid off. Kane was fast becoming a permanent fixture in the team and in the hearts of the Spurs fans, who now sang of him as 'one of their own'. And he was still only twenty-one – Tottenham had certainly hit gold on their own doorstep after years of trying to find a striker who could live up to past legends.

Kane paid tribute to those very same supporters after the Chelsea game, saying, 'The fans were brilliant. They'll be buzzing going into the new year after beating one of their London rivals, who we have struggled against in recent years. I am delighted for the fans and delighted for the club as well. Hopefully we will take this into the games ahead.' He also admitted that his first goal, the strike from twenty-five yards out, was his 'best so far'.

He then added to *Spurs TV*, 'I am delighted to score against one of the best teams in the world. To get us back in the game and win the way we did is obviously a great night for us. We stayed in the game after they scored and whenever I get the ball on the edge of the box I always look to shoot. Thankfully it went in and then we really pushed on, built a bit of momentum. We finished the game and obviously got five goals against a really good defence.'

The good times were starting to roll. Harry grabbed another

brace at the end of January, 2015, as Spurs won 3–0 at West Brom and followed it in the next match with yet another double – one that would earn him a place in the fans' hearts for ever. Yes, against bitter local rivals Arsenal – and his goals won the match, too, as Tottenham held on for a 2–1 victory. You couldn't have scripted it any better – the local boy scoring the winner in the match that all Tottenham fans ached most to win, and in his first ever derby against Arsenal. The boy Kane had made their dream come true and was hailed by Spurs fans around the globe that night after Spurs had come from behind to beat the Gunners. The victory pushed them up to fifth in the Premier League table and they were now only just behind Man United for that all-important fourth spot – the final Champions League spot – on goal difference. Kane's goals were typical of his predator instinct as he sneaked in to stab the first one home from a corner and was on hand to head home the winner late on.

After the game Pochettino told reporters, 'Harry showed today that he is a great player, with a great performance, but my idea is that he can improve still and we need to push him to develop his potential because his potential is massive, but it was a fantastic performance today.'

While Kane himself told *BBC Sport*: 'It's my first north London derby and it was incredible. I watched so many as a kid and the feeling now is one I can't describe and won't forget. I'm happy for the team and the club. It is a special day. I am working on all aspects of my game and when I get in those areas I am confident. I am enjoying my football at the moment and playing with a smile on my face.'

The smile widened when it was announced he had been named Premier League player of the month for the second successive month – only the fourth player to achieve the feat. Collecting the award, he told the Press, 'I'm very happy, very pleased. It's an honour. To win this award once, let alone twice in two months is special. Against Arsenal, winning 2–1, and getting both the goals was a special day for myself, for my career and for the club itself.'

Such was his ambition, he added he hoped to become the first to win it three times on the trot. 'To make history would be something very special. Obviously I've scored a couple so far this month. Still a few more games to go, so hopefully I'll get a few more goals and we'll see what happens, but I'm looking forward to the games ahead. Everything has happened quite fast but I have always said I had belief in myself. It was just waiting to get the chance and being patient and being ready to take it. I've been able to do that. I have loved every minute of playing and have loved my football so much at the moment, playing with my mates, in a great team and a great squad. I am looking forward to the rest of the games.'

There were further good tidings that February when Harry's rapid progress was rewarded with a new deal by the Tottenham hierarchy. At twenty-one years old, he signed up for the Spurs project for another five-and-a-half years, committing himself to the club until 2020. There was no confirmation but sources said the contract was worth £60,000 a week. He followed it up by tweeting, 'Very happy to have signed my new contract at Spurs! Excited for the future ahead!'

But winning the Player of the Month award for a third

successive month would not happen and Harry's smile would disappear temporarily over the next month as he and Spurs now embarked on a five-game run which would see them fail to win and, more distressingly, see them lose a cup final at Wembley, a moment Harry would admit was 'his lowest in his career so far'. It was of little consolation that he would still hit two goals in that barren results spell – in the match following the win over Arsenal, a 3–2 loss at Liverpool, and a 2–2 home draw versus West Ham United. The team would also exit the Europa League in disappointing style after drawing 1–1 at home to Fiorentina and crashing 2–0 in the return leg in Italy.

But the biggest let-down was defeat at Wembley in the Capital One Cup final against London rivals Chelsea, on 1 March 2015. Goals from John Terry and Didier Drogba saw Chelsea to a 2–0 win with Harry unable to get on the scoresheet. Spurs looked weary after their exertions in the Europa League in Italy a few days earlier and could not pick up their usual pressing game to any effect. Harry was distraught after the game and said, 'I am gutted for the players, for my teammates, for the staff, for the club itself. It's the worst feeling in the world – losing, and losing in a final on the big stage is even worse. I'm always disappointed when I don't score. But it's tough, Chelsea are a good side, they've got one of the best defences in the league.

'When you see them lifting that trophy it makes the fire in your belly burn that you want to be back and you want to be lifting that trophy and that's what we've got to do with the squad we have. I think everyone's proud of themselves. We gave it our all. We played the way we wanted to play and it just didn't go for us. Both their goals you could say were a bit scrappy, a bit lucky, but that's the difference in the top games on the big stage and it went Chelsea's way. We've got to dust ourselves off and move on as quickly as possible.'

Spurs were also now out of Europe and the FA Cup so they only had the league to focus on, which meant the bid for a Champions League spot was all the more vital. Harry added, 'That is the aim. We've got a lot of games to go now. The Premier League is the only competition we're in so we've got to get back to winning ways as quickly as possible and see where it takes us in the league.'

It was good positive thinking from a young man who had already shown he had his feet on the ground and did not have his head in the clouds, either. But even the aim of finishing fourth in the Premier League at the end of the 2014–15 season would prove just beyond Tottenham. In the final match of the campaign, they would win 1–0 at Everton – a result that left them in fifth place, one outside the qualification zone. It did guarantee them an automatic spot in the group stages of the Europa League but it was something of an anticlimax after they had great hopes of the top and a cup win at one stage of the season.

Yet Harry ended the season with that winning goal at Everton and it had been a quite remarkable rise after he had started it as third-choice striker at Tottenham. It was his thirty-first goal of an incredible season – one which had seen him not even become first-choice striker until November 2014, almost three months into the campaign. That he would still hit so many goals is almost beyond belief, especially at such a tender age, and it meant he equalled a Premier League club record. The truth of it all was simply that Kane was a natural-born goalscorer.

He showed that by putting the disappointment of the Capital One Cup final loss behind him as he hit his first Premier League hat-trick in a 4–3 victory over Leicester City within three weeks of the Wembley let-down. He left the pitch with the match ball tucked under his arm and beaming like the Cheshire Cat as he lapped up the adulation of the home fans, who had finally found a home-grown hero to idolise. The hat-trick also served as celebration for the fact that he had been called up for the England squad before the match. He was also the first Spurs player to hit a league hat-trick since Gareth Bale in 2012 – and we all know what would happen to the Welshman's career after that. Signing for Real Madrid, Bale became one of the world's top three players along with Ronaldo and Messi.

Harry admitted he would love to be lumped in with that elite level of company and was doing all he could to achieve it. Time was on his side and Pochettino was delighted with the progress his boy was making in this first proper season of action. After the hat-trick, the Argentine said, 'His hat-trick was great. I am happy for him and the team. Now to look forward and keep going. We need to improve because we conceded three goals.'

While Harry told *Standard Sport*, 'I'm absolutely delighted and to get the three points as well is the most important thing and it caps a good day all round. It's been a special week and one I definitely won't forget and hopefully if I keep working hard and keep progressing I'm sure I'll have many more weeks like this.'

No one at White Hart Lane doubted that would be the case. Harry Kane was a special talent who had been found on the doorstep. Tottenham had nurtured him and brought him on gently and then given him his big chance in this special season. Now they would benefit immensely as Kane repeated his fantastic form – and even lifted the prestigious Premier League golden boot the next season. He had certainly earned a damned good summer break in 2015 and would come back even more determined to leave his mark after it. The good times were ready to roll for Kane and Spurs. And for Kane and England, too...

CHAPTER SEVEN

ENGLAND CALLING

When he was sixteen, Harry got the first call to help his country – and he was delighted to oblige. In January 2010, he was called up to play for England's Under-17s in the Algarve Tournament in Portugal. He was the only new name in boss John Peacock's squad and was 'honoured' and 'privileged' to be chosen. England faced a tough test if they were to triumph – they would have to negotiate their way past France, Ukraine and the hosts over four days. But there was no doubt this was a talented bunch – the squad minus Harry had been working together brilliantly since the previous season's successful Victory Shield campaign.

The strength of the squad could be gauged by simply casting one's eyes over some of the names within – names who would go on to become Premier League and full England team stars. Players like Everton's Ross Barkley and Stoke's Jack Butland (at the time playing with Birmingham) and Will Keane of Hull City (then with Manchester United). There were other players who had great potential – including West Brom's Saido Berahino, Everton's Luke Garbutt, Liverpool's Andre Wisdom and Arsenal duo Chuks Aneke and Benik Afobe. Harry knew he was going to work with players who had star quality but, as always, was confident of his own ability and felt sure he would fit in well.

Harry would later admit being picked for this tournament was one of the five pinnacles of his whole career, saying, 'This was the first time I pulled on the England shirt. Playing for your country is a magical moment and for me it was the start of everything I dreamed of achieving as a senior player.'

It was also a successful competition, with Harry heading home with a winner's medal after England triumphed in Portugal. A 0–0 draw with hosts Portugal in the Algarve's Parque Desportivo da Nora in Ferreiras meant they were champions.

And even the locals enjoyed the footballing fare served up by the young English players including Harry. The local Portugal Resident website, *portugalresident.com*, commenting that: 'England's Under 17 men's football team came out victorious in the Algarve Tournament for the second time in three years, following a 0–0 draw with Portugal on Tuesday. During the tournament, which was hosted at the Parque Desportivo da Nora in Ferreiras, Albufeira, England also beat the Ukraine 3–0 and drew 1–1 with France.'

Meanwhile, the Spurs official website, *tottenhamhotspur. com*, paid tribute to Harry on his international baptism, adding that, 'Harry Kane has made his debut for England

Under-17s in the prestigious Algarve Tournament in Portugal. Our Academy skipper and top-scorer for the Under-18s this season Harry, a First Year Trainee, played for 63 minutes as the Three Lions opened the tournament with a 1–1 draw against France at Estádio Municipal Bela Vista, Parchal on Saturday. Harry, whose performances also earned a place on the first-team bench against Everton in the Carling Cup, then came on as a 70th-minute substitute in an impressive 3–0 win against Ukraine at the Estádio Algarve on Sunday.'

His bosses even at under-17 international level were already convinced he would be a winner. Kenny Swain, who was John Peacock's assistant, told *The Guardian* that Harry was 'on the radar' but had to battle because his route into the team was blocked by other strong attackers like Connor Wickham, Berahino and Afobe.

He said, 'When Harry first joined up with the Under-17s for the Algarve tournament… the most outstanding thing for me was his character – his drive and determination… a thirst for goals and wanting to learn and do better.'

And Peacock himself was similarly enamoured with the boy's determination to succeed and his strong work rate. He said, 'Harry's attitude was excellent. He was very enthusiastic and always itching to get on the pitch, the potential was always there with Harry.'

Those tributes showed how far Harry had come by 2010. He was clearly making his mark among the younger versions of the national team and was battling for a starting spot in the Under-17s. But fortune, which had been favouring him as he climbed the international ladder, suddenly took a wrong turn. Illness thwarted him just as he was set to appear in a major international finals for the Under-17s. It was a great pity, as the squad would go on to claim the title and he would surely have played some part and ended up with a winner's medal of his own. He was upset at missing out but still urged his teammates on and wished them all the very best as they departed without him for the event in Liechtenstein. It was very much a case of redemption for the team after they finished bottom of their group a year earlier and exited at the initial stage of the competition.

In 2010, as Harry cheered them on from his sick bed, they won their Group B with maximum points after seeing off Turkey, the Czech Republic and Greece. In the semi-finals they came up against the French and the quality of the opposition would give an indication of just how Harry was missing out on testing himself against potential world-class players. Two first-half goals from Connor Wickham earned a 2–1 win but the identity of France's goalscorer highlighted just what a valuable tournament this would have been for Kane, but for his illness. For no less than Paul Pogba, who would become the most expensive player in the world when Man United splashed £93 million on his services in 2016, was the man who gave the French hope with his second-half goal.

Victory over the French then set up a final with Spain, another big miss for Harry, as they had won the event in 2007 and 2008 and their senior national team won Euro 2008 that same summer. Again, their team oozed quality as they showed by destroying Turkey 3–1 in the semis, with two goals from Paco. Harry would have enjoyed meeting the

Valencia youngster who finished top scorer in the finals with six goals, and whose fourteen in qualifying and the finals was a competition record. It would have given Harry an up-close-and-personal opportunity to see what he was up against as he aimed to become Europe and the world's number 1 striker.

Of course, England had their own ace striker in Connor Wickham, whose efforts in Liechtenstein earned him the top award of Golden Player of the tournament. But would he have won it if Harry had been there? Maybe Harry would have been playing up front with him, or even instead of him? But full credit to Wickham for taking his chance and proving he, like Harry, would be one to watch for the future.

In the final at the Rheinpark Stadion (Liechtenstein), England minus Kane got off to a bad start when Andre Wisdom put through his own goal, the defender deflecting a cross by Spain's Gerard into his own net. Wisdom made amends by heading the equaliser to make the score 1–1. And Wickham grabbed his third goal of the tournament just before the break. Plucky England held onto their 2–1 lead in the second half and that was enough for them to lift the trophy for the first time since the tournament began in 1982.

Captain Conor Coady, of Liverpool, paid tribute to all the boys who had worked so hard within the squad over the past year – including Harry – and said it was a moment of glory he would never forget, whatever his senior career brought. He told the press, 'It was unreal to lift the trophy. I couldn't believe it was happening. I've dreamt about the day I'd do it and now I've done it; they can never take that back, I've always got that memory. They had a quality side and in the last twenty,

twenty-five minutes they battered us, it was an onslaught. But I thought we defended well in the end and came out as champions. I know how good a player Andre is, he shows it week in week out for our club – he's absolutely superb. The goal today capped off his tournament, he was fantastic in the second half, he showed what his defensive qualities are.

'And when you have a player like Connor up front you know he'll score; if you give him the ball he'll do something with it, and that's what he did today. This has just capped off what the U17s have achieved this season, it's been absolutely fantastic. We've got great individual players and great team spirit, it's unbelievable.'

It was ironic that the skipper could well have been talking about Harry, rather than Wickham, but for Kane's illness. But Kane was, nonetheless, still delighted at the boys' success: as we have noted, for Harry the team would always be more important than any individual. So even though he was absent through illness, he was there in spirit, although it remained a fact that it was a damned shame he had to miss out on such a prestigious event that could only have boosted his personal development in the game.

Soon he was on the up himself, moving smoothly from the Under-17s to the Under-19s with his country. Harry made his debut for the latter on 8 October 2010, in the 6–1 romp over Albania. Being Harry, of course, he scored on this debut, hitting the back of the net twice against the hapless Albanians in a European qualifier in Vise, Belgium. Connor Wickham also scored on his Under-19 debut in the same match: the duo were already earning headlines for their prolific goalscoring.

In 2012, Kane finally made his debut for his country in a major international tournament, starring for the Under-19s in the European championships after helping them qualify. He did exceptionally well, especially when you consider the man who would become England's number 1 striker started some of the games… in midfield! Harry recalled later, 'It was my first [major] tournament as an England player so I was naturally excited to experience such a situation. I scored against France but played in midfield a bit as well. We got to the semi-final but I was rested for the game against Greece – and we lost.'

Was Harry saying they lost because he was rested? I doubt it, probably he was merely stating a fact and disappointment that the lads went out in the semis, when he would have loved to have been involved in the final. Kane was complimented on his work in the tournament, especially when he scored the winner against France, which took England into the match against Greece. After the win, he told the *thefa.com*, 'It's good to be off the mark now, but more importantly, for the lads to help us get the win. It's my third game of the season and funnily enough, I got the goal from midfield. The celebration is obviously a personal thing, but that meant a lot to my family and everyone back home so that's something for everyone there.'

The *hotspurhq.com* website summed up how good Harry had been in that victory, saying, 'Harry Kane scored England's second goal in a win that sees them top of their Group and qualify for the semi-final where they will play Greece. England took an early lead against France but after the French drew level Kane scored the winning goal when the French goalkeeper flapped at the ball from a corner. It fell to Kane who displayed good technique as he scored from a position in the centre of the penalty area. Kane was playing in a deeper central midfield role but with freedom to get forward. He worked hard and successfully pressurised the French to regain possession for England. He showed good distribution and nearly had a chance to score a second goal from a long throw to the back post but the ball just eluded him.' England had drawn their opening match against Croatia and then defeated Serbia 2–1, with Harry involved in both goals. For the first, he had put the keeper under pressure and forced an error that led to the goal and he played a part in the build-up to the second.

The part Harry was playing in the tournament was also stressed by organisers UEFA on their own official website. They pointed out, 'England set up a UEFA European Under-19 Championship semi-final with Greece after goals from John Lundstram and Harry Kane gave Noel Blake's side victory against France. Needing a point to make sure of progress, England claimed all three with an assured display. Les Bleuets – who briefly levelled in the first half through Jordan Veretout – were already assured of a place in the last four regardless of the result, but finish second in the Group B standings, meaning they face holders Spain in the last four on Thursday. France [had a] fine equaliser but parity was short-lived, though, as England regained the lead before the break. This time Millieras could only help Robert Hall's corner into the path of Kane, who drove in.'

England head coach Noel Blake paid tribute to his goalscorers, Kane and Lundstram, for their willingness to keep battling and determination to score but also praised his team as a whole for holding out against a talented French side, who once again included star man, Paul Pogba. Blake said, 'It was a very tough game. France had a lot of possession and dominated the ball in front of our back line to a certain extent. At the same time, I thought we played some really good football. We had a game plan in terms of what to do when we didn't have the ball and the players carried it out to the letter. We only conceded one goal and that was something we should have dealt with if we're honest. I can't fault the lads though. I made some changes because I feel you have to maximise your squad and I believe in each and every member of ours.'

That helped explain why he rested Harry. The aim was to keep the boy fresh, hopefully, for the final, although it did not quite work out, as England exited against the Greeks in the semis. Pogba, who skippered the French during the tournament, also stressed the importance of a talented overall squad rather than a couple of individuals, before he took on the English. He said he was well aware of the likes of Kane and that he could damage their hopes of glory, but added, 'I am confident that we can get a positive result against England and secure first place in the group. There will more than likely be some changes in our team because our last match against Croatia – when we were lucky to score near the end – was physically demanding. We trust in all of those who will come in, because we know this is a squad where anybody can replace anybody. We are a solid bunch and there is no such thing as first and second-string players in this group.'

Harry had certainly enjoyed the tournament and the chance to test himself against such burgeoning talents as Pogba. Not that boss Noel Blake was at all surprised that Harry had taken his chance when he had given it to him. Blake would later tell *The Guardian* how Harry had stamped his personality on him early on when they first met, saying, 'We trained at West Brom, ahead of our first qualifying game in 2010–11, and he blew me away. I said to the group, "What he has said to us with that performance in his first training session is that he is not here just to be in the squad." His performance warranted that he actually started in the team. And he did. People talk about his work ethic in matches but he trains that way.'

In total, Harry made three appearances for the Under-17s at national level, netting twice, and fourteen for the Under-19s, with six goals to show for his efforts. He was still not a regular at Tottenham; indeed, he seemed to be permanently out on loan. It would not be until 2013 that he really started to force his way into the Spurs squad, let alone the starting eleven. But the loans were clearly doing him no harm as far as the international arena was concerned: he was continually developing and making an impact at each different level. At the time, the FA would mark him out as one to watch as he climbed through the age groups towards the England Under-20 and Under-21 squads. They stated, 'The Tottenham Hotspur ace is a clever forward who was first capped at U17 level in April 2010 when he helped John Peacock's squad through the Elite Round and into the European Championship Finals.

Unfortunately, he wasn't able to take his place in the squad for the ultimately successful trip to Liechtenstein due to injury, but he remained on the radar and Noel Blake selected him to feature in the U19s for their Euro First Qualifying Round in Belgium in October 2010. He was then part of the U19s squad which reached the semi-final of the Euros in 2012, helping them to qualify for the U20 World Cup with his goals and link-up play.'

The FA could see that this was a player who could provide great service for his country if he was nurtured properly when involved with the England teams. And he was well looked after by the likes of John Peacock and Noel Blake, who had plenty of time for him given his determination and total commitment when he joined up with the various squads. Harry felt wanted and gave his everything in return. The FA also realised that his reputation as a goalscorer was growing, even though he had started some games in midfield, and predicted he would have a major role to play in the FIFA 2013 Under-20s World Cup in Turkey, adding that, 'After being named in the England U20 squad for the FIFA World Cup in Turkey, he will also be looking to keep his reputation intact on the international stage.'

Like one of his heroes, David Beckham, Harry loved playing for England and being around the squad and he and his family were immensely proud when he was chosen for the tournament in Turkey, at the end of May, 2013. And what a squad it was... laden with youngsters who would go on to become Premier League names. Harry was delighted to be included and said he was looking forward to working with a third manager at international level in Peter Taylor, the man who had made Beckham captain in his one and only game in charge of the senior England team as caretaker boss. That decision was one of the key ones in Taylor's career, as it laid a path for Becks to become full-time skipper. It also showed Harry that he was a man who would push youth to the fore and who he could work well with.

Harry trusted Taylor and his instincts from day one and was impressed that the boss had stuck with many of the players who had worked so hard in the Under-19s in the Euros the previous year. Then, they had frustratingly gone out in the semis when Harry was rested but now the men who moved up an age group were determined to go one better in Turkey. The squad included the following from the Under-19s: Sam Johnstone, Tom Thorpe (both Manchester United), Eric Dier (Sporting Lisbon), Ross Barkley and teammate John Lundstram (Everton), Conor Coady (Liverpool) and Harry Kane (Tottenham). There were some impressive names there and that made Harry believe that, yes, they could go far in the forthcoming tournament.

Interestingly, in the make-up of the squad Harry was featured in the forwards, not as a midfielder. It looked as if his efforts to be seen as an attacker had paid off. He had never complained when asked to work from midfield but had shown when he powered forward that he was more effective in an advanced role. The full squad read like this: Keepers: Johnstone (Man United), George Long (Sheffield United), Connor Ripley (Middlesbrough). Defenders: Sam Byram (Leeds), Dier (Sporting Lisbon), Jon Flanagan (Liverpool),

Above: Above left: Harry Kane celebrates after scoring during a 2015 U21 Championships Qualifying match between San Marino and England in Serravalle, Italy.   © *Giuseppe Bellini/Getty Images*

Below left: Kane gestures during a Europa League group match between PAOK FC and Tottenham Hotspur in Thessaloniki, Greece in September 2011.

© *Vladimir Rys/Getty Images*

Below right: Kane playing for England in a friendly against Italy at the Juventus Stadium in Turin.   © *GABRIEL BOUYS/AFP/Getty Images*

Above: Kane fights with Milan Badelj for the ball during Tottenham Hotspur's Champions League contest against Fiorentina in February 2016.

© ANDREAS SOLARO/AFP/Getty Images

Below: Kane celebrates scoring the first goal during the Champions League Round of 16 match between Juventus and Tottenham Hotspur at the Juventus Stadium on 13 February 2018.   © Giuseppe Maffia/NurPhoto via Getty Images

Above: Kane defiant in celebration after scoring an equaliser for Tottenham Hotspur against Borussia Dortmund in the Champions League in November 2017.

© *Kieran Galvin/NurPhoto via Getty Images*

Below: Then-England manager Roy Hodgson chats to his players before their international friendly against Italy in March 2015.

© *Laurence Griffiths/Getty Images*

Above left: Ronaldo and Kane speak after the Champions League group match between Real Madrid and Tottenham Hotspur at the Bernabeu in October 2017.

© *Laurence Griffiths/Getty Images*

Above right: England manager Gareth Southgate gives instruction to Kane during the international friendly between France and England at the Stade de France in June 2017.

© *Ian MacNicol/Getty Images*

Below: England players, many of whom would be in the famous 2018 World Cup team, salute fans after the National Anthem before the France vs England friendly kicked off.

© *Aurelien Meunier/Getty Images*

Jamaal Lascelles (Nottingham Forest), Dan Potts (West Ham), Adam Reach (Boro) John Stones (Everton), Thorpe (Man Utd). Midfielders: Barkley (Everton), Gael Bigirimana (Newcastle), Coady (Liverpool), Larnell Cole (Man United), Lundstram (Everton), James Ward-Prowse (Southampton). Forwards: Chris Long (Everton), Kane (Tottenham), Pritchard (Tottenham), Luke Williams (Middlesbrough).

So from being a fringe player who would be up against the likes of Connor Wickham to lead the attack in previous, younger age groups, Harry was now clearly THE man for the number 9 shirt. He was a better striker than the other three named for the tournament and was confident he would deliver the goods for his country, if chosen. It was going to be a tournament that would severely test the progress of the young England stars: a tournament that would see them up against many differing styles of play with teams from across the globe. Kane and Co. met up at England's national training ground, the outstanding facilities at St George's Park, in Burton-on-Trent in the Staffordshire countryside and had a few days to practise set pieces and fine-tune tactics before flying out to Turkey on Wednesday, 12 June. They were then based in Antalya for their first two group games against Iraq on 23 June and Chile on 26 June. Three days later the squad would move on to Bursa for the final group game against African champions Egypt on 29 June.

The opener against Iraq should have been a formality given that they had struggled to even put together a squad due to the troubles inside the war-torn country. Yet, embarrassingly for England, they drew 2–2 after going two goals down. The official FIFA tournament website for the Press summed up what a let-down it had been for England, meaning their barren winless run in the competition continued, despite an enterprising opening in which Kane featured prominently. The website account continued: 'Ali Adnan scored a dramatic 93rd-minute equaliser as Iraq secured a 2–2 draw with England in the sides' FIFA U-20 World Cup opener at Antalya's Akdeniz University Stadium. The Three Lions had looked on course for their first victory in this competition in exactly 16 years, but their tournament record run now stretches over 15 successive winless matches.

'Peter Taylor's team had begun in purposeful style, with Ross Barkley surging forward after six minutes and forcing a fine save out of Mohammed Hameed [Farhan]. Iraq might have scored themselves with eight minutes of the first half remaining when Mohanna Abdul-Raheem drifted in from the right, eluded a couple of challenges, and curled a left-foot shot just over from 20 yards. But England remained on top and, soon after, Harry Kane showed great pace and power to break through the Iraq defence and force another good instinctive stop from Hameed.

'From the resultant corner, England moved in front. Kane was again involved, flicking on James Ward-Prowse's cross, and charging in at the back post was captain Conor Coady to direct a well-placed header into the far corner of the net. The game looked to have been decided in the space of a few second-half seconds, when Samuel Johnstone pulled off a magnificent double save and play immediately flowed to the other end. Alert and alive to possibilities, Kane rampaged down the right flank and claimed another assist with a low cross that Luke Williams side-footed firmly beyond Hameed at the far post.'

So Harry had clearly played his part, providing two assists for the two goals, but it had not been enough. Slack defending allowed the Iraqis to draw level when they should have been comfortably defeated. England could only draw their next match, too, and this time Harry was on target. He brought his country level on the hour mark after Chile had taken the lead. Ross Barkley set Harry up after a fine run and Kane made no mistake, drilling the ball home from the left.

England had two points from two draws and would need to beat Egypt in their final group game to have any chance of progressing. But it was not to be. In another disappointing outcome, they lost by two goals to nil. Harry's dreams of returning home a hero with the trophy had bitten the dust. Yet again, he was industrious and almost scored in the first few minutes, only to see his powerful header go agonisingly close, but still wide.

England had finished bottom of their group and headed home in extremely low spirits. They had been one of the favourites but seemed to suffer the anxiety that had long held back the senior team at major tournaments. The expectations had been high but, as is often the case with the seniors, had not been met. Having said that, we had been warned by the bookies that the team might replicate the seniors and struggle – precisely because of that weight of expectation on their shoulders. As the Football Tipster website succinctly pointed out before the event got underway: 'The two favourites in Group E have to be Chile and England although Egypt can potentially spring a few surprises and Iraq are very likely to finish bottom of the group. England are helped by their team being full of players that are on the books of massive clubs, but the problem that they have is the weight of expectation that is always on their shoulders, even at youth tournaments such as this.'

Perceptive words, indeed, as were subsequent comments pinpointing Kane as the key man for England if they were to progress as comfortably as expected.

Afterwards, inevitably, the barbs started to fly with the national papers bemoaning how a nation with so much money invested in football, and players of genuine quality, could fail so abysmally against the likes of Iraq and Egypt. In a damning indictment that summed up the general feeling in Fleet Street, *The Independent* did at least mention Kane in dispatches, saying, 'The most talented player in the England team has been Ross Barkley, the Everton 19-year-old who tends to blow hot and cold. Eric Dier, the Sporting Lisbon academy boy who is the grandson of the late Football Association secretary Ted Croker, has played well. Harry Kane and Alex Pritchard of Spurs have had moments of promise, although the former should have scored against Egypt.'

Taylor himself tried to find positives with his team's showing, but admitted the defeat by Egypt was disastrous, adding, 'I thought we would win tonight, to be honest, because I thought we were improving as a team, I thought it was probably our worst performance since we've been here, even though we created a lot of chances. If you don't play as well as you can and you don't take chances, you get punished and that's what happened tonight. Egypt showed good character to win the match tonight having lost the previous two games. We still feel we could have scored more goals and that's the mistake that we made. Their first goal was very well taken and the second came when we were trying to get back into it.'

Taylor said it had been a worthwhile experience for Kane and his teammates. They had lost but had also at least savoured the workings of an international tournament which, hopefully, would help them in future when they stepped up a notch. Taylor added, 'The experience of playing in the Under-20s World Cup will have been fantastic for everybody. It's a brilliant competition, but we're disappointed.' The defeat also meant England had now gone sixteen matches without a win at this level.

Harry was down, but far from out. In fact, he was still on an upward trend. England might fail from the weight of expectation at more than senior level, but Harry Kane had signalled his intent in Turkey. He had played for his country at Under-17 and Under-19 level, and now wanted to have a go with the Under-21s. He knew he had to keep on delivering at club level, and his chance would surely come.

On 13 August 2013, it did: Kane made his debut for the Under-21s in the match with the 'Auld Enemy', Scotland. Harry came on as a substitute almost on the hour-mark as England romped to a 6–0 victory in Sheffield. Remarkably, given the scoreline, Harry failed to score, although he did test the trembling Scottish backline with a few strong runs towards goal. But he made up for drawing a blank in the team's next match as he grabbed a hat-trick against San Marino in a

UEFA Euro 2015 qualification encounter, England winning 4–0 away at a canter. Harry left the field with the match ball and told pals he was thrilled to have hit a hat-trick for his country and that he hoped it would be the first of many.

His Under-21 boss Gareth Southgate praised his centre-forward for the hat-trick, saying, 'It is always memorable to score a hat-trick for your country and he should be very proud of that. He had some good service. There are things that we can take from this. All you can do is try to do the right thing and keep learning.' England followers were also impressed with Kane's prolific nature, with one Spurs and England fan saying, 'Great to see the Spurs youth system continues to produce quality talent. Kane looks to be a great solution to our long-term striker problems, with both Soldado and Defoe around their 30s. He took his chances brilliantly.'

Now Harry had hit that hat-trick, the goals continued to flow for the Under-21s. He would also score a brace against France, which took his total to a remarkable thirteen goals in twelve games. The match in November, 2014, ended in a 3–2 defeat for England but Kane at least could be pleased with his night's work. His two goals had put England 2–0 ahead in Brest, but poor defending cost them dear. Harry was disappointed with the result – as was boss Southgate, since it was his first loss as England Under-21s supremo. He told reporters, 'We knew they were a powerful and athletic team and a different test to what we've faced before, which is why we came. With the weather the way it was, that made it more of a physical game and there were so many misplaced passes with people struggling to stay up on their feet. I thought we were fortunate to be 2–0 ahead and, in the end, we haven't really done enough to win the game. That said, it was exactly the sort of test that we wanted and had we hung on for 2–2 away in France then that would have been an outstanding result.'

Then he added a line of praise for Kane, who had proved once again that he could handle the pressure of leading the line for his country. Southgate added, 'What we have shown is that we can score goals.' It was a nice comment for Harry, who had actually only started the match because Saido Berahino, England's top scorer in qualifying, had been moved up to the national team's senior squad. Harry had certainly given Southgate something to think about if the West Brom striker returned to the Under-21s. By the end of the Euro 2015 qualifying games, Harry had given Southgate even more to contemplate. He had netted six times in eight qualifying matches and was now a certainty to make the squad for the finals in the Czech Republic in June 2015. Kane had emerged as the group's top marksman, overtaking Saido Berahino in the process, and Southgate was enthusiastic about the player's progress in such a relatively short period since he had joined up with the group.

And let's not forget that Harry had also made his SENIOR England debut just two months earlier – and had scored too, but more of that in the next chapter. Harry was also keen to play in the Under-21s finals – he considered it an honour to represent his country at any level and would never reject a call-up – but his club manager Mauricio Pochettino was less impressed that Southgate had chosen his man as one of the three strikers in his squad, along with Berahino and Danny

Ings. With his country, the same as with his club, Kane had come a long way in a short time and by now was indispensable to Pochettino's plans for Premier League domination. The days of loans and sitting on the bench were over for a striker who was now regarded as the main man up front at the Lane.

And the Tottenham boss made his displeasure clear at the time, saying Harry would benefit more from a rest than additional hours of football. He would comment further when Harry got off to a barren start at the beginning of the next Premier season, almost saying, 'I told you so.' He said, 'Did Harry do too much in the summer in hindsight? Yes. Not only on the pitch, but off from the pitch as the pressure – he is a hero for Tottenham and England – was unbelievable. The way that the people see him, it's not easy to recover because it's not only physical or mental. It's true that, maybe, the summer did not help him.'

In the event, it was good experience for Kane to play in a major international tournament abroad, but the outcome was less than enjoyable. He played every minute of England's games but left feeling deflated as they jetted home early due to finishing rock bottom of their group after disappointing results against Portugal and Italy.

Harry and Co. got off to a bad start in the opener against Portugal despite strong hopes from the players, the manager and the press and TV pundits that this could be their year. The England team certainly looked strong on paper – what with Butland in goal and the likes of Harry, Nathan Redmond, Jesse Lingard and James Ward-Prowse dotted throughout the ranks. And the bench boasted Danny Ings, Ruben Loftus-

Cheek, Calum Chambers and Michael Keane, all top-notch youngsters who would go on to have fine club careers after the tournament. Not that the Portuguese were no-hopers – not by a long way, in fact. They had the brilliant defensive midfielder William Carvalho with creative genius João Mário and striker Ricardo in their ranks. But the bookies still predicted England to come out on top.

As is usually the case with England and major tournaments, things did not go to plan. Southgate's boys crashed to a 1–0 defeat, with Mario on target on the hour. It was the first time in eighteen matches that England had failed to score and Southgate argued his team deserved at least a draw, telling reporters, 'I think a draw would have been a fair result. We said at half-time maybe one goal decides the game and the goal we conceded was very unfortunate but that's football. I've said to the players it is easy to be really down after a defeat in a tournament but if you don't pick yourselves up quickly, you are not ready mentally for the next game. We have to do that because I don't think there is any disgrace in the way the players have performed. We created lots of decent openings and looked great going forward. The majority of the game we defended pretty well. It was a good game against a very good Portuguese team. I still believe we are good enough to get through.'

Harry was particularly disappointed to have drawn a blank. He had several attempts on goal in the first half, only to be denied by the keeper in the form of José Sá. Harry then almost broke through with two shots late in the game, only for the dominant Sá to thwart him again. Kane walked off head held high and convinced England could still qualify, telling his teammates they 'had deserved better, it was just one of those games you get now and again when the ball won't go in the net.'

Skipper Butland echoed those thoughts, saying, 'We deserved more from the game with the chances we had – we got between them and created chances and their keeper's pulled off some big saves. On another day, two or three of our chances get deflected and go in and it was unfortunate for us that the goal that did us fell kindly for him and he hit the post and it rebounded out to João Mário. There is no shame in the way we played and we have to take the way we played and the chances we created forward. If we can reproduce that against Sweden and Italy, I am hopeful we will get the points needed.'

The next match pitted them against the Swedes and this time they benefitted from a 1–0 win, with Lingard securing the points that kept them in the competition with a strike five minutes from time. Lingard took the glory, but it was Kane who took the official honours, being named Man of the Match for his ninety-minute display of powerful, centre-forward play, continually threatening the Swedish backline and only missing out on a goal himself due to goalkeeping heroics and plain bad luck as he hit the side netting rather than the goal itself.

The winning strike was England Under-21s' first tournament win in ninety minutes since they beat Spain in 2009. Lingard's goal also ended a five-game wait for a goal from open play at a tournament. For this event, it meant they were back on track for a place in the semi-finals – a win over Italy in the final group game would confirm that position.

'That was more like it,' Harry said after the win. 'We played well again and this time got what we deserved… the three points. Now we can look forward to the final game in the group and know that it is in our hands whether we progress or not.' He was 'delighted' with his Man of the Match award but, as always, stressed it was a reward for the team as much as him, because the team had played together so well.

Southgate was as much relieved as pleased that his team had finally nailed down a victory, saying, 'We had faith we had players on the field that could get the goal. We started to create more chances as the game went on and we had to hold our nerve. In the end it was a wonderful piece of skill that wins us the game, but we had dominated possession. Sweden are always a threat because of the way they work, but today I thought we deserved the victory, although maybe we weren't as fluid as we were the other night.'

And Lingard echoed Harry's thoughts, that the team had grafted and earned the win, and could now prepare for the Italy game with 'great hope'. Jesse said, 'We had to keep our heads – we knew the goal would come eventually. We just had to wear Sweden down and it would come in the end. Our spirits are up and our confidence is up and we'll now go into the Italy game fully focused knowing we can do the job and qualify.'

So all Harry and the lads had to do now was beat Italy – and they would be in the semis. But once again England would fall when under pressure; whether the seniors or the Under-21s, it was the same old story. A mental barrier as much, if not more, than a physical barrier – a lack of belief, and a crumbling when the stress hit peak levels. Harry played his final ninety minutes for the Under-21s but left the field defeated and 'a bit numb' as England lost 3–1 to the Azzurrini. It left England bottom of their group and out of the competition; Italy, too, exited, losing out to Sweden on second place on goal difference.

Kane had set up Ings for what should have been a goal early in the game, only for the Liverpool hitman to find the side netting. It summed up England's night of frustration as Harry was then thwarted by the Italy keeper after brilliantly controlling a ball that dropped from the air and firing towards goal. England had twenty goal attempts, but only four of them were on target. Southgate was upset that his team were heading home, but tried to focus on the positive that Harry Kane and some of the others, who would now go on to senior recognition, had at least tasted the atmosphere of a major international tournament, commenting that, 'We created a lot of chances and have not been able to take them until the last minute. Two minutes of madness in terms of our defending has cost us the game but that is the harsh reality of tournament football. The experience has been a brilliant one for our young players but we've not been able to get through to the semi-final.'

Southgate also refused to condemn Ings for missing that simple early chance that Kane had created for him, pointing out that, 'It would be wrong to single that out. We've created a lot of chances and had some good attempts on goal that the keeper has saved. On another night we'd maybe score three or four and have a scoreline that is completely different but it is at both ends that we haven't been able to do the job tonight.'

Harry Kane thoroughly backed that view, echoing Southgate's mantra that it was as a team that they would win, and as a team they would lose. No one individual should carry the can for defeat, or the glory alone for triumphs. Skipper Butland readily agreed with that analysis, telling *uefa. com*: 'It doesn't matter how well you play, you've got to be ruthless at either end. Two sloppy goals against a team like this is something you can't accept and that was the end of our tournament. You have to perform at either end and make every chance you have count. At the back you have to be just as ruthless, we weren't that. It was in our hands to get through and we didn't perform.'

Harry flew home to London from the Czech Republic, disappointed but hopeful that there would be more tournaments, and at a higher level, to come. He had completed his national service at Under-21 level and now graduated full-time to the senior squad; his international apprenticeship was over and he was ready, determined and more than able to now make his name with the big boys of world football.

CHAPTER EIGHT

SENIOR SERVICE

Despite taking part in the doomed Under-21s championship in June 2015, Harry Kane would make his mark at senior level before and after the tournament. The event in the Czech Republic that summer was his young England swansong – and rightly so. The man who was destined to become the Premier League's Golden Boot holder within twelve months should clearly have been playing for the seniors, full stop. It was really a goodwill gesture from then England boss Roy Hodgson, and a special request from Under-21s supremo Gareth Southgate, that led to Harry's being on the plane to the finals in the first place.

Harry himself was much too humble to say he should not be playing for the youngsters, indeed he had been looking forward to the tournament. His club manager, Mauricio Pochettino, had no doubts, however, that his star man should not have been with the Under-21s, and made his views apparent in press briefings both before and after the event. He said Harry was too good for the young England team, and that it did not serve his advancement by him being part of the set-up. He insisted Kane should automatically be in the senior set-up now. That would be the case, but not until after the Under-21 finals.

Southgate would get his way – and Harry would experience the atmosphere and the highs, and more of the lows, as England stumbled to a swift exit from the competition. As we have seen in the previous chapter, no one would be blaming Kane for the team coming up short. No, he was Man of the Match in one game and a constant threat in the other two. It was more a case of defensive deficiencies costing the side dear.

Even though the team's finishing bottom of their group had been a massive let-down, Harry had no regrets about making the trip with the Under-21s. He had enjoyed the experience, but not the results and was proud to have represented his country in the finals. He was even prouder when it was made clear to him that his time with the group was up afterwards, precisely because he would now become a fully paid-up member of the seniors. He left the Under-21s with many fond memories after fourteen appearances and spoke about what he had learned from the tournament, saying, 'Sometimes, we have to be braver. Just a bit more ruthless and clinical. We could have done better in their box and a bit better in our box too. There are a few things in all three games that we could have done better. I don't think we reached our top form and we got punished. It hurts now and we have to see what we could have done better and learn from it.'

He remained optimistic about the future of the seniors, insisting they COULD win a tournament in his lifetime, and during his time in the team. He said, 'I believe that. That is always the aim, the dream to lift a trophy for England and it still is. No one can say we don't have the ability. We have amazing young talent coming through. Amazing talent in the senior squad. It is just putting the dots together during a tournament and seeing what happens. We have to forget about the pressure and expectation. We have to do what we do in qualification and not falter in the groups. That happens over a period of time.'

He reckoned Southgate had done a good job steering the team in the Czech Republic and ended his chat with reporters by stressing once again that the future was bright for the seniors, if only they could lose the stress factor, and be more ruthless, including himself, 'I think Gareth has done a great job. All the lads have been right behind him. He picked the players he thought were the best players and that's it. I don't think anyone has let him down, it's just periods and patches over the three games that have kind of not gone our way.

'It is great for us to play in the Champions League and Europa League for European experience. That doesn't change the fact that there are a lot of senior players who have Champions League experience. It is something that has to change. We have to be more ruthless in tournaments and forget about the pressure and go for it.'

He would now take that determination into his full England career – a career which started BEFORE the Under-21s finals when he made his debut in March 2015 against

Lithuania at Wembley. And it was a debut he would never forget as he scored just seconds after joining the action as a second-half substitute.

Harry had joined up with the seniors for the first time after Daniel Sturridge suffered another injury setback and impressed regulars in the squad as he was put through his paces in training at St George's Park in Burton-upon-Trent. Some even believed he would make the team straight off, such was his impression in training, although ultimately he would come on as a substitute for Wayne Rooney, rather than starting alongside him against the Lithuanians. England vice-captain Gary Cahill was sure that if Harry did start, he would let no one down. He told reporters at St George's Park on the first day of training, 'I've played against him three times this season and he's a real handful. He's a fantastic talent. For me he's got all the attributes. He's had a terrific season, his confidence must be sky high and he's a real top player. Whether he starts or not is down to the manager. We've got four top strikers here, all chomping at the bit to play and Harry's in that bracket. I'm sure he feels he's ready to play but it is up to the manager.'

And what of Kane's temperament? Cahill added, 'He comes across as a top professional and I'm sure whatever he gets asked to do he'll go ahead and do. He's got his taste of the seniors in this meet-up and I'm sure there'll be many more squads that he'll be involved in in the future.'

Man United's Michael Carrick was just as positive about Harry and how refreshing and determined to be a part of it all the boy had been at Burton. He said he believed Kane was a big-game player and, as such, would be a key component in any success England were to enjoy in the future, adding that, 'As the spotlight's grown he seems to have grown and his performances have improved and improved. He looks like a real deal and I'm sure he's got a big, big future ahead of him.'

The day before the Lithuania match, even a former hero for Tottenham's biggest rivals, Arsenal, made the case for Harry to get the nod and start. Paul Merson reckoned he had earned the right to be given a chance after his exploits in his full debut season at the Lane. Merson, writing in his SkySports pundit blog, said he also saw glimpses of another Lane legend in the manner in which Kane played. Paul said, 'He reminds me of Teddy Sheringham. He drops off, comes looking for the ball. He has an unbelievable future in the game.'

And former Spurs striker Paul Walsh went a step further and advocated Kane as worthy of not only an England spot, but the Player of the Season award after his unbelievable exploits. Walsh told the *Express*, 'He has been magnificent. At the start of the season – I'm quite happy to hold my hands up here – I wasn't sure he was going to be the answer to Tottenham's prayers. I'd seen him on loan – he did OK but he hadn't pulled up any trees. I didn't see him having an impact but every credit to the player. He has shown great appetite for the game. He has nice feet, runs well with the ball and he scores all sorts of goals.'

Given that both Merson and Walsh were masters of their trade up front for the North London teams in their own playing days, the compliments meant something. Fellow strikers appreciating your worth, and blowing your trumpet, was something that Harry Kane truly appreciated. He knew he was on the right track when such talented former exponents of the art of attacking football went public with their backing and accolades.

And even Lithuania coach Igoris Pankratjevas got in on the act, telling his Press conference how he feared Kane after watching him at work in the Premier League. He said: 'Statistics speak for themselves. I know Harry Kane has scored twenty-nine goals in all competitions so that fact speaks for itself. I've seen him play at international level for England Under-21s, he played in Lithuania recently and he is a strong forward.'

In the build-up to the game, Harry was also led to believe that he WOULD start when the Press revealed they had caught a glimpse of boss Roy Hodgson's notepad as he attended a training session. The pad had Kane up front alongside Rooney and speculation now could only grow that Harry would start. But he was wise enough to know that names on a notepad did not equate to the team on the day: in fact, Hodgson's pad merely outlined options that would be worked upon in training. It made good sense to try out a Kane/Rooney partnership in training, even if the team on the day did not work out that way.

So Harry was neither disappointed nor feeling surprised nor let down when Hodgson took him to one side to tell him he had done great in training but that he would be on the bench when the game kicked off, with a view to coming on as a sub later.

Rooney would start without Kane alongside him but he too had words of comfort for Harry, telling reporters how he believed the boy was good enough to start and that he had an incredible international career ahead of him; that this was only the start of a long, long journey. Wayne said, 'His season has been incredible, it's his first year in the Premier League and to score the goals, his performances have been excellent. He fully deserves the call-up. We've seen that he's a goalscorer, if he gets a chance he can finish. It's great for English football. He's been on a different route to me and he's having a tremendous season. If there's anything I can help him with then I'm here but at the minute he's doing well. I'm sure he's got family and friends around him to keep his feet on the ground. If he keeps doing what he's doing, he'll have no problems.'

Hodgson also made it clear to Harry that he could now consider himself a bona fide member of the senior squad; that his days at Under-21 level were officially over and that he envisaged a very bright future for him at senior international level. He hinted that Harry's debut was indeed imminent, saying, 'I've been very happy with Harry Kane this week. He's done well. He's not in any way damaged his chances of playing in the senior teams and I am sure over the course of the two games we will see him make his full debut. We'll see if that's from the start against Lithuania or on Tuesday or coming on as a substitute.'

All he needed to do was keep his head down and work hard in training, and keep the goals coming at club level, and his time would come. Indeed, the time would come – and it was not far off at all – that Harry could consider himself a regular starter and one of the first names on the England team sheet. After finally breaking into the Spurs first team, his rise had been inexorable – and the same would now be true with England.

Harry would soon become a goalscorer feared at international level as well as club level – and the subject of much speculation about the world's biggest football clubs keen to sign him, including the major players in both Spain and Italy.

Not that any of the gossip would go to Harry's head. He was 'one of our own', as the fans at the Lane continually sang, and had no intention of leaving his beloved Tottenham. He remained grounded and wise for his years – even when he made all the back page headlines by scoring within two minutes of coming on for his senior England debut. My pal at *The Sun*, Charlie Wyett, summed up how amazing a feat it was – and yet at the same time how it could have been predicted, saying, 'The biggest cheer of the night was for the arrival of Kane. Unbelievably, ridiculously, he scored at the far post after more fine work from Sterling. Kane really cannot stop scoring. While he will head to the Czech Republic with the England Under-21s, he will be a major part of Hodgson's senior team after that, you can be sure of that.'

After the game, Harry would speak of the goal moment with pride, saying, 'It was amazing to be just out there at Wembley. So then to score so quickly was crazy. It honestly felt like a dream when you are in a moment like that. I had visualised that my entire life.'

The only debate over his goal was about the timing. Some media groups had it as seventy seconds, some at seventy-five, some at seventy-nine and some at eighty. Whatever, it was less than a minute-and-a-half and was executed with Harry's third touch at senior level as he headed home a Raheem Sterling cross on seventy minutes. That rounded off a fine 4–0 win and had Kane's name across all the headlines on the back pages of the papers the next morning. He had arrived as a full England star – and in some style, too. Harry expanded upon his debut joy, telling BBC Radio 5 Live, 'I'm just proud. A dream come true. It's a special night and definitely one I won't forget. It's what you dream of as a kid, it's a bit of a daze and I am enjoying every minute of it. I've worked hard to be here. It's been a great week. I was excited to play and to score is a dream come true. The boss made his decision and I had to get on with it and when called upon be ready. To be able to repay the fans is amazing.'

Rooney added his own tribute as skipper: 'It's a great lift for the nation. He's scoring goals in the Premier League and now he's doing it at international level. We're a close group of players, we're all excited to have him with us and we want him to do well.' While boss Hodgson declared himself 'absolutely delighted' for Harry and that the player had deserved his chance to shine and taken it brilliantly. He added, 'It's nice when fairy tales come true. It has come true for Harry.' Kane had put himself at the forefront of Hodgson's thinking in terms of who should now be England's number 9, pushing his claims ahead of Jamie Vardy and leaving Sturridge a worried man.

Would he now start in the team's next match, a friendly in Italy? Hodgson refused to be drawn on that and Harry was as modest as ever, saying, 'That's up to the boss. If I am called upon that would be great. I'll just recover for the next couple of days and look forward to it.'

It was Harry's thirtieth goal for club and country in a remarkable season and was celebrated around the globe as almost 12,000 tweets were posted involving him within two minutes of him scoring. Yet his header was not the quickest goal ever scored by a debutant in an England shirt – that honour remained with Spurs wing-half Bill Nicholson, who hit the back of the net in just nineteen seconds. What was it with Tottenham players on their debut and England records? Bill's goal came in 1951 against Portugal and was his first touch. In second place remains Huddersfield's John Cock, who scored after thirty seconds against Ireland in 1919.

Hodgson now tried to slow down what had become an inevitable bandwagon demanding Harry start against the Italians in Turin. He said, 'We're not going to hold him back, there's no question of that. But I'm rather hoping I've got Harry Kane for a long period to come and I don't want to be the one who throws him in and he flies too close to the sun.' He said that he did not envisage any burnout but that it was his responsibility as the national manager to ensure Harry was treated correctly to aid his development, elaborating that, 'When someone has shone quite so brilliantly, that's always in the back of your mind. But from what I've seen of him, from what I know of the apprenticeship he's already served, when I look at the qualities he possesses as a football player I've got no fears that will happen. But I still think it's prudent of Tottenham Hotspur and Mauricio Pochettino and myself as the England manager not to stand here in front of you singing his praises.'

In the build-up to the Turin encounter, Rooney, in his role as skipper, also added his voice to the Kane pandemonium, saying, 'It's incredible really. You can feel the excitement around the country and you could hear when he came on everyone wanted him to come on. He probably didn't even think himself that he'd score so quickly. Through speaking to him, you can see he's a level-headed guy and I'm sure he's got good people around him and he'll have the ability to be able to cope with what comes.'

If you'd imagined that after all that holding back expectation stuff, Hodgson would have used Kane as an impact sub again, you'd be wrong. Just days after his plea to the Press to not build Kane up too much, Roy then picked him to play up front against the Italians. He announced it in this way to the Press pack: 'I'm able to name my team but I'm not going to. I can tell you that Harry Kane will make his full debut, playing from the start and Wayne Rooney will captain the team. I think it's nice to see the two of them on the field together. They've played a lot in training and the other night they could have but they didn't because Harry took Wayne's place. So I am pleased to see them playing together in this game and Harry certainly deserves his chance.'

Rooney echoed those sentiments and admitted he was looking forward to striking up a partnership with Kane, 'It's exciting for English football that Harry has come through and has been scoring goals for Tottenham. I hope that continues. It's a big night for him, his first start for England. I'm sure he'll be excited and will go out and give his best. Obviously I'm excited to play with him and hopefully we can do well to try and help the team win.'

And the new link-up went well, or at least it did when Hodgson finally put Rooney up front with Harry in the second half. Having a man with him helped ease Harry into the game and he showed off his physical strength and constant ability to frighten a backline with a strong performance. Let's not forget that he was up against arguably the best centre-back combination in the world with crack Juventus pairing Leonardo Bonucci and Giorgio Chiellini to contend with. But contend with them he did, and admirably, forcing the usually composed duo into unflattering errors and last-ditch attempts to thwart him as he bore down on goal. A flyer of a shot by Andros Townsend earned England a 1–1 draw and when the whistle went veteran Italian stopper, and skipper, Gianluigi Buffon, headed straight over to Kane and embraced him. It was a symbolic moment: a genius of former days approaching the end of his international career saluting a player who was just beginning his, and who had such hopes for the future.

Harry said he appreciated the keeper's gesture and that he would be proud if he achieved half what Buffon had achieved in a glittering career with Juventus and Italy. All the pundits agreed that Harry had made a solid, confident start with the only thing missing being a goal. They were also in unison that he had massive potential to become a fixture in the England team and a goalscorer of repute at this level. The *London Evening Standard* summed that up best, commenting, 'The goalscorer sported an impressive quiff and a trendy beard, but the look was dark and Latin rather than the blond of Harry Kane. The best that could be said for England for the first half of the evening was that Graziano Pellè delivered the kind of impressive headed strike Kane might one day trademark for his country. Let us hope so. After all, Kane certainly did enough in the 1–1 draw to suggest that he is headed that way.'

In a two-week period Harry had come on as a sub for his England debut, and scored, made his full debut in Italy, and caused world-class defenders all sorts of problems, and would follow it a few days later by being named Spurs skipper for the first time. He was twenty-one years and 251 days old, so it was little surprise that he shook his head and smiled when asked what he thought of everything that had happened in that fortuitous fortnight. It had been a dream come true and the best two weeks of his life, he would tell the press after the match against Burnley in which he took the armband for the first time. Harry admitted, 'Yes you could say it has been the best week of my life – to score, to make my first start and score for England, and to be captain. It has been an unbelievable couple of weeks and one I won't forget for the rest of my career. It's a huge honour and to lead the lads out was a very proud day for me, just a shame we couldn't get the win.'

After all the hullabaloo there were, inevitably, dissenting voices who argued that Kane was being lauded to the heavens, but had achieved 'nothing'. The brilliant Martin Samuel, quite rightly, gave short shrift to such notions in the *Daily Mail* – and spoke for the majority of us – when replying to a reader who had suggested just that, 'Why is being top goalscorer in English football "nothing"? If Kane still holds that position at the end of the season he would join – just in the Premier League era – Thierry Henry, Alan Shearer, Michael Owen, Jimmy Floyd Hasselbaink, Didier Drogba, Robin van Persie, Andy Cole, Dwight Yorke, Chris Sutton, Dion Dublin, Kevin Phillips, Ruud van Nistelrooy, Nicolas Anelka, Carlos Tevez, Dimitar Berbatov, Luis Suárez and Cristiano Ronaldo.

Some fair players in there, I'm sure you'll agree. Some better than others, obviously, but nobody should dismiss Kane's achievement as "nothing".'

Certainly everyone I knew in Fleet Street was of the opinion that Kane was now here to stay in the England team. He was the number one striker now Rooney's plundering was on the wane and would take some shifting by Sturridge or Vardy. Kane's claim also encompassed the fact that he was a playmaker as well as a goalscorer, something his two rivals could not claim to be. Harry could pass the ball and set up a teammate; like Teddy Sheringham in a previous era, he had that clever ability to see the game developing around him and to float a pinpoint pass before an opponent had worked out what was going on. Add that to his phenomenal goals rate and you had a modern day striker of the highest quality.

Certainly England were happy – and relieved – that Kane had not fallen prey to Irish charms now his talent and full array of skills had been seen on the senior international stage. There had been some talk that Harry could represent Ireland since his dad was born in Galway. In November 2013, new Ireland boss Martin O'Neill told reporters he was interested in the idea of bringing in players who could represent the Republic, even if their claims for doing so were tenuous at best. He said, 'Jack Charlton went back to someone sharing a drink with someone, you know, and it didn't do him any harm at all. I will have a look at it to see.'

Luckily for England, Harry was never tempted to cross the water. He was a Tottenham player and an England player, simple as that. He had already starred for the Under-21s and wanted to become a regular at senior level, as he explained in August 2014, 'There's no decision there. Obviously I'm playing for England's Under-21s. I want to break into that senior squad.'

O'Neill would bring the matter up again six months later, claiming that Harry's 'people' HAD approached him initially over a possible switch although he now accepted it would not happen as Kane had insisted on record he wanted to stay with England. O'Neill said, 'I was talking to somebody about this last night and we were just saying that Harry himself always wanted to play for England. Really, it was as simple as that. The order of events – though I don't think it's really important any more – is that initially the agent got in touch and said that he would have a keen interest, and we wanted to go and chase it up.

'But then I noticed in the newspaper where he said he wanted to play for England. And that has remained the same. Someone was even speaking to him recently and that was exactly the same conversation. Fine, if that's the case.'

Having said that, Martin then went on to say how Harry would have benefitted under his guidance – at least in terms of the number of caps he would have won! He added, 'Sometimes what agents do is they have someone who looks after the player who is not actually licensed to buy or sell or be involved as an agent but they look after the player. And he was the one who called. But he happened to call me on a day when Harry Kane said he wanted to play for England. It would have been really nice, absolutely. There's a fairly decent chance he might have had a few caps for us before he actually makes his debut for England, considering the way he's playing.'

Well, he decided he would bide his time and wait for England to come calling rather than throw in his lot with the Irish. He had wanted to play for England ever since he had got into football and would not change his mind at the last minute just so that he could earn more caps with Ireland. Not that he was not grateful that O'Neill had come knocking, mind you. He considered it a compliment, sources told me, not only to him but to his Irish dad. Both were proud of the family's Irish roots but Harry was an Essex boy, brought up with kids who also dreamed of England, so it was no surprise he instinctively chose to play for the country in which he had been nurtured both family and football-wise.

Harry was pleased with the way his first two games for his country had gone and felt he had done enough to warrant selection for the next squad. His boss Pochettino was of the same frame of mind but worried that the call-up had affected his top man after a couple of lacklustre displays by Harry and fellow squad debutant Ryan Mason in the club games directly after the Lithuania and Italy matches. Pochettino felt the games and involvement with the squad had taken a lot out of the duo physically, mentally and emotionally, as he explained to reporters at a Spurs press conference.

Pochettino said, 'When players get their first call-up, they try to show they are good enough and try to impress the national manager, and because they are over-motivated they expend a lot of energy. When you come back to the team, the consequence is that for two or three weeks you are a little bit down. It is normal and this happened at Southampton [where he was manager previously] too. I remember that we were third in the table and we went to play against Arsenal in November. If we won, with three points we'd have been first in the table. The performance wasn't good. Why? Because we'd spent a lot of energy and it was difficult to keep our focus on the normal life.

'I remember my first call-up for Argentina against Holland. I was up on a cloud for a month after it because it was unbelievable to play for the national team. When I got back to Espanyol it was difficult. I'd been away for fifteen days with my national team and I came back and I said, "Oh, but now I play with Redondo, Batistuta..." You feel like a superstar and then you have to go back to Espanyol.'

Many Spurs fans also back the England team, too, turning up at Wembley and abroad in force, and they did not agree with the boss on this one. They felt Harry had done the club proud with England and refuted the idea that it had (and would) affect his form at the Lane. One fan, Freddie, said, 'What a load of nonsense. It's not as if Harry was running around like a lunatic to have expended so much energy. He did not get injured. He's a young, fit lad and that should not have taken much out of him. Just accept his form has taken a dip and not blame it on England call-up.'

While Kino said it was a weak argument by Pochettino, 'He failed to mention that he also chose to give Harry the [captain's] armband which no doubt added pressure. Also either Kane and Mason can handle the responsibility of being an English national or they can't. What is it with the fragile psych of these English players? I'm sure there is more or similar pressure in other countries.'

Another fan also put the boot in on the manager, saying, 'Nonsense, you burnt them out with all your double training sessions from earlier in the season. We've been awful since the cup final and you need to sort your selection out and start playing players in their actual positions. Oh, and seeing as you always refer back to your playing days, and considering you were a defender, try getting them to actually defend!'

While another Tottenham diehard argued that it wasn't the stress of international football that had derailed Harry for a couple of games, but the weight he felt at club level of having to lead the line alone with no other striker at the club good enough to help him out, explaining that, 'We need two new strikers in the summer to take the weight off Kane if Adebayor and Soldado are not going to survive. We blew our chance of top four with two lousy results and it seems the whole team are suffering from a long season. You have to take into account we have a young side who haven't experienced this amount of matches before so they will feel some effects. Poch needs to mix it up and bring some experience into the side for next season.'

It would be six months before Harry next had a chance to show his worth for his country and, almost inevitably, he would prove the naysayers wrong by scoring – and then hitting form for Spurs afterwards. The idea that playing for his country blunted Harry was nonsense; what we have seen is that playing too many games was the major concern in that it left him looking jaded, and in need of urgent rest. Mr Pochettino, take note!

CHAPTER NINE

SAN ENCHANTED EVENING

AFTER all the hullabaloo about Harry looking jaded and tired after his England debut as a sub against Lithuania (marked with a goal) and full debut in Italy, the spotlight was on him once again as he joined up with the squad six months later for the traditional autumn international fixtures. He dismissed claims by his club manager that he had faded after his debut and said he would always look forward to playing for England whenever he was chosen. Now the talk was that he NEEDED to score for England, as he was still without a goal for Spurs a month into the new season. It seemed he couldn't win either way when he pulled on the England shirt!

Even though he had scored on his debut and put in a powerful showing in Italy, he in no way took it for granted that those markers he had put down guaranteed him a starting spot for any of the six matches England faced in the two-month period between 5 September and 17 November 2015.

Which was probably just as well, since Roy Hodgson would go for an experimental looking line-up for the first of the games, a Euro 2016 qualifier away in San Marino. Up front was Jamie Vardy, with Wayne Rooney tucked in behind, or as his partner, depending on how the game went. Of course, it was a fixture no one expected to prove troublesome for England, for San Marino, along with the likes of Luxembourg and Liechtenstein, were perennial whipping boys for the big lads of world football. A category which England, for all their failures in major tournaments, surely considered themselves in still.

Harry was not called upon until the fifty-eighth minute, when he replaced Rooney as a substitute. By then it was 3–0 to England and by the end of the game the visitors had won comfortably by six goals with no reply. Harry got on to the scoresheet for the fifth goal. He chipped the ball home beyond the despairing San Marino keeper after a fine pass from Jonjo Shelvey. It was Kane's second goal in three games for his country – a brilliant return even allowing for the quality of the opposition in two of those goals. Not only that, his arrival as a sub gave England much more of a balanced look as he plugged into the traditional centre-forward role, freeing up Vardy from it and allowing the whippet-like striker more space in between the lines and the wings, to better utilise his pace and torment the San Marino back line.

The win guaranteed England qualification for Euro 2016 and Harry celebrated with the rest of the squad as they returned home that night. He was a newcomer to the scene and still only twenty-two, but he played his part. After the win, he tweeted his delight at the goal and praised Rooney for also scoring, as the skipper was now just one short of becoming England's all-time top goalscorer. Harry tweeted, 'Delighted to get the goal and most importantly qualify for the Euros! Well done to @WayneRooney Hopefully break the record on Tuesday night!'

Kane then told *ITV Sport*, 'It's great to get on the scoresheet. A lot has been said about me not scoring this season but I came off the bench and, thankfully, scored. It is a great achievement by Wayne Rooney to equal the goalscoring record and we are all buzzing for him but the whole team did well and we don't want to stop here as we want to keep moving on.'

The reference about discussions over his 'not scoring this season' was one that would become something of a regular one: he had failed to score at club level for one month since the new season began – and it would be a case of same again when the next campaign started one year later. So the goal against San Marino was his first of the season for club and country.

That would get the doomsayers going, querying whether Harry's goals of the previous season were those of a one-season wonder. Harry would also be labelled 'a late starter' as it seemed he needed a few games of a new season to get totally into his stride. It had nothing to do with playing for England, or the prospect of upcoming international matches. It was just the way he was – although I have no doubt that as the years roll by he will get off to fliers, rather than waiting a month to hit top gear, as he develops further.

But honest as he always is, Harry admitted that he had dwelt upon why he had not scored at club level for the first month of the season. But a chat with England goalscoring legend Alan Shearer at a charity match had helped make him realise it was no big deal – and that the goals would start to flow again. He told the press how the chat with the *Match of the Day* pundit had put his mind at ease, explaining, 'We shared some things because he's been in the same sort of situation as I am now and he gave me some good tips. It was great to hear what he went through sometimes and what he did about it. He just said that you are going to go through games without scoring but the best strikers in the world just put it to the back of their mind and focus on the next chance or goal. Talking to players like that can only help me – players who have been there and done it at the top level for years. That's what I'm aiming to do.'

The chat certainly seemed to help him with England as he now added to his tally. Kane hit the back of the net in his very next appearance – a 2–0 victory over Switzerland, which was also memorable for Rooney becoming his country's top goalscorer after he converted a penalty for the second goal of the night.

Harry had found the net to open the scoring after coming on as a second-half substitute. Luke Shaw set him up at the far post after a fine segment of play involving Rooney. Kane did not hesitate as the ball reached him, hammering it home low. It meant Harry's record in Euro 2016 qualifying now read three goals in three appearances from the bench, an impressive triple in just over eighty minutes' playing time for England. Harry wasn't just banging on the door for a regular starting spot now, he was hammering it down with goal after goal.

The Sun's Charlie Wyett summed up how ridiculous it was to have suggested Kane was a one-season wonder and made a pertinent point that no one else had about his scoring feats for England: 'The night was in danger of becoming a massive disappointment until Harry Kane once again delivered. He scored after 79 seconds on his debut against Lithuania, after 18 minutes against San Marino and within ten minutes of coming on last night. The only time Kane has not scored for England was when he started. Those who have tipped him to become a one-season wonder will end up being proved wrong. England have now won all eight of their qualifiers and look certain to deliver the perfect ten.

'Tougher tests are to come – at least Roy Hodgson's team will play France and Spain in some decent friendlies in November – yet Rooney cannot do everything on his own. Him aside, the starting XI had mustered just ten goals between them and while Hodgson has not been helped by injuries, at least Kane's continued goals presence should ease the burden on the record scorer.'

Hodgson would now put his trust in Kane, starting him for the next four games which brought wins against Estonia, Lithuania and France but defeat by Spain, the latter match in which England were outclassed and Harry was starved of service. He would go those four games without scoring but his next goal would come in momentous circumstances, in Berlin. Any game against Germany is a pivotal one for the development of an England team in different eras and this one would prove to be no different. Harry was excited about the game, even more so when he learned he would be in the starting eleven. This was a game every England star wanted to start in and Harry was determined to prove he had what it took to keep his place in the team. And where better an opportunity to do that than against England's biggest rivals and the reigning world champions?

With Rooney missing injured, Harry knew he had a good chance of making the starting eleven. Boss Roy Hodgson told him a couple of days beforehand that indeed he had and that he had total faith in him. And even Germany boss Joachim Löw admitted he feared the Spurs striker, saying he would be a big threat if chosen and that the spine of young Spurs players, including Kane, Dele Alli and Eric Dier boded well for England's future. Löw told reporters that because of such young stars England, were 'interesting and one of the favourites to win Euro 2016' and that it would be 'a good test' for his brilliant team. He added, 'This will be a taste of what we can expect at the Euros.'

And that also proved to be the case for Harry and his teammates, too, as the hosts roared into a 2–0 lead in Berlin, with goals from Toni Kroos and Mario Gomez. Low had paid compliment to the test he expected England to pose by starting with his virtual first-choice eleven and they had dictated the early pace and rhythm of the game. But Harry settled England's nerves by pulling one back just after the hour mark, a goal that will always be remembered as much for its delivery as its execution. He deceived a hapless defender with a 'Cruyff turn' and then lashed the ball home past the world's top goalkeeper, Manuel Neuer.

It was a sensational goal and one that was appreciated by

many football fans across the globe as it served as a special tribute to Johan Cruyff, the legendary Dutch footballer who had passed away just four days before the game. He had given his name to the 'Cruyff turn', which Harry pulled off so well, after debuting it in the 1974 World Cup finals. Cruyff worked the turn by initially befuddling a defender by pretending to be about to pass or cross the ball. Then he would drag the ball behind his planted foot with the inside of his crossing foot, turn through 180 degrees, and accelerate away from the defender.

Harry had pulled off the same feat forty-one years later, and with similar aplomb. Indeed in some ways it took the skill one phase further on as he scored directly after completing it.

The young player's goal was also applauded by Löw after the game. 'Kane caused us a lot of trouble,' he would say, 'and that goal was something else. It was impossible to stop him because of the turn and difficult for Manuel as the turn took everyone by surprise and created time and space for the shot.' Hodgson also nodded his head and said, 'Fantastic goal. I always knew Harry was going to be a special player for us and he has showed that he can be tonight. To see an England player score a goal like that gives us all great hope and encouragement that we are on the right path.'

Harry himself was on a real high after the game and the toast of the dressing room. Little wonder given the nature of his wonder goal. He would later admit it was 'a dream to score and to score such a goal' against the Germans. He said, 'This was the best goal I have scored in an England shirt so far, especially as it was against one of the best goalkeepers in the world. I used a Cruyff turn and then struck the ball into the corner. At that moment I didn't think about the symbolism of scoring after the use of a Cruyff turn – but afterwards I did!'

And at the time he said he believed the result would be a major boost for England's hopes of doing well at Euro 2016 (which, however, would not be the case as they crumbled in the tournament), 'To go and win that game in the manner we did – to come back from 2–0 down away from home to the world champions – was such a big boost. Psychologically that can help us further down the line. It's good to have experiences like that to draw on for when you are next in a losing position.'

Follow-up goals from Vardy and Dier secured the win for England in Berlin after Kane's effort had instilled them with renewed hope. It was also telling that England had nineteen goal attempts to Germany's ten; this appeared to be a team moving forward with style, with Harry as its fulcrum. This was also Harry's first goal since starting for England, making it four in all.

England fans were cock-a-hoop not just with the remarkable result but with the performances of Kane and his new international partner-in-crime, Vardy. On social media many commented on their displays by suggesting the partnership represented the beginning of the end for Rooney as first-choice striker. One England fan, Arundeep, said, 'Rooney should not be anywhere near now, Kane and Vardy are too much.' While Najaf added, 'Wayne Rooney's [England] career is officially done tonight. It would be a disaster if Roy played him ahead of Vardy and Kane.' And Marty added, 'Vardy and Kane ruining Rooney's England career.'

It was a mite over the top, given that Rooney was now England's top scorer ever and that he still inspired the squad as leader. He still had a lot of appearances ahead of him. But it showed just how far Kane had come in his rush to the top. Still a young man and arguably one of the first names on the team sheet. OK, Vardy was also in with a shout but he was pushing thirty and surely of more use as an impact sub with his speed to run at tiring opposition defenders.

Kane also played in the next match, another prestige friendly, this time against the Netherlands at Wembley. But it would be a frustrating night as he and England struggled for cohesion in a match they should have won against an experimental Holland. It didn't help that Hodgson dropped him to the bench, only bringing him on after seventy minutes for Adam Lallana. It was 1–1 at the time but the Dutch won it seven minutes after Harry emerged. The outcome was a massive disappointment after the wonderful result in Berlin and Harry and the boys trooped disconsolately off the pitch.

It was not the result they needed as Euro 2016 loomed but perhaps it was a good thing in that it cooled expectations after the win against Germany. This was always the way with England – the fans either believed they were good enough to win a tournament or that they were overrated, pampered stars who were not good enough to get past the group stage. Harry Kane soon learned not to get too excited if England won, or too down if England lost. He had been an England fan as a boy and experienced those very same emotions as the traditional supporter of the national team. But now, as a player and an intelligent, mature one at that despite his tender years, he analysed his own and the team's displays with a much more rational, considered set of values.

It was England's first defeat at Wembley since November 2013 and Hodgson bemoaned a 'lack of creativity' after the match, although he said his team did not deserve to lose. Rooney, meanwhile, to his credit, took the more optimistic view that the breakthrough of players like Kane and Vardy was good news in that it created for stiffer competition and could only be good for the team in the long run. It was a generous analysis given he could be the victim if Harry did start at Euro 2016 as the main striker. Wayne said the argy-bargy for a starting role had 'not been there' in previous tournaments and added, 'Now if everyone is fit, no one knows. The manager can play three or four teams, different combinations. For the country it's going to be an exciting tournament. It's an opportunity for us to do really well. I want to be there and be involved and hopefully lead this team as far as possible.'

Euro 2016 was looming ever closer and Harry was relieved to learn he would start the next friendly, against Turkey at Manchester City's ground on 22 May. It was a case of sweet-and-sour as he scored once again for the national team, but then missed a penalty. Harry opened the scoring swiftly, hitting the back of the net with a well-drilled shot after Spurs teammate Dele Alli set him up on four minutes. Harry was offside but the ref ruled a goal and he wasn't about to argue. The penalty miss took the shine off the day for him, although the team still won 2–1, albeit with several worrying performances in defence. Vardy won the penalty but Kane hit the post with the spot kick, much to his dismay as he held his head in his hands. Luckily, Vardy won the match with England's second goal.

Harry had proven once again that if selected he would not let his country down – and could be relied upon to score the goals that would surely be needed if the team were to progress at Euro 2016, given the backline's obvious deficiencies. Kane had been voted Man of the Match but a stat linked to the penalty miss was one he would rather not have warranted. He had become the first England player to miss a penalty, apart from shootouts, since Frank Lampard erred against Japan in May 2010.

There would be one more friendly for England before their opening game against Russia in Euro 2016, against Australia at Sunderland's Stadium of Light. England triumphed 2–1 but Kane was not involved in the game, spending the whole match on the bench as Hodgson tinkered with his line-up. Still, he had been assured by the boss that he would play a part in the tournament opener the following month. Harry Kane would excitedly pack his bags for the event in France, with great hopes that he could be part of an England team that would buck the trend of relative failure at major tournaments. Yet, as we will see in a later chapter, he would leave France with his tail between his legs, his optimism dashed by another disappointing failure by England, and claims that he himself looked jaded and fatigued. But before focusing on Euro 2016, we should examine the season that led into it, and Harry's feats for Tottenham in his remarkable 2015–16 club season.

CHAPTER TEN

THE MAN WITH THE GOLDEN BOOT

If the 2014–15 season had been the one when Harry Kane had arrived seemingly from nowhere to hog the back-page headlines in the nationals, the 15–16 campaign would be one in which he would prove he was no flash in the pan. Indeed, he would do much, much more than that – he would prove that he was a striker whose proficiency in front of goal could stand comparison with the Premier League's best. It was remarkable to watch him during the season, considering he had only become a Spurs regular in November 2014. Yet twelve months later he was scoring for fun and would continue on his goals spree to win the coveted Premier League Golden Boot award in May 2016.

Many fans wondered how he had exploded on to the scene from seemingly nowhere but that, of course, was a fallacy as any Tottenham fan would tell you. Only twenty-two, he had been around a good while, learning his trade in the lower leagues on loan and then the Championship and returning to the Lane and finding his feet as third-choice striker, being patient and waiting for his big chance. He had been nurtured by Tottenham and, when his chance finally came, had taken it with open arms. So much so that he had hit thirty-one goals in his first season in the Premier League for the club – and that after becoming first choice only three months into the season.

He had also played for his country at senior level and was raring to go in pre-season after a well-earned summer break with his long-term girlfriend, Kate Goodland. Despite his heroics that first season, some critics still wondered aloud whether Kane could repeat his goalscoring feats in his second season. This would be his first FULL season as Spurs' number one striker, since Pochettino had decided to sell both Soldado and Adebayor. The pressure was on in the sense that he was now the ONLY top-class striker at the club, and that some pundits believed he would fall victim to 'second season syndrome'. That is football's equivalent to the record industry's 'second album syndrome', whereby a recording artist delivers a stunning debut but then struggles to reproduce the magic on their second album. Inevitably, a panning awaits from the critics and doubts are raised to whether they will ever hit the heights again.

But Harry would avoid that scenario with an even BETTER second season portfolio – although he would get off to what would become known as his regular slow start before the goals started to fly in. Having said that, there would be no sluggishness on the club's summer 2015 tour, which would see him among the goals and highlight just how far he had come in terms of popularity and renown after that incredible first season.

The first sign of his new-found stardom came in Australia when Harry was mobbed at a shopping mall in Sydney when fans spotted him. Spurs had to send a minibus to pick him up, otherwise he might still be there signing autographs! He said, 'It was surreal!' And regarding that wonderful first season, he added, 'I don't think what's happened this season has sunk in still. I've not had a chance to look back, but I've loved every minute of it. I've always wanted to be a player at a top club, starting week-in, week-out in the Premier League, playing against the big teams, playing in a cup final as we did this year, and playing for your country. I've managed to achieve that in a small amount of time, which has been crazy but great. I don't want it to stop! What I've got to do now is work hard to maintain it.'

He showed he was doing just that when the tour hit Colorado. Legends Kaká and David Villa had given the American hosts a 2–0 lead, with Harry pulling one back just before the interval. And some goal it was, as he sped through the backline before dispatching the ball into the net. When Harry was taken off late in the second half he received a rapturous ovation from the crowd, a further sign of his growing acclaim, although some Spurs fans would point out that he might do even better if he had some help in attack from another forward. They feared he might struggle to repeat his goals feast if he had to forge a lone furrow all season.

And as the Premier League campaign got under way in

August, 2015, it seemed their fears may have foundation as Harry struggled to find the net. Of course, with it being his first full season as first-choice striker, we had not yet had the advantage of knowing that the boy was a slow starter. That he took a little while to fine-tune his goal instincts – and that it would be exactly the same twelve months later.

But what we did learn straight away was that Harry meant business – that he was determined enough and confident enough to believe that he deserved his place in the team. That became loud and clear when he demanded he be given a new shirt number for the season – and it was one that came with a heavy load. After having the number 18 on his back the previous season, he now told Pochettino he felt confident enough to take the number 10 shirt. That was the sign of a player who believed he was ready to not only stay in the team, but one who also felt ready to make a claim for legend in the club's illustrious annals. It had been the domain of Adebayor, but few Spurs fans believed he had deserved to wear it; he had no special place in their hearts and had failed dismally to live up to the giants who had worn it with pride in yesteryear. It is debatable whether Adebayor even knew the great importance of the number 10 shirt at Tottenham.

But Harry Kane was certainly well aware of the aura surrounding it. He was well versed in the history of the club and how its legendary 'number 10s' over the years were held in reverence by the supporters. Harry told *The Telegraph* just why he wanted the shirt and just what it meant to him: 'It's such an iconic number at Spurs. When you look at the players who have worn it – Sheringham, Keane, Hoddle, Ferdinand,

Greaves. When I was growing up Keane and Sheringham were my idols and they wore 10. So it was always my dream to wear it. Obviously 18 was great to me and [Jermain] Defoe gave it to me. But when I knew 10 was available I just wanted it. I love this club and to be wearing number 10 for Tottenham is amazing for me. I could not resist.'

But some reckoned the weight of the shirt contributed to his goal drought at the start of that season – he went 748 minutes without netting, although Harry laughed off the suggestion. His first club goal in the new campaign came on 26 September 2015, as Tottenham thumped Man City 4–1 at home in the league. Of course, he was relieved to have scored but denied that he had been under intense pressure to do so. He had simply continued to play his own game the best he could in the knowledge that the goals would flow eventually. All the world's top scorers have hit a barren patch some time – it just seems that Harry's goal-less periods come at the start of the season. Which is surely better than them coming at the end, when the pressure is really on, and the goals are needed to hit end-of-season targets, such as a cup win or a Champions League spot. Harry would add that one day – and soon – he also anticipates winning those targets, including the Premier League crown.

Harry crashed the ball home from what seemed an offside position, but maybe he was due for his luck to turn after so many of his efforts had somehow evaded the goal so far that season. He certainly was happy to claim it on the hour mark and confirmed to BT Sport after the game that he had never been over worried by his twelve-hour barren spell, explaining that, 'There's been a lot of talk but I'm a confident man and have faith in my ability. I'm delighted. It was a very good victory against a team who were top of the table.' Pochettino was also pleased for his star man, saying, 'It is never easy to play against a club like Manchester City, as they have so many great players. I congratulate my players because they were brilliant. We fully deserved the victory. We are all very happy for Harry Kane. As a striker, you want to score. It is very important for the team and him. We believe in his talent and quality.'

City boss Manuel Pellegrini was inevitably less charitable, merely saying that he had no comment on Kane's talent or otherwise, except to add that his goal was definitely offside! This was hardly surprising, also given that the defeat ousted his team from the top of the table and pushed Tottenham up to fifth.

And to show just how unpredictable football can be, just over a week later Harry was on the wrong side of scoring, with an own goal in the 2–2 draw at Swansea. *Wales Online* (*walesonline.co.uk*) made a big thing of Harry's misfortune, saying, 'After Montero pressurised Walker into giving away a corner, Shelvey's swinger saw Kane, alone at the near post, attempt to clear on the edge of the six yard box try to volley a clearance but sliced it into the top corner of his own net.' And then crowing that: '"Harry Kane, He's one of our own..." Swansea fans offer up their contender for chant of the season moments after Tottenham's hometown hero puts Monk's men 2–1 up.'

The *London Evening Standard* was, predictably, much more sympathetic to Kane's plight, calling his own goal 'a horrible mistake'. Harry himself simply shrugged and said he would not let it weigh him down – in Kane's balanced, measured world view you take the bad and the good in equal measure. That way you keep your feet on the ground when you hit the heights and don't fall into despondency when the lows come around. It is a philosophy that has served him well over the years as he battled for his place at Tottenham, via loans and the subs' bench, and become 'an overnight sensation' with the club and England, after finally being given his chance at the expense of more experienced pros who had failed to deliver.

Harry showed his resilience and got on with his own game. At the end of the following month he scored a hat-trick in the 5–1 away win at Bournemouth, a resounding answer to those who had said he had lost his goals touch and those who had sniggered that he hadn't lost his goals touch as he had scored at Swansea (with that own goal). Afterwards his boss said he had never doubted that the boy would hit the goal trail in devastating form once again. Pochettino told the press pack, 'We put them under pressure with the way that we pressed high. The effort was fantastic and I'm very pleased with Harry Kane's hat-trick. It's important for us, for the team and for him. We always believed in him.'

Harry was his usual stoical self when he told *BBC Sport*, 'You're never going to just be on a high, you're going to have ups and downs. It's about maintaining your focus, not getting too carried away and trying to stay patient. That's what I've been doing. I don't think I've been doing that badly overall. Today the ball dropped for me nicely and I was able to put it in the back of the net. I'm obviously delighted to get a hat-trick, but the most important thing is that we won comfortably.' And Gary Lineker, one of Harry's heroes, tweeted his congratulations: 'Welcome back. A nice little hat-trick. It was only a matter of time.'

Harry was truly back and proved it by scoring in the next five Spurs games – the 3–1 league win over Aston Villa, the 2–1 Europa League victory over Anderlecht and the 1–1 league draw with Arsenal, the 4–1 win over West Ham and the 1–0 win in Azerbaijan against Qarabağ FK. Naturally, his goal in the latter match against Tottenham's north London rivals gave him the greatest joy. He put Spurs ahead at the Emirates, with a sweet sweep of the ball past Petr Čech. It was his fifth goal in his last three league appearances and his sixth from twelve games that season – one in two and not a bad return for a man who some pundits claimed had lost his goal touch. Plus it was the first time he had played at the Emirates and he would admit that made the goal extra special.

After the game Harry told reporters, 'I was absolutely buzzing with the goal. It was my first time playing at the Emirates and I wanted to score so badly and wanted to win. We played so well and had chances to go 2–0 up so we're disappointed we didn't get the win in the end but perhaps in a couple of days we'll probably say it's a good point. We've had a tough week and I thought we played well. It's just the way football goes. We're also undefeated since the first game of the season, which is great. I'll keep working hard and keep trying to do my best for the team.

'We've shown that we can be up there with the big teams. We probably deserved to win against Liverpool, we beat

Manchester City and maybe deserved to win at Arsenal as well. We're not just drawing where we're hanging on, we're drawing where we're playing well and there are chances we could be winning these games. We've just got to keep doing what we're doing – there are lots of games still left to play. There's still a long way to go and we're not going to come out and say that we're title contenders but we're in a great position and we've played a lot of tough teams – but there's still a long way to go.'

Harry headed off to join up with England during the international break and when he teamed up again with Tottenham it was for another huge clash in London, this time against West Ham United at the Lane. After his goal against the Gunners, Kane now went one better with a brace in the 4–1 win over the Hammers. The goals were once again rolling in and those who doubted him now came over all shy, while those why stood by him simply nodded as if to say, 'We told you so.' The optimists far outweighed those pessimists and the question now being asked in pubs near the Lane was whether Harry could better his output from the previous season and challenge for the Golden Boot award.

The double against the Hammers was fair reward, as Kane tormented their defence all afternoon and earned himself the customary chants of affection from the fans. They loved nothing more than beating local rivals, and Arsenal and West Ham were at the top of their wish list. Even Hammers boss Slaven Bilić departed from the norm to praise Kane, admitting the player 'had caused us big problems' and that Spurs had been 'quicker and stronger' than his own team. The victory meant that Tottenham were now twelve league games unbeaten, equalling a club record, and snapping at the heels of Arsenal for a place in the top four. Pochettino's decision to work with a young English core and to continue to back Kane was paying dividends.

Kane took his goal tally in London derbies to twelve in fourteen games and, after scoring just once in Spurs' first thirteen games of the season, now had eight in his last five. He said afterwards that it was the team's best performance of the season so far and that he was pleased with his own form, but that he had never once doubted that he would be back among the goals in a big way as the season progressed. He was voted Man of the Match and left the Lane once again on a high. Kane would draw a blank when yet another London outfit, Chelsea, turned up at the Lane a week later but at least he did not have to suffer the bitter taste of defeat as the two teams battled to a 0–0 draw.

Christmas saw him back in business with goals in consecutive games against Southampton and Norwich. The 2–0 win at Southampton marked Harry's hundredth appearance for Tottenham and he admitted after the game that it had given him great pleasure to mark the occasion with a goal – and to see the obvious joy it brought to the fans he loved. It was also his tenth goal in his last ten matches.

The 3–0 win over the Canaries on Boxing Day was a particularly pleasing festive prezzie as Harry grabbed yet another brace to complete his scoring for 2015 in some style. He scored from the penalty spot after being set up by Dele Alli for his second of the game, a result that kept Spurs well on target for a Champions League spot. They were fourth in the table and both Kane and Pochettino were convinced that not only could they stay there, but they could even improve on that position by the season's conclusion. The two goals meant Harry had scored twenty-seven in the league in 2015 and had beaten the club record set by another of his heroes, Teddy Sheringham. Pochettino led the plaudits for Harry's record feat, telling reporters after the match, 'It is difficult to speak more about Harry Kane. For me, he needs to keep working hard and keep showing his qualities in the games. Dele Alli is another player we are very happy with but it is about the team and they showed confidence in how we played.'

Landmark games and records falling were now becoming the order of the day as Harry consolidated his position as Tottenham's number-one striker and continued to push his claims to be the first name on the England team sheet, too.

No sooner had 2016 dawned than he chalked up yet another milestone with his fiftieth goal for Spurs in the 2–2 draw at home to Leicester in the FA Cup third round. Typical of Harry the team man, he bemoaned the fact they had not been able to put the tie to bed before conceding, but he was pleased to have hit the fifty-mark with a last-gasp penalty after a Nathan Dyer handball in the box.

Harry had come off the bench to net that goal as both teams rested key players, with Vardy out of the match completely for Leicester. Pochettino also rested Hugo Lloris and Érik Lamela while City boss Claudio Ranieri felt able to drop Danny Drinkwater and Riyad Mahrez to the bench. It underlined just how important the Premier League was now – even a top

FA Cup clash was deemed losable if it meant success in the league and a possible Champions League spot. The players had been left out as both managers decided the league match the following Wednesday – when the teams would meet again – was of much greater importance. Both were pushing for the title and so it made sense to give preference to the league, even if that meant exiting the FA Cup.

In the event, both would get another chance in the cup with that draw leading to a replay a couple of weeks later. But the Wednesday result would leave Pochettino the loser in terms of laying down a marker in the league. All the key players on both sides who had not started in the cup match returned, but it would be Leicester who gained an advantage and major psychological booster as they returned to the Lane and won 1–0. It was a victory that left City in second place and Tottenham in fourth and opened the gap between the teams to six points. If Spurs had won, they would have been just a point behind them and so it is clear that many pundits are correct in saying that it was a win that gave Leicester belief that they actually COULD go on to lift the league crown.

Even in January 2016, the sceptics were still predicting that the bubble would burst and City would end up probably seventh or eighth. But the win at the Lane made most realise that this wasn't a continued lucky spell; that City could well win the league if their players continued to defy all odds. For Harry and Co. it was a sickener – as Harry would concede afterwards. Sure, he was ever optimistic that ground could be made up and it was, after all, only the start of January but it was a match he had felt could be won and it was only natural that he and his teammates felt low. It had looked as though the match was heading for a 0–0 draw, which would have been disappointing in itself, but up popped Robert Huth to head home a winner, just seven minutes from time. It was a killer blow. Spurs had had the better of the game and the better chances, with one Kane effort being tipped on to the bar by Kasper Schmeichel but it was the result that counted. Pochettino tried to play down the defeat saying, 'I'm disappointed. We created the better chances. You need to score. We need to keep calm and try to improve. All the stats are positive for us. It's difficult to explain – we deserved more and to win the game. In football you can get punished for one little mistake. We are going to try to analyse the game. We were unlucky tonight.'

And, sure enough, Tottenham now went on an eight-match unbeaten run with Kane contributing another five goals. It showed how resilient he and his teammates had become. A loss like the Leicester one could have led to even more trouble a few seasons earlier, but now Kane dusted himself off and showed the power of positive thinking. There was no moping by him or his teammates – they simply worked extra hard in training and gave their all in the matches, starting with the very next one against perennial relegation battlers, Sunderland. Inevitably, Harry scored as Spurs put their Leicester blues behind them by thrashing the Black Cats 4–1 at home. It was just what 'the Poc' ordered and had the confidence oozing back through the veins of his young team.

Once again Harry was on target from the penalty spot, after Danny Rose was fouled. It was his twelfth league goal of the season and his fifty-first in ninety-one games for the club. He did not manage to find the net but found revenge was oh-so-sweet in the next match, as Spurs won 2–0 at Leicester in their FA Cup third round replay. But Kane was back on the scoresheet in the 3–1 win at Crystal Palace, the 3–0 win at Norwich, when he grabbed a brace, and, most importantly, the 2–1 victory at Manchester City. Given the Blues were one of their main rivals for a top four spot and, indeed, the title, this was a major shot in the arm for Harry and the team. To win at City showed they had the ability to shoot down one of their biggest rivals and that they were definite contenders for the league crown.

Once again, Harry would convert a penalty, after Raheem Sterling handled the ball in the box. Coolness personified, Kane fired the ball past Joe Hart in the City goal. City levelled but Eriksen won the day. It was another one for the history books, too, this time for the team as they notched their fifth consecutive Premier League game for the first time since they won six in 2011. The win kept them in second place, just two points behind Leicester with everything to play for. City were four points behind Spurs in fourth, with Arsenal two adrift in third.

Kane told reporters the win was a statement of intent by Tottenham – that they were going all out to lift the league title and were not just a team who played pretty. That they could dig in and battle when necessary, adding that, 'To come here where City are very good and get the result how we did is great. It was a different performance to the 4–1 win at home and it shows what we're capable of. It's not just one way of playing – we can adapt, battle and everyone worked very hard for each other so it's very rewarding to get the three points. There's always a tough game here on a big pitch. City, at home, have the incentive to go forward and try to get the result. We got ahead but then dropped off a bit too much, they got the goal back but to go again and get the goal for 2–1 shows the character and ability in the team. It was a great ball from Erik Lamela to put Christian through for the winner, he took a great touch to set it up and then he did what he does best – put it in the back of the net. It was a cool finish in a pressure situation so I'm delighted for him. To get the victory in the end is an amazing result and we have to build on this going forward.'

Harry admitted he was enjoying taking – and scoring – the team's penalties, and that the success rate was not simply down to good luck. He practised long and hard on the training ground and saw the results in games. He also tweeted his thanks to the fans after the City win, saying, 'A massive win! To score, celebrate and win together with the fans was unreal!'

The games were coming thick and fast and the pressure was unrelenting. But Kane kept his cool and, in an incredible four-week run from 5 March to 2 April 2016, he scored seven goals, six for his club and one for England. The national team goal came in an international friendly in Germany as England stormed to a brilliant 3–2 win over their biggest rivals. But it was in the competitive club world that his goals really mattered at this time of the season, those six starting with a goal in the 2–2 home draw with Arsenal on 5 March and culminating in the 1–1 draw at Liverpool on 2 April. The Arsenal draw was something of a disappointment, since a win would have put Spurs top of the league and the Gunners had to come from behind with ten men, with Alexis Sánchez salvaging an unlikely point. Harry's goal was a belter; he won the ball in the left-hand corner, moved inside and struck it home from what seemed the most unlikely of angles.

The goals glut continued that March with a brace against both Aston Villa and Bournemouth and helped to earn him the Premier League March Player of the Month award. He had racked up twenty-two league goals, three more than nearest rival Jamie Vardy, and was leading the race for the Golden Boot award as the run-in to the end of the season loomed. Amazingly, given those stats, it was Kane's first monthly award of the season. The previous season he had won back-to-back awards in January and February. Harry was delighted to win it again that March, saying, 'I scored one of my better goals against Arsenal and we built on that performance against Villa and Bournemouth. I was delighted to score the goals in those games. Hopefully I'll get a few more goals and continue to push on, continue to do well for the team and we'll continue to keep winning games.'

Which he did, and they did. His goal against Liverpool on 2 April was his twenty-second league strike of the season and put him clear at the top as Spurs' highest ever scorer in a Premier League season. It also meant he had scored twenty in a season twice, joining nine others and only behind Les Ferdinand (three seasons), Ruud van Nistelrooy (four), Thierry Henry (five) and Alan Shearer (seven). Michael Owen never managed it – which highlights Kane's feat in doing so in his first two seasons.

Harry continued his fine form as he now closed in on the Golden Boot, all the while knowing that if he faltered, the prolific Vardy and Agüero were waiting to pounce. Kane grabbed yet another double in Tottenham's 4–0 win at Stoke on 18 April, and was on target again as Spurs fought out a 2–2 at Chelsea on Monday, 2 May. His final goal that May would come with a strike for England as they beat Turkey 2–0 at Wembley in a pre-Euro 2016 friendly. But by then he had already got the Golden Boot in his holdall, finishing with twenty-five goals, one ahead of Vardy and Agüero, and helping Tottenham to third spot in the Premier League. Sure, Harry and the team were disappointed to lose out on the title to Leicester but it had been some campaign: a campaign in which both he and Spurs had come a mighty long way. They had all progressed yet again under Pochettino and it would now surely be only a matter of time before they DID lift the league title the whole club craved.

They had signed off with two disappointing results – a 2–1 home loss against Southampton and a 5–1 going-over at Newcastle – but that could be put down to sheer fatigue and the pressure finally taking its toll. This was a young team and they could only learn from that double bitter taste of defeat – and the final disappointment of finishing third, a point behind Arsenal. Harry and the boys had given their all to finish above the Gunners for the first time since 1995, but it was not to be.

Harry had another consolation in that he was named in the PFA Team of the Year for the second consecutive campaign while his goals had propelled Tottenham into the Champions League. He was the so-called 'one-season wonder' who had fared even better in his second season. Now all he had to do was repeat it all over again in his third season, and help England to glory in Euro 2016. Which was a big weight on the local lad who was still only twenty-two years old, but one that he was more than happy, and grateful, to shoulder. But the Euro 2016 weight would turn out much heavier to lift than the Tottenham one…

CHAPTER ELEVEN

CORNERED AT THE EUROS

It would be viewed as one of the most puzzling, not to say foolish, decisions of the 2016 European Championship in France – and would also play no small part in the ridiculing and parting of the ways between the England football team and their hapless manager, Roy Hodgson. Yes, we're talking about the nice but out-of-his-depth boss's dastardly plan to get his top striker to take the corners for the team. Instead of causing havoc in the penalty area, Harry was out wide or left, sending balls in to players who were not as deadly as him in front of goal. If any one instance summed up the sometimes potty nature of the Hodgson era, it was this. Why, oh why, would you lose such a potentially lethal impact in front of goal from your main man? No wonder rival teams were grateful to Hodgson, for this was much more of a blunder than say Glenn Hoddle's introduction of a faith healer in the England camp at the 1998 World Cup Finals.

Hodgson himself explained his thinking like this, claiming that Harry had the accuracy and pinpoint ability to get the ball to the right spot that apparently no other man in his squad possessed. He went on: 'I don't need to apologise for Kane taking a corner. Especially if you've got a player with his quality striking a ball and no one else in the team who comes up to that level of striking a ball.'

At the time, Harry did not complain, he simply got on with the job and tried to steer the corners into the most dangerous positions, even though he was the only striker of any team at the tournament to be put in such a position. But later in the tournament he told reporters how it had come about, saying, 'Me taking corners was something we tried when we first met up for the warm-up game against Turkey. We had a lot of tall players and they saw the delivery I had, and wanted me to put it in the box. We did it then and it stuck.

'I've taken a few for Spurs now and again when we have been chasing the game. I've even scored goals from corners, but they've rarely been direct with a header. There have been knockdowns. I've been sniffing out areas where the ball falls, and putting it in the net.'

A couple of months later he would confirm to *The Sun* that it had been Hodgson's dictat at Euro 2016 although, Harry being Harry, he refused to criticise the boss. He has never been one to denigrate a fellow football man in public and is generally free of spite and resentment privately, come to that.

Harry said of his boss's 'masterplan': 'It was the manager's choice and I always listen to the manager and follow instructions. The issue got blown out of proportion a bit because we weren't winning games like we wanted to. But, that's football. You have to take the bad with the good.'

Others within the game were less generous. His club boss Pochettino said during the tournament, 'I don't want to criticise but I think Harry is a top scorer, so why is he taking free-kicks or corners if his skill is to score? You need to stay in the box, not outside.'

And Alan Shearer stirred the ever-growing hornet's nest of criticism by tweeting, 'I have to say that if a manager asked me to take corners, my answer would be, "Ask someone else to take them!"'

But Shearer, of course, became established as an England legend and had enough presence and clout to have told his manager that he would not be cajoled into taking corners. Harry had only just started his England career and was hardly in a position to be laying down the law to a manager who was sixty-seven years old and set in his ways – and who had the power to leave him on the sidelines if he felt the player was speaking out of turn. A source confirmed this, saying, 'Harry Kane had only just broken into the team and was trying to establish himself as an automatic starter for Hodgson. Would you have questioned his judgment if you were in that position? Would you have jeopardised your place in the team by telling the boss that he was wrong?

'Let's be clear here, it's OK for Shearer to play the big man, but Harry was not in any position to do that. He was a newcomer and was reluctant to speak out; he was wary and maybe a bit fearful, which is perfectly understandable. Plus he is the sort of guy who will always "take one" for the team and who puts the team first, rather than personal glory. The boss is the boss and Harry respected Roy in that role and would have played anywhere or adapted to any tactics for him.'

That makes a lot of sense: a young newcomer who did not want to rock the boat, and who put the collective before self. Admirable traits from one of football's good guys and someone who has his feet firmly on the ground.

Having said that, other former footballing stars were quick to also put the boot in on Hodgson's baffling decision. Jamie Redknapp told *Sky Sports News*, 'We're allowing one of our best players to take corners – and it's not good news. I can't understand it. We've got some very good technical players – Alli, Wayne Rooney – so why are we letting Harry Kane take them? He can deliver a good ball and he has that cross where it dips into the box, but I'm sure most players can do that. We need Kane in the box. To have our best striker taking corners doesn't make any sense.'

And Ray Wilkins added, 'It baffles the life out of me. If you're a midfield player playing at international level and you can't kick a ball forty yards, unopposed, and stick it in an area of ten yards at a height where you have an opportunity to score, you shouldn't really be playing.'

A month after explaining why he had been pushed to take the corners, Harry did admit that it had become a point of laughter in the England dressing room, telling reporters, 'I will probably never take another corner. It's obviously a laugh and a joke now. We had a bit of a laugh and a joke with the manager about it, but it's something that happened.

'I am happy to be in the box and hopefully I will get a goal for it. It has become a bit of a thing now on social media. You have just got to laugh with it. Of course, it was a disappointing moment in the summer but it's football. It's what makes and breaks you as a player. It's what grows you up as a player and that is what I have got to use to help me.

'As a striker I want to get goals, it doesn't matter who I am playing. Hopefully if I am picked for the next game or the next squad hopefully I can get a few goals and see what happens.'

He admitted that despite his relatively poor showing in the Euros he was determined to push on with England – and that his club form over the previous season gave him all the confidence he needed to do just that, adding, 'What happened last season has given me confidence. Unfortunately there was a lot of talk last year and I managed to prove a lot of people wrong so people will talk this year as well. It's part of football. I am confident in my ability. I know that if I continue doing what I am doing the goals will come that is all I can do.

'I won the Golden Boot and I am a confident player.'

In an interview with his sponsors, Nike, he expanded upon how his self-belief and commitment helped him to maintain his remarkably swift rise to the top. Harry said, 'Of course it has all happened quite quickly for me. It is hard to get to be playing in the Premier League – but it is even more difficult to maintain that and stay at the top level when people are trying to get your place or work out your game to stop you. So that's something I need to work on in future years but if I keep scoring more than twenty goals a season it won't be a bad thing.'

And analyst Peter Smith summed up the farcical nature

of the move by pointing out how effective, or not, Harry had been with his corners in England's first game at the championships, against the Russians, saying, 'Kane took six corners against Russia on Saturday night, with two particularly poor efforts flying over the box, forcing Dele Alli to dash after the ball to keep it in play on the other side of the field. In the Premier League this season [2015–16], Kane took just seven corners for Tottenham, where Christian Eriksen is the dedicated set-piece specialist. And all seven of those Kane corners were taken short.'

Prior to Sam Allardyce's first (and as it would transpire, only) match as England boss in September 2016, skipper Rooney admitted that he had personally decided to relieve Kane of corner duties, against Hodgson's strategy, after the match against Russia. He did not consult with Hodgson, but felt it was within his remit as captain to make such a bold move. He said, 'Harry was taking corners. Roy decided for Harry to take corners but I felt at the time that he was the top goalscorer in the Premier League. He's a big lad in the box.

'It was Roy's decision but after the first game (against Russia) I don't think Harry wanted to take the corners so I went over and took them. I felt I probably should have been taking them anyway. Harry is probably better in the air than me and for the last season he had been scoring a lot of goals. So that was it really. I think players have the right to make decisions on the pitch. You make a decision on what you see on the pitch. Nothing was ever made of that. I don't think Roy had an issue with that.'

The fans were just as disappointed by Hodgson's move –

and made their opinions clear. They wanted Kane back in the box and well away from the edges of play. One fan, Mick, said, 'If the chosen wingers can't cross a ball, dead or otherwise, they shouldn't be there. Period! Kane or any other forward should be in the box because that's what he is there for, to get in and score. Idiotic decision and excuse by Roy.'

While Chris said, 'It was really ridiculous stripping the attack of a vital player when a full-back can easily take a corner kick.'

And Jude added, 'I couldn't understand why Harry Kane was out there taking the corners for England. He is a great striker and should have surely been on the end of the corner, knocking the ball in the net? It was such a waste having him do something that full-backs or midfield players could surely have managed? It's not a big deal to get a ball over precisely. England lost a valuable asset through Roy Hodgson's stubbornness and short-sightedness with Kane.'

When Allardyce did take over, he made it quite clear that Kane would no longer be on corner kick duty. Big Sam knew full well that the Spurs striker was best suited in the middle, where he could cause most damage to the opposition. He had no intention of giving his rivals a head start by holding Harry back from the thick of the action.

The business over the corners – and Harry's taking of them – summed up his impact at his first major international tournament. In a nutshell, they and he were disappointing. He had headed for France with massive optimism and belief, but left, if not shattered, then certainly a little bruised. Harry is an optimistic guy, who always sees the positives rather than the negatives, but even he needed to draw breath as England returned home, yet again from an international tournament, with a feeling of failure and let-down. He had set off as part of the new generation: the players who had never experienced the traditional despair at tournaments that had supposedly blighted them mentally. The likes of Lampard, Terry, Beckham and Co. were long gone. Only Rooney and Joe Hart remained from the really bad old days. Kane, Dele Alli, Danny Rose and Eric Dier were at the heart of the new brigade who would usher in a fresh, successful era, because none of them were tainted by the crushing disappointments of previous eras.

It was perhaps telling that they all played for Tottenham, too. Much to his credit, Mauricio Pochettino had created his vibrant young team with an English spine – and that was to his advantage and, we hoped, England's. It was not to be. Like previous generations, younger England seemed to struggle to live up to expectations, as if the weight of bringing success for the nation was just too heavy a load to carry.

Of course, it wasn't as simple as that alone. No, Hodgson's tactics and his meddling with his team's formation also played a significant part. If he hadn't made wholesale changes against Slovakia in their final group game, for example, England could have topped the table and got a far more comfortable set of fixtures, including a 'typical Brit encounter' against Northern Ireland in the round of 16, a fair chance against an underwhelming Belgium in the quarters, and the chance to make amends for previous let-downs against the Portuguese in the semis.

As it was, Hodgson's choices sent the team down a far trickier road – with the pugnacious Icelanders lying in wait in the round of 16, and a calamitous defeat into the bargain.

But Harry was certainly not at his best in France that summer. For me, he looked tired and jaded at times – no doubt the effect of his non-stop football at club level during the previous season. If one criticism could have been levelled at Pochettino that season, it was that he did not bring in a top-notch addition up front. It meant Kane had to play almost every match: if he had not, Spurs would have been a striker light and could have struggled. It put an enormous weight on his shoulders – which he was more than willing to carry, but which left him looking in need of a damned good rest when, instead, he was playing as England's number one striker in a major tournament.

Yet Harry had arrived in France full of hope and looking forward to making his mark on his first major international tournament. He had certainly come a long way in a short time – just fifteen months after his debut against Lithuania in March 2015, he was recognised as the main man up front for his country. Fleet Street's finest tipped their hats to Hodgson for having the courage to name five strikers in his squad; an attractive, confident, even daring move given his inherently conservative nature as a coach over the decades. Back at Euro 2012, his first tournament in charge, he had seemed keener not to lose, rather than to win, but he had realised since the World Cup of 2014 that England's more dazzling options were in attack, rather than defence, and had come around to the way of thinking that attack was, therefore, the best form of defence given the talented band of young forward players now at his disposal.

The sports desks in London credited Hodgson for his conversion and then started to debate the relative merits of the 'famous five' – Kane, Daniel Sturridge, Jamie Vardy, Rooney and the eighteen-year-old starlet Marcus Rashford. The latter was expected to make up the numbers or maybe come on as an impact sub, and as Rooney was skipper he was more or less bolted on as a starter. So that meant Kane would be fighting with Sturridge and Vardy for that automatic starting spot next to Rooney. He and Vardy were top scorers in the Premier League the previous campaign while Sturridge was still trying to regain maximum fitness, so it looked like a straight battle between Vardy and Harry.

Most commentators agreed that Harry would get the nod, as he had rather more variations to his game than Jamie, and he looked the more natural choice to link with Rooney. His vision meant he could also swap spots with Wayne and sneak into that number ten role so loved by his idol Teddy Sheringham in an earlier era, and Wayne could easily move into the centre-forward position. The *Daily Mail* best summed up Harry's right to claim a starting role, saying, 'The Premier League's top goalscorer who almost led Tottenham Hotspur to their first Premier League title, and he did it by playing up top in a 4-2-3-1 system too. Kane ranks first for minutes played (3,368), goals (25) and dribbles (104) out of the five this season, and he is second for shooting accuracy (61%) and chances created (44). As England's most recognisable centre-forward, Kane will, in all likelihood, be first choice in France and rightly so.'

But they came up with a rather more revolutionary idea of playing Kane WITH Vardy, with Alli in the number ten role, and Rooney in midfield.

That was all conjecture but there was no doubt that the excitement within the country, and among the players, was real and increasing. Harry tweeted his delight at making the squad on 16 May, saying, 'Delighted to be in the England squad. Looking forward to meeting up with the boys.'

The boys arrived in France on 6 June after posing on the runway in England prior to their flight. The majority looked grim – with just Kane, Vardy and Kyle Walker breaking the solemn mood with natural smiles. The trio were clearly looking forward to the event and possibly not as nerve-hit as other members of the squad, which was a young one compared with England squads of previous years.

I was told some were a little concerned after the terrorist attacks that France had suffered, but they would be tucked away and safe in Chantilly, in the north of the country, where security measures were said to be the most stringent England would have experienced at any major tournament, given the threat. As *The Sun* pointed out, Hodgson wanted the training camp to be just as secure – but for another reason, reporting that: 'England will set up camp at their Chantilly training base, where Hodgson has installed Fort Knox-style security. The Three Lions boss is so concerned about opposition scouts spying on his training and tactics ahead of the Euros, he insisted that seven-foot tarpaulin screening was erected around the entire perimeter. The secluded spot north of Paris is now the most secure in the history of the national team at a major tournament.'

I suspect Hodgson's concerns may have added to the worries of his young squad and I am not so convinced it matters whether the opposition see you train or not. Certainly, the likes of Brazil never worried about being hidden away when they won their series of World Cups; no, they more often than not welcomed people to watch, including locals, and their players appeared to enjoy the freedom. And in England's case at Euro 2016, it hardly seemed to have paid off as they struggled to hit their stride and their play and tactics were often as predicted by the Press beforehand.

The following day Hodgson did allow a group of invited local children to watch his squad train after they received a warm welcome in Chantilly. The youngsters even sang the English national anthem to make their visitors feel at home! Kane was seen at the head of the group as the players embarked on a run and was happily chatting with Jack Wilshere and Rooney. So, clearly, if he was going to find the tournament hard going it would not be because he was feeling low in any way. A source told me, 'Harry was bright and fit as a fiddle at that first session. He was enjoying being in France and enjoying being part of the England set-up. You've got to remember that this is a player who always dreamed of making it as a footballer at the highest level, and you don't get much higher than representing your country in a tournament abroad. Harry always dreamed of playing for England – now he was doing just that and he couldn't wait to get going and for the first game.'

That first game was just four days away, in Marseilles. It was vital that England should get off to a good start, with a win, to keep spirits high and ease the pressure for the other two

Group B games, against Wales on 16 June in Lens, and Slovakia, four days later, in Saint-Étienne. There was a little room for error as the top two sides would automatically qualify for the knockout stages and the third-placed side would advance if they turned out to be one best four teams of the six third-place finishers. That meant you would have to be pretty poor not to make it through to the next stage, but it was important to finish top of the group so that you would hopefully avoid the big guns, and tougher assignments.

But England got off to a disappointing start in Marseilles, being held to a 1–1 draw by the un-fancied Russians. Harry didn't score but he did have his hands tied behind his back at set pieces – particularly corners! Yes, this was the game that ignited the debate about him having to vacate the middle for the edge of the pitch during corners. He took six corners in total, just one fewer than he managed in the thirty-eight Premier League games he played in the previous club season. One fan, Anthony O'Connell, summed up how farcical the situation was, saying, 'As an Irishman Roy reminds me of that great tactician Steve Staunton. He came up with the very tricky play people out of position plan! I'm sitting in Amsterdam and at half time I hear, "Playing well and should be two up. Need Vardy on for Sterling and someone else taking corners." The decision to put Kane on corners does seem a bit like an ageing guitar band doing a synth album to try to make themselves look cool when they should just stick with guitars. "Here, look everyone, I can do this." Don't.'

England had looked to have won the game after Eric Dier put them ahead but ended up deflated when Vasili Berezutski equalised in injury time. It was two points lost, rather than one won and, from Harry's point of view, that caused problems, as the press and public began to question his right to an automatic starting role. Typical of the general consensus among the press, *The Guardian* said, 'England weren't terrible, but perhaps Kane and Sterling were below par.'

To be fair, Harry was no worse than the rest of the team and he did have the ball in the back of the net, midway through the first half. Unfortunately, but quite correctly, it was ruled out as he was offside.

A couple of hours later, after England had skulked back to their hotel, the recriminations truly began to mount, with Harry proving to be the main scapegoat. *Football365.com* used facts to justify their claim that Hodgson should consider dropping him, saying, 'Thirty-three touches – the fewest of any starter aside from Aleksandr Golovin, who was substituted in the second half. Three shots, all of which were off-target. A passing accuracy of 73.3%, better than only Cahill and Hart in England colours. Too many corners. England have been faced with numerous decisions in the build-up to Euro 2016: who to start in any of the four defensive positions? Who to start in midfield? Where to play Rooney? How to fit in Jamie Vardy? Few questioned the inclusion of Kane, only debating where to place him in the XI. After 90 minutes of anonymity against Russia, his starting place should be in jeopardy.'

After the game, the England team could at least rest in luxury at their hotel. The Auberge du Jeu de Paume was a five-star establishment with every conceivable spa facility and pampering services. The ninety-two-room hotel described itself as 'the very expression of fine French living' in which 'every detail exudes timeless elegance and comfort'. And as England had booked out all ninety-two rooms there was no chance of other guests disturbing them… as there were no other guests. All the players were given Spotify accounts for downloading music and a personal Xbox or Playstation console.

Harry, as a keen golfer, was looking forward to getting out on the course to banish the blues after that disappointing opener. He was glad of the sanctuary the hotel and training provided away from the glare of the media and TV cameras, as the debate over whether he should play in the next match against Wales intensified as the days went by. No one was saying he was not good enough to play against Wales, the consensus was that he was jaded, that he was simply too tired after not having a decent break from the game for some considerable time. As the *Daily Mail* pointed out during the tournament, 'Kane played in every Premier League game for Spurs last year and only missed four league games the season before after breaking into the first team. He also took part in the Under-21 European Championship last summer, meaning a period of over two years without a true break.'

Put that way, it did indeed seem a persuasive argument that the boy did need a damned good rest. He looked jaded and lacking a yard of pace and no wonder, given that he had played so much football in a two-year period with no time to recharge his batteries. As previously stated, his club boss Pochettino must take a large chunk of the blame for that situation because he did not invest in a class striker at Spurs to help poor Harry shoulder the burden.

It was also claimed that 'senior figures' within the England camp had argued that Harry should not play against the Welsh, but my sources said this was 'mischief-making' by the press and that no teammates or management would indulge in such underhand briefings against Harry, who was 'a really well-liked and well respected figure in the camp'.

There were media figures who believed Harry should be dropped, chief among them one of his biggest admirers, former England striker and the man to whom he is often compared, Alan Shearer, who is now a respected analyst on *Match of the Day*. He argued that Kane had had his chance and not taken it, and that he should therefore be left out.

Writing in *The Sun*, he said, 'When you're a striker your neck is on the line in every game. If you get a chance and miss it, that is what will be highlighted by pundits like me. It is even harder in tournament football because you only have a month to prove yourself – actually forget that, probably a game or two.

'But I do feel slightly sorry for him as he was up there on his own for both games, whereas when Daniel Sturridge came on he had Jamie Vardy with him. Then Marcus Rashford came on late on as well to give the Welsh defence even more to think about.

'Kane has not had that same support. But his chance might be gone as in the next game Roy Hodgson now has to start with Vardy and Sturridge up front. For all the goals Harry Kane has scored for Tottenham over the season, we were all looking for an impact in these opening two games of England's group – and he could not make it. I'd have a diamond in behind with

Rooney at the peak of it, Dele Alli on the left, with Adam Lallana right and Eric Dier at the base of it. Now that will concern any team in this tournament.'

And former Ireland striker Tony Cascarino, writing in *The Times*, added, 'Harry Kane is one game away from being dropped. International football is an unforgiving stage but that is the reality for the Tottenham striker after he struggled against Russia. Having been a star for Tottenham for two seasons he was probably England's poorest player on Saturday.'

Another international striker of a different era, this time Scotland's Charlie Nicholas, contended that Kane should keep his place – and that Raheem Sterling should instead be dropped, with Jack Wilshere coming into the team. He said this would help provide the ammunition for Kane to work with, since Wilshere could feed Harry.

The idea that a change of tactics and shape would get Harry firing was also strong. Surely Hodgson could see that if he played Dele Alli directly behind Harry that would help his game? After all, the duo, with Dier as a defensive midfielder had been the spine on which Tottenham had enjoyed such a successful season. It felt to me that Kane was starved of service, hence his drifting out on to the wings in the game against Russia to look for the ball.

Wales would be no walkover: they had Gareth Bale as their star man and Kane knew from personal experience just how good the Real Madrid superstar could be on his day. He had seen him in action when the pair were together at Tottenham and told his England teammates that they would have to be at their best to contain him. Bale had lit the touchpaper for a potentially explosive clash by claiming England lacked the passion of the Welsh. Wales had beaten Slovakia in their first game in Group B and Bale was in a mischievous mood.

He then turned the screw even more by suggesting Wales were actually a better all-round team than England. At a press conference before the game, he turned the tables on reporters and asked, 'How many English players would get in our team?' He then smiled and answered rhetorically, 'None!' England boss Roy Hodgson had previously accused Gareth of disrespecting his team when he had said a day or two earlier that Wales had 'more pride and passion' than the English.

Fortunately, the talk did not translate to victory for the Welsh. The match in Lens did not go Gareth's way as England squeezed home with a 2–1 win. Once again, he was on target, sending Wales 1–0 in front at the interval, but goals from Jamie Vardy and Daniel Sturridge won it for England. Sturridge scored in injury-time when Wales looked to be heading for a deserved point.

For Harry, the match was another personal disappointment. Of course, he was happy that England had won but such was his struggle to get going that Hodgson hooked him at half-time and replaced him with Vardy. Raheem Sterling also suffered the same ignominious fate at the interval. Harry had started brightly enough, threatening the Welsh defence with his runs and ball control but he seemed to tire as the first half wore on. Clearly, he was jaded and, I would contend, simply suffering burnout from too much football with no break to recharge. In that sense, Hodgson taking him off did him a favour, as it gave him a rest! But it probably wasn't the wisest move by the manager in terms of helping the boy psychologically.

Yes, Hodgson had finally proved to his critics that he could be ruthless and daring when the need arose. But that hardly provided a confidence booster to Kane at a time when he needed one; a traditional substitution on the hour would have saved Harry from the indignity and of being taken off when the match was halfway through. Or Hodgson could have brought on Vardy or Sturridge to give Harry a bit of much-needed support in attack – and then sacrificed him if that didn't work out.

The Telegraph's Paul Hayward also picked up on the idea that Kane had been given a raw deal, in that he was foraging up front alone because of Hodgson's systems. He said, 'It would be a surprise if Sterling kicked another ball at this championship. But there are mitigating factors for Kane, beyond fatigue (he has played 65 games in 12 months). With Sterling and Adam Lallana mostly wide, the Premier League's hottest striker often looked isolated in his centre-forward's role.'

England now moved to the top of Group B with four points; with Wales a point behind in second place. But it would be the Welsh who ended up topping the group and England who finished second after the final matches. England could only whimper to a 0–0 draw with Slovakia, while the Welsh dragon roared to crush the Russians, 3–1.

The Slovakia match was a disaster for Hodgson. He dropped six players – including Harry and Rooney – and paid a price as a disjointed performance led to that 0–0 draw. Harry came on in the seventy-sixth minute, with Wayne arriving as a sub twenty minutes earlier. By the time Harry arrived, it was difficult to make an impression and to mould in with the team, especially as the Slovakians defended en masse, and defended stoutly. A draw for them felt like a win, and meant they progressed too as one of the best teams to finish third in the group stages.

Harry and the boys trooped off disconsolately, knowing a win would have left them top of the group rather than runners-up and facing a potentially more difficult task in the next round against the winner of another group. Hodgson tried to lift spirits and defend himself against criticism of his wholesale changes by saying, 'If we had won the game people would say we didn't miss the players I left out and when we don't they say the team selection is wrong. But I am used to that one. Finishing second is a disappointment but we are still in the last sixteen and who is to say the team we will play will be that much stronger? You just don't know, the way we are playing I am not frightened of anybody.'

They were defiant words from a man who knew his position would be untenable if the team crashed out in the next stage, the round of 16. Luckily (or at least it seemed that way at the time) England found themselves up against Iceland, who had finished runners-up in Group F. But it would have been an even better draw if Hodgson's men had won Group B – as they would have faced Northern Ireland. It would have meant a clash against a team who played with passion and no mean determination, but would have been a game they would surely have won if it had indeed turned out to be a 'typical blood and thunder UK derby'.

Instead, it would be Wales who would enjoy that encounter

while England would face a tougher, but still winnable, encounter against the Icelanders, who had a couple of skilful, creative star players but also a resolute defence that would take some breaking down.

After the failure to break down the Slovakian backline, destroying the even tougher Iceland defence would be no easy task. Harry had hit the golf driving range soon after England returned to their Chantilly base, trying to put the disappointment of the 0–0 draw behind him and to work out some of the frustration he was feeling. Then he and Vardy hit the golf course itself, raising their spirits with a game and taking it in turns to drive the buggy around!

The following day the duo were joined by their skipper Rooney after Hodgson decided to give his squad a second successive day off. Harry was still working damned hard on his game when training resumed, in the hope it would help him hit the heights in games. As Alan Shearer had once said, after reaching a similar drought with England in the build-up to Euro 96, all you can do is keep grafting and getting yourself in the right positions. There was no magic wand: strikers often hit the wall and the goals dry up. But, just as inevitably, they start to go in again and continue to do so. Harry's problem was more deep-rooted in that he was suffering fatigue, although he would deny that was at the bottom of it. Never one to complain or moan, he just kept on pushing himself.

He himself admitted hard work and self-belief were the fundamentals he upheld more than any others in his pursuit of football greatness, adding that, 'I have always said that hard work and self-belief have been two very important things for me along the way. There will always be ups and downs but as long as you know you have got what it takes to make it, you should be able to do it.'

But would his efforts on the training ground be enough to earn him a starting place against Iceland? On the Wednesday afternoon after the Slovakia draw, he and his teammates were glued to the TV as the final games in Group F were played. There was a general relief in the camp when it emerged they would indeed be up against Iceland. This was, after all, a game they could win and were expected to win. Iceland were playing in their first major tournament and their lack of experience at this level would surely count against them in the England match, wouldn't it?

Hodgson said he was taking Iceland seriously and, as if to substantiate that, sent out a team that could be viewed as his first-choice eleven starters, including Harry in the number 9 shirt. Harry had been given a nod that he would return to the side after he was put up for interview duties by the FA before the match; it would have certainly been unusual for a man who was not going to start to be in the glare of the cameras and Fleet Street's finest.

He was asked why he was struggling to make an impact on the tournament and his answer suggested he had indeed been starved of service. Harry told reporters, 'I probably haven't had a clear chance where I'd say, "I'm disappointed I missed that. I wish I'd scored that one." But you have to be ready when that chance comes. When teams are defending deep, it's difficult, especially as a striker. You always have two centre-halves behind you and maybe a sitting midfielder as well.

'It's a bit more difficult creating chances. But we can do better as a team in the final third – crosses better, final passes better and slipping players through. We can get better on that and, if we do, it'll be all right.'

It was suggested to him that his form could be suffering because of fatigue – and that Hodgson had actually done him a favour dropping him because it had at least allowed him to rest. But Harry was unwilling to buy into that scenario, telling the press conference, 'I don't think burnout is a worry. To progress in major tournaments, you need to rotate. I do a lot of recovery, whether it's ice baths or in the swimming pool, massages and soft tissue work. Eating right is a big part of it. Of course if you want to be at the top of your game for years to come, you have to look after your body.

'The gaffer made his choice in the Slovakia game and we all stick by it. He chose to change a few players, but that's tournament football. Of course I want to play every game but when you have Jamie Vardy up front and Daniel Sturridge on the other side, there's competition for places. I've only played around 115 minutes of football. As a striker I want to score a goal or two in every game. But it doesn't always work like that. I'll keep my confidence up and, if I'm playing on Monday, I'll do my best to score and create chances.'

And what of Iceland, and was he confident England could up their game at last and convincingly see them off? Harry nodded and ended the press conference with his reply, 'We know Iceland will try to make it difficult. But last season was a lot different for me to my first year in the Premier League. Defenders maybe get a bit tighter when I get the ball. But if you want to be one of the best in the world, you have to learn to cope with that – and you learn from tournament football.'

And with that confident statement of intent about his own ambitions and determinations, the boy was off, and back down to the serious business of training in Chantilly for the showdown in Nice. The bookies were confident Harry would hit form and score against Iceland, with Ladbroke's predicting: 'England hitman Harry Kane has struggled to find his feet at Euro 2016 but he and the Three Lions' all-time top scorer Wayne Rooney are 7/1 to both find the net against Iceland in Nice. It's proving a very popular bet, with the Tottenham man having won last season's Premier League Golden Boot.'

But when it came, the game ended in humiliation for Kane, who did return to the team, and his teammates as England crashed 2–1 to the tournament minnows. It was a result as unexpected as it was disastrous and spelled the end for Hodgson and his backroom team, including Gary Neville. Kane would live to fight another day for his country but he would not be able to look back on Euro 2016 with any particular fondness or pride. He was one of several stars who simply looked as though there was nothing left in the tank after an exhausting Premier League season's football. If any recruiting sergeant was needed for a winter break in England, this latest international let-down would provide a more than adequate case for it to happen.

It was England's worst humiliation since the 1–0 defeat by the United States back at the 1950 World Cup. Keeper Joe Hart was at fault for the winner, allowing a shot to go through his hands. Harry played the whole ninety minutes and was no better or worse than his teammates; it was a collective failure from a team who looked tired, nervous and unusually short of inspiration. Plus they were up against a rival who defended as if their lives depended upon it. Captain Rooney tried to explain why Harry and Co. had not delivered, telling the BBC, 'It's a sad day for us. Sometimes not always the best team wins. Once they got in the lead we knew it would be difficult to get the goal back because they are well organised. Going into the last sixteen facing Iceland we were confident we could win the game. It's disappointing but we have to move on.

'It's tough. There are always upsets in football – it's not tactics, it's just unfortunate. We know we're a good team. I can't stand here and say exactly why it's happened. Roy Hodgson will look back and think what he could have done differently. I'm still available to play. It'll be interesting to see who comes in.'

Rooney – and Kane – would live to see another day while Hodgson would call it quits immediately after the game. He had failed to revive England. Daniel Sturridge was adjudged to have been England's star man, with *The Guardian* giving him six out of ten for his performance. They were not so generous to Harry, marking him just four out of ten and commenting, 'His evening was summed up by the free-kick he hit over the penalty area and straight out of play with three minutes remaining. His touch was leaden, his radar off and his passing poor.' At least Harry wasn't bottom of the class – the paper also gave marks of three out of ten to Joe Hart, Eric Dier and Raheem Sterling.

It was a sad end to a tournament that had promised so

much for Kane and he would head home to London with a heavy heart. But then he would shake off the blues by taking a well-earned holiday and returning to Tottenham and throwing himself into training for the new season. There would surely be many more international tournaments for him to prove he was one of the world's top strikers: in international terms, it was a beginning, not an end, however painful the overall experience, for Harry Kane.

CHAPTER TWELVE
SWEET 2016

After the disappointment of England's Euro 2016 debacle, Harry Kane was glad to return to the welcoming arms of Tottenham – and to have a go at retaining the Golden Boot award he had won the previous season for those twenty-five goals. He had spent time away with childhood sweetheart Kate Goodland and Spurs teammates Dele Alli and Eric Dier, and their girlfriends Ruby Mae and Daniela Casal. The trio, known to many Tottenham fans as the 'Three Amigos' because of their close friendships at the club and with England, managed to dispel the gloom of their France nightmare with the national team. They enjoyed meals out together after relaxing, swimming and generally unwinding with their ladies.

The three lads returned to pre-season training later than many of their colleagues after their exertions in France for England. They arrived at Enfield on Tuesday, 2 August and were welcomed by boss Pochettino and the rest of the squad. Everyone was glad to see them and their arrival boosted morale after a couple of defeats without their services in the International Champions Cup (ICC). Pochettino was particularly keen to get them reintegrated as he plotted for another successful campaign. His public aim, as always, was to finish in the top four and ensure Champions League football at the Lane, but privately he admitted he would love to go one better than last season and finish runners-up and maybe, just maybe, champions, although he knew that was a long shot.

The Argentine was a realist as well as a brilliant manager, coach and motivator and felt that the boys would push for top spot but that it may take a little longer as they were still such a young team. Experience and further development would take them ever closer to the summit, so he set himself a personal target to win the league within another two or three years, sources suggested. Harry, Dele and Eric threw themselves into training at Hotspur Way that Tuesday morning, keen to completely banish the cobwebs of France 2016 for good, and to get up to speed as soon as possible with their teammates – and back into the first team.

Without the magical trio, Spurs had lost 2–1 to Juventus and then 1–0 to Atletico Madrid at the Melbourne Cricket Ground in the ICC. And Mauricio had felt it necessary to apologise to the thousands of Spurs fans in Australia, who had been upset that Harry and his pals had not travelled to play, especially as they had forked out good money to see them. He said, 'I am sorry to our supporters in Australia. It would be great for all the players to be involved in the tour in Australia. We saw last year, it was amazing to see our supporters in Australia. I think they understand that it's very difficult – they only arrived back a few days before we came here. It was a very difficult decision for me.

'It's important that they build their fitness after the whole season. A very stressful season, the Euros were difficult. We always say the same – they are not machines, they need to rest, they need to recover after only maybe fifteen or twenty days holidays. It's very important to be fit for the whole season.'

Kane and Co. would finish their pre-season work with a match against Inter Milan in Norway's Ullevaal Stadion in Oslo – and it was a match Pochettino was desperate to win to lay down a marker for the new Premier League season, which would begin at Everton's Goodison Park in eleven days' time.

Harry met new boy Vincent Janssen, the Holland international striker, who had been brought in by Pochettino from Alkmaar for £17 million. Pochettino's plan was to play the Dutchman up front with Harry to help relieve the pressure on his number one hitman. The omens were good – Janssen had scored a fantastic haul of twenty-seven goals in his final campaign in the Dutch top-flight, the Eredivisie. Add to that Harry's twenty-five-goal collection in the Premier League and you had the makings of a potential fifty-two-goal partnership!

Harry would admit he was excited by the prospect of working with Janssen and about the potential results their link-up could bring. He said, 'Vincent is a great player. He likes to hold the ball up and bring others into the game and I'm sure we'll play together this season. He's strong and has a good finish when he gets the chance. He's a great addition to the squad.'

He also made it clear he would not have any problems playing slightly behind the Dutchman if it was to the benefit of the team, pointing out that, 'I've played number 10 before and I'm not too worried going in and playing off him.'

For the prestige encounter with Inter Milan, Pochettino recalled all three of his amigos, along with fellow England international, full-back Kyle Walker. And what a difference their return made to a team that had fallen to Juve (Juventus) and Atletico earlier in the ICC. Tottenham hit the Italians for six, with Harry bagging a brace on his return to the team. Yes, the boy was back – and in some style, too. He opened his account on just five minutes from the penalty spot. Harry crashed the ball home into the top corner of the net past a despairing Samir Handanović in the Milan goal. Harry sent the keeper the wrong way after the spot kick was awarded for a foul on Kyle Walker in the box.

Harry grabbed his second of the game on the hour mark, rifling home after Érik Lamela set him up nicely for the shot.

Pochettino was delighted with Kane's contribution and those of his fellow returning England teammates. He told Spurs' official website, 'It was important to finish our pre-season in a very positive way and important to win. It was the first time the players involved in the Euros played and it was fantastic to see them all together. Now we have another week to prepare for the game against Everton and we will arrive ready to compete.'

The London football reporters were also pleased Kane had

shown he still had what it took after the summer of discontent. They were en masse big supporters of Harry and many had been angered that he had appeared to be the main scapegoat for England's poor showings. The capital's *Evening Standard* newspaper led the way in praising him, at the same time taking an indirect dig at those naysayers who had questioned him, saying, 'The 23-year-old failed to score during Euro 2016 but needed just four minutes to get back into the groove this afternoon. The striker's first goal may have "only" been a penalty but he dispatched it past Samir Handanovic with aplomb to get Spurs off to the perfect start. While Kane appeared to be jaded at times during the tail end of last season he looks all the better for recharging his batteries and linked up with Dele Alli as well as ever. Kane's second effort was the strike of a man unfazed by the criticism he received with the Three Lions.'

And a readers' poll at the same time showed that the fans also believed Kane was still THE man as far as goals were concerned. Out of nearly 8,000 votes by far the largest proportion – 36 per cent – said they believed Harry would once again grab as many as twenty-five goals in the coming season. It was a vote of confidence from the London Press boys and the fans who knew a talent when they saw one, despite the criticisms levelled at Harry by certain TV pundits during Euro 2016.

Harry had arrived back at training and for the Inter Milan match in a bubbly mood, hardly as if the Euro 2016 fiasco was still weighing him down. Naturally, he was glad to be back in the welcoming atmosphere of his club, but there was another reason he had such a spring in his step. He announced he was going to be a father for the first time, with the baby due to be born in January 2017.

He told how long-term girlfriend Kate Goodland was pregnant, tweeting: 'So happy that @KateGoodlandx and I are expecting our first child! Exciting times ahead! Can't wait!'

The tweet was accompanied by a photograph of their two Labrador dogs with signs around their necks. One sign said, 'Mum + Dad are getting us a human!' The other read: 'Guard dog duty starts January 2017.' Harry and fitness instructor Kate had been together since their teenage years when they met at school.

Harry had told the *London Evening Standard* before the Euros in France that he would love to be a dad one day. He said, 'Yes, it's something I'd like to do in the future. It's not on the agenda now, but you never know with these things. Obviously I've got a girlfriend who I've been with for quite a long time now, almost five years, we're settled and we live together.

'There's been a few elbows here and there, she's mentioned it a few times, as normal, but I'm happy with the way things are going and we'll see where it takes us – one day, definitely yes.'

And another reason to celebrate was that he would be twenty-three a few days after the revelatory tweet – no wonder he was walking on air when he arrived back at the Lane prior to the Inter clash.

After the win over the Italians the whole Spurs team geared up for the Premier League opener against Everton, with Harry particularly focused on getting off to a good start. He had not hit peak form in terms of goals for a few games the previous season but resented the claims by the press that he was going to be a habitual slow starter; or that he was a striker who could only really get into his true stride when he had a few games under his belt. His aim was to hit the ground running this season, and that, hopefully, meant hitting the back of the net against the Merseysiders. Not that it would be easy: they were now managed by the meticulous and demanding Dutchman, Ronald Koeman, who had left Southampton to join them in the summer. Koeman was a renowned defensive midfielder in his playing days and, as a manager, had come to build his teams from the back. Defence was key in his eyes and, to that end, he had splashed out on Swansea's tough-tackling, Mr Reliable centre-back, Ashley Williams, to shore up a backline that had leaked goals towards the end of the previous campaign.

But as *The Telegraph*'s excellent chief football correspondent Jason Burt previously pointed out, Kane was the type of man and player who would work relentlessly to up his game – and that his club manager had even designed a special training programme to help him in his admirable quest for improvement and perfection. He went on to write: 'It is all part of Kane's insatiable appetite for self-improvement, which is evidenced in the way he has reshaped his body as well as his game to become an England international and a key component of Hodgson's team. Spurs manager Mauricio Pochettino tailored a specific "power programme" for Kane to develop him, while the player himself has used a sprint coach to develop a yard of pace that he naturally does not possess. Kane is also a very honest and positive character, one who will confront issues head-on and does not shirk away.'

Pochettino showed his faith in Harry after that Euros setback by starting him as a lone striker in the match at Goodison Park. Janssen would come on to join him in attack on the hour and they would show glimpses of forging what could be a top-class partnership. Harry's England colleague Ross Barkley had put Everton ahead, with Érik Lamela rescuing a point for the visitors. After the game Pochettino admitted his boys had not been on top form, and that keeper Hugo Lloris's withdrawal with a hamstring problem just before half-time may have unnerved the team. He told the BBC, 'The first half was difficult for us and we did not play well. Hugo Lloris got injured and that was a big impact on us. In the second half we played as we usually play. They scored early and they believed they could win the game. They were very motivated. Lloris has a hamstring injury and we need to assess tomorrow to see what happens. We tried to correct the problems we had in the first half. With another striker, the team felt comfortable. Vincent Janssen brought good energy on the team and he gives us a different option.'

He was asked by reporters if Harry would manage another full season of games given that he still looked a little jaded at Goodison, in addition to his struggles in France, and answered: 'Harry needs to be ready for every game and then it is my decision whether he plays or not.' The fans, like the manager, were standing by their man. They were equally adamant that Kane should be given the chance to recuperate fully and have a worker alongside to help him out, in Janssen. And they were equally indignant that the boy's ability seemed to be being questioned when it was clearly simply a case of working back to form after exhaustion. Given time, they knew he would return to the majestic form that propelled him to that coveted Golden Boot. One fan, George, said, 'Harry must have Janssen alongside him, he cannot always do it by himself.' While Dave added, 'Nothing to worry about… for the last two seasons he doesn't start scoring goals until October.' And Steven added, 'Give the boy a chance, for God's sake! He has hardly had chance to draw breath for two seasons and yet has proved again and again that he is the best striker we have had for years. Give him time and he will soon be back to his best, and knocking in the goals for us.'

Harry himself then stepped forward to claim that he was not physically exhausted, but suffering from mental stress because of Tottenham's collapse at the end of the previous season and England's poor showing in the Euros. He told the *Mirror*, 'It's hard not to think about it. When you're away on holiday, it's all you think about, wishing it went better and what you could have done better. But football is going to be highs and lows throughout your career and it is how you deal with that which makes you the player you are. You have to put stuff like that behind you. That has got to go to the back of the mind and focus on this season.

'We want to do better; we want to improve. We have been through it together, learned from that experience together so hopefully we can push on this year and do even better. It was a disappointing end to what was a great season. You have to learn from that and be stronger. We know what we did wrong, we have to work on that for this season and hopefully we will do that and do well.'

It would be a month before Harry opened his goalscoring account for the new season. There had been whispers that his burnout from non-stop football had taken the edge off his game and that he was suffering from England's showings in France. But it was probably much less complex than that: he was a slow starter, as had been evidenced the previous campaign when he did not hit the net for his club until the end of September. And that season hadn't ended too badly, had it? What with him ending up with a remarkable thirty-two goals in all competitions!

By 5 September 2016, his goal drought actually spread across nine games for club and country, including drawing a blank in the recent World Cup qualifier in Slovakia, which England still managed to win 1–0 in the one, and only, match under the disgraced Sam Allardyce's tenure.

And talking to the press before the next Spurs game, the Premier League encounter at Stoke, he said he was not worried because he had been through the same drought the previous season. He remained convinced in his ability and trusted that the goals would flow once he truly got into his stride. Harry said, 'As a striker I want to get goals, it doesn't matter who I am playing. I didn't score in Slovakia but I felt we all put in a good shift for the team and worked hard for each other. Hopefully if I am picked for the next game or the next squad hopefully I can get a few goals and see what happens.

'What happened last season has given me confidence.

Unfortunately there was a lot of talk last year and I managed to prove a lot of people wrong so people will talk this year as well.

'It's part of football. I am confident in my ability. I know that if I continue doing what I am doing the goals will come that is all I can do. I didn't score in my first seven or eight games last season and then to go on and win the Golden Boot proves that it was just a matter of time. People might talk now or if I don't score in the next five or six games, it doesn't bother me.

'I am a confident player. I know if I keep doing what I am doing I will score goals and that is what I am going to do.'

And, lo and behold, he then went and scored in the match at the Britannia Stadium! Harry led the attack for seventy-three minutes against Stoke, before being replaced by Janssen as Tottenham roared to an impressive 4–0 win. The Britannia is one of the toughest grounds to play at, never mind emerge victorious with an uncomfortable, often bitter wind raging through the gaps in the stadium's corners, and many a fine team has come a cropper there over the years. The home support is also unremitting, fiery and passionately loud to add to the general feeling of not being made at all welcome. So Spurs' victory was especially sweet for Harry and his teammates.

Harry slotted home the fourth of the day and was in celebratory mood, as it was not only his first of the season, but his fiftieth goal for Tottenham. The first of, no doubt, many scoring landmarks he was destined to pass on what was only the start of his incredible journey from local lad to international star and first-choice number 9 for his country.

As Fred Nathan of *The Sun* pointed out while commenting on Harry's feat, 'Welcome back Harry Kane! He clocked up 50 Premier League goals from 87 games with a simple tap in. He is the quickest Spurs player to reach that landmark, beating Robbie Keane and Jermaine Defoe by four games – and it ended a goal drought which had lasted five league games.' It was also a statistical fact that Harry had become the fourth Tottenham player to score fifty Premier League goals (after Sheringham, Defoe and Keane).

The away fans continually chanted Harry's name and his own joy at getting off the mark was clear as he spoke after the game, saying, 'All you can do as a striker is keep working hard and getting in positions to score. Sometimes you need the ball to fall for you – and it did today.'

The relief and euphoria of the Spurs fans was also clear – they loved Harry, he was their local hero and they had urged him on from the stands. As the *Express* noted, 'Harry Kane is one of their own and now Tottenham fans can hail him their most prolific Premier League marksman. In breaking his duck for the season with a tap-in, he also notched up 50 Premier League goals. And he has reached that milestone in 87 games – four fewer than it took Robbie Keane and Jermain Defoe in their White Hart Lane heydays.'

Even boss Pochettino spoke of his own relief that his main man was back on the goals trail, saying, 'I am very happy for Harry. It's always good for a striker to get that first goal. Now he's got it – and the record – he can play his normal game. It was an outstanding, perfect performance by the team. It's true that we started the game a little sloppy but after fifteen or twenty minutes we got on top, scored the goal and started to handle the game. In the second half, we fully deserved the result. I'm very pleased for the players and for our supporters as well.'

It was Tottenham's second successive 4–0 win in the Potteries and gave them a massive confidence boost as they prepared for their first Champions League group game four days later. The first match saw French outfit Monaco arrive in north London but it would not be staged at the Lane. Wembley would be the prestige venue while the club's new ground next to the Lane was being built. It also provided those fans who often could not get tickets for games at the Lane to cheer on the club as Spurs were given the entire capacity of the national stadium by Wembley bosses. Spurs admitted they were thrilled at the prospect of playing to such crowds as they returned to the Champions League, saying back in July, 'We are delighted to confirm that we shall be opening the full stadium capacity for all of our Champions League fixtures next season. We shall be launching a Group Stage Multi-Game Ticket that will be on sale shortly. Not only will this ticket ensure your place at all three Group Stage matches, it will also secure you the same seat for these and for any subsequent matches in the campaign that you buy tickets for.'

There had been suggestions that far from being a plus, Wembley could be a negative for Spurs in that rivals Arsenal had struggled to find their true form when they competed in the tournament when they played there temporarily in the 1990s. But Harry was more than happy with the prospect and made it clear he believed he and the England contingent at the club could help make it a fruitful phase in Spurs' history. He told the Press after the win at Stoke, 'If there are 85-90,000 Tottenham fans in there it's only going to make you play better. A lot of us have played there already, so it feels like even more of a home. Everyone knows how iconic Wembley is, but that's what we've got to be careful of, Monaco are going to come here and it's a big occasion for them as well. We have to make sure we're ready for that.

'The lads are excited after we got a good result here at Stoke. Now we can go there on Wednesday and enjoy the record-breaking crowd; it's going to be an amazing atmosphere and the lads cannot wait to play in that one now. There's a buzz about that one and coming off the back of a 4–0 win you can't ask for much more. We have to prepare well for Wednesday now.

'We're not there just to participate. We want to go as far as we can, we feel we have a group that we can definitely qualify from. A good start is important.'

And Pochettino had no fears that it might all go pear-shaped for his team at Wembley. He said, 'It is not a problem for us. We need to go to Wembley and play, behave naturally and not try to find an excuse, that's never good. We need to play and try to beat Monaco.'

He explained that he had two pitches specially made to the same size as the one at Wembley at Spurs' Enfield training ground to prepare his men for the game and added, 'With two pitches, we designed the same dimensions as Wembley. We change between the pitches to keep the grass at a good level. We use different pitches on different days during the week. You have more space to play, it's more difficult for the opponent to press you when there are more metres to run, but it is the same for both. We believe in the way we play and it's a good chance to play on a big pitch. We need to adapt our game. We feel good at White Hart Lane because it's our home and we need to feel good at Wembley.'

It might well have been important to get off to a good start, as Harry said, but it wasn't achieved, as Spurs stuttered to a disappointing 2–1 defeat at the hands of Monaco. Was Wembley going to jinx them as it had Arsenal, who lost three out of six Champions League games at the national stadium in 1998–99 and 1999–2000, which meant they did not even make it out of the group stages? Arsène Wenger had called their Wembley experience 'a nightmare' and Tottenham fans were wondering if the same word would be applied to their matches after the team got off to such a dreadful start. Wenger had pointed out that the team suffered a physical disadvantage in that their normal game was tailored to a different stadium, and that the iconic nature of Wembley had provided more of a boost to their opponents rather than his own men, as had been anticipated.

Former Spurs ace Gary Lineker had also hinted that Tottenham could find it more difficult than expected at Wembley, telling *The Telegraph*, 'It's different. Your home ground gives you comforts. You get in the dressing room which you know and you're comfortable, and all these things add up. So if you are playing your home games kind of "half away", you suspect it might be a disadvantage.'

Harry and his teammates could hardly complain about

the lack of atmosphere – a remarkable crowd of more than 85,000 turned up and did their best to lift the team. But a disappointing night's work was best epitomised by the fact that the only stat Harry left with was a yellow card, a booking for a late tackle on Fabinho. And, in fairness, he had escaped the same fate earlier for a similar indiscretion on the same player. It was one of those nights when nothing seemed to go right for Harry. After his goal at Stoke, he had high hopes of adding more to his haul, but he struggled to make a major impact. He was not alone; the team as a whole had an off night as Monaco punished them. Toby Alderweireld grabbed their consolation – and gave them hope – after the French had powered into a two-goal lead. It would not be enough and the thousands of Spurs fans traipsed away from Wembley shocked and grim-faced.

The stats showed it maybe should not have been such a shock, as the club had lost their previous three games at Wembley – two FA Cup semis and a League Cup final. And they had won just one of their previous five Champions League games – a 1–0 win over AC Milan back in 2011.

So maybe there was a Wembley jinx after all; it certainly appeared that way after the loss against Monaco. Let's not forget that the previous year Spurs had coasted to a 4–1 win over the same team in a Europa League clash… at White Hart Lane.

After the game, it was generally agreed that Tottenham had played OK but that defensively they were not on top of their game. UEFA reporter Daniel Thacker summed up the problems, explaining that, 'While there are plenty of positives for Mauricio Pochettino and Spurs to take from their second-half display, the reality is that this is not the start to their UEFA Champions League campaign that Tottenham would have wished for. The hosts' lapses in defence in the first half cost them dear.'

While Pochettino himself admitted, 'You pay when you make mistakes and we paid. They only had two shots and like to counter. We created chances but weren't clinical. We need to look at ourselves. We need to be more aggressive in front of goal. It was only the first game but we need to improve and fast.' And Dele Alli rued the loss as a game they should have won – a viewpoint shared by Kane, who told pals, 'It's a blow, it was just one of those nights where the ball wouldn't go in the back of the net for us.' Alli added, 'We started poorly and they punished us for it. We did enough to win the game but we did not take our chances. Monaco are a good team but we weren't ruthless enough. The fans came out in numbers and never stopped singing. We need to pick ourselves up and win the next game.' Harry also agreed with Dele that the fans had been the major plus-point of an otherwise disappointing night, saying, 'They were brilliant and kept us going, like they always do.'

Harry also admitted he and his team should have been more ruthless with the numerous chances they had – but refused to concede that they had lost because of a Wembley jinx. He said, 'We actually started well. We had a couple of early chances but at this level, we should have been more ruthless. We got caught out and punished. At 2–0 down in the Champions League it's very difficult. We were the better team in the second half but we just couldn't get that second goal.

'I don't think Wembley was a factor. If anything it was a positive. There were more fans, the pitch was bigger, it suited us. We had more space on the ball. It's a level where you get punished for mistakes or for not being that little bit more ruthless. We've got to learn from that, got to get better and quickly, because the Champions League will soon go.'

Harry and the boys needed a lift after the defeat and started preparing for the next match, a home fixture against Sunderland, who were struggling towards the bottom of the table but who had, in David Moyes, a new manager determined to prove himself after his struggles at Manchester United and Real Sociedad in Spain. But he was up against a team just as determined to prove that the Monaco defeat was an aberration in a season that had otherwise started well and promised so much.

Before the game Harry had laughed off, and criticised, FIFA 17 for their latest ratings. Despite winning the Golden Boot, he had only received a shooting rating of 84 and a passing ability of 71. He told website *Copa90.com*, 'I think my shooting has got to be in the 90s. Passing should be a bit higher; higher than 71. And it looks like my defending has gone down since the last one!'

Harry was confident they would beat Sunderland at the Lane – and that he would keep scoring now he had started. He told reporters, 'People said that this time last year and I went on to win the Golden Boot and score thirty goals for club and country. People are going to talk. It doesn't bother me. I'm fit, I'm ready to go. I'll be ready on Sunday against Sunderland if called upon and hopefully I can get on the scoresheet and win the game. As a striker you've got to be confident. I will never lose my confidence in front of goal. I'll be there on Sunday, shooting and making the keeper work.'

And he would do just that. In the end, it would be Harry Kane and his cohorts who won the battle – and a battle it was as the Wearsiders dug in as if their very existence depended upon it, which in a way it was starting to look once again as if it did, in terms of Premier League survival anyway. It was to Harry that Tottenham looked for inspiration in a grinding match that should really have been won at a canter rather than relying upon a single goal – and it was Harry who provided it, with his second goal of the season, and his second in three games. Clearly, those shooting boots were started to fit nicely once again for the perennial seasonal 'Slow-start King'.

His goal was a simple enough tap-in after errors in the Sunderland backline. Black Cats' boss Moyes admitted you cannot afford to make such blunders when you have a predator like Kane waiting to pounce. He said, 'We had a chance to clear the ball for the goal. That was a mistake and, of all the chances Tottenham got, that was a soft one and we gifted them that. It's not something we want to be doing, especially when there's a top-class striker like Harry Kane close by.'

The victory put Spurs third in the table and maintained their unbeaten domestic run. But while he hit the winner, there was also pain among the joy. For Harry was carried off on a stretcher in the eighty-ninth minute amid fears he had suffered an injury that would sideline him for some time. Harry had lunged bravely into a tackle but was left on the ground, holding his ankle and clearly in some pain.

The hosts' superiority was reflected in that they had nineteen attempts at goal in the first half to Sunderland's miserly three. And if it had not been for keeper Jordan Pickford's heroics Harry would have had two goals to his credit before the break, as the keeper foiled him twice at close range.

After the game Pochettino admitted he was worried about Harry going off injured and said he did not yet know the extent of the injury. He added that he was pleased with the win as it had blown away the cobwebs of disappointment from the Monaco loss, but confirmed that it should have been by a bigger margin, telling the BBC, 'Sometimes it's difficult. We fought a lot and tried to score. I'm happy with the three points and it takes away the feeling from losing against Monaco. I want to create chances and play well – sometimes you need a lot of chances to score. Today we always tried to go forward. We feel disappointed because we created a lot of chances in the first half.'

Spurs' official website spoke of the relief in the stadium when Kane finally ended the visitors' stubborn resistance, pointing out that, 'It had been coming to be fair! After sustained pressure after the interval, Walker sent over a cross which Son headed towards goal. The ball wasn't going in but Papy Djilobodji chested it down and then mis-controlled on the edge of his six-yard box, the ball rolling straight to Kane who gleefully tucked home. That was our 22nd shot of the game.'

Paul Jiggins at *The Sun* also commented on the relief the goal brought, but added that it was followed by groans of worry when Harry was carted off the pitch on a stretcher.

He said, 'Harry Kane finally penetrated Sunderland's pink and purple wall to send Tottenham up to third. But he was then carried away on a stretcher with a nasty looking ankle injury late in the game. Kane pounced to leave his own team unbeaten in the Prem and the Black Cats with just a point from five games. But he was replaced after his ankle buckled when lunging to make a challenge.'

A couple of days later Pochettino confirmed what Tottenham fans had most feared – that Harry's injury was not one that could be easily put to bed. He said, 'He has injured his ankle ligaments. We will continue to assess him every day but don't want to put a timeframe on it.' But analysts predicted he could be out for up to two months, which would be a very severe setback for the club and Harry himself, after he had just started hitting the back of the net again.

At the same time, stats kings Opta focused on Harry and came up with results that suggested he could indeed have suffered burnout with non-stop football. They pointed out his appearance against Sunderland was his seventy-first consecutive Premier League start and that he had run thirty-one miles more than any striker in the top-flight, with Watford's Troy Deeney that distant second. Those stats also did not include his minutes for England since the start of last season (982), or in the Europa League (359), the FA Cup (165), the Champions League (90), or the League Cup (90).

Fitness coach Raymond Verheijen had no doubts that exhaustion had been a major contributing factor to Harry's injury and argued that Pochettino had been pushing Kane and the others too hard. He told *Metro*, 'He's demanding so much from his players. He's pushing them hard. If you look at this team's consistently fading away in the last months of the season, you can say that he's pushing them too hard, especially when you have so many players who have had a long season. What probably had happened is that Pochettino has trained them too hard, too soon in pre-season given the long season and Euros, and twisting your ankle [as Kane did] is a typical injury when you have accumulated fatigue.'

Harry's replacement would be Dutchman Vincent Janssen, but he was sad that Harry would be sidelined as it meant he would have to wait longer to form a potentially lethal partnership with the man he considered one of the best strikers in the world: Harry. Janssen said, 'He is a very good player. We played some games together and it went very well. He has a lot of qualities – he is one of the best strikers in the world so it is nice to play together with him. I can learn a lot from him but at the end I want to play a lot with him. It is nice that he is here.'

Those were decent comments from a man who was incredibly decent. Of course, Janssen was glad to be getting a run in the team but his selfless comments showed he was a good fit for the 'team-rather-than-self' philosophy Pochettino was determined to drum into his squad.

Spurs skipper Hugo Lloris also chipped in, saying how he hoped Kane would be back asap and that the injury would prove not to be as bad as feared, and that, 'We just hope it is not too bad. It is true that, if you look at the images, we can be a bit worried, but all the medical staff are going to try to bring him back as quick as possible. We have a competitive team and are fully confident in every player. When one player is missing, it gives an opportunity to another player to bring his skills, energy and quality. This is the story of the season and that's why we need all the players involved to be committed to the club because when the manager needs you, you need to respond well.'

But at the end of the month, Pochettino stepped forward and said he believed Kane would not be out for two months, that the boy was responding well to treatment and he was positive he would return ahead of schedule. Pochettino told reporters, 'I always try to be honest with you. Just half an hour ago we received the report about the scan and it's much, much better than we expected. Maybe we can reduce the time he misses. We are happy, the scan was very positive, we are very happy about this news but still we cannot give a time for how long his recovery will be.

'We are happy because the scan was better than we expected. I am not a doctor, it's difficult to say how long but it's true that it's much, much, much better than what we expected and that is very positive.'

All the worry, all the talk, all the hopes of a quicker recovery only went to show just how important Harry Kane was to Tottenham… and to England. For he would also miss three World Cup qualifiers, much to the regret of interim England boss Gareth Southgate. Kane had become THE key man for club and country – and he was still just twenty-three years old.

CHAPTER THIRTEEN

IN THE FOOTSTEPS OF LEGENDS

I t is a sign of Kane's impact at White Hart Lane that by the end of the 2015/16 season he was already fourth on the list of Tottenham's top league goalscorers in the era of the Premier League. On 2 May 2016, Harry netted in the 2–2 draw with Chelsea, his twenty-eighth goal in all competitions for the club that season – and his forty-ninth in just two years in the league. True, the gap between himself and the third highest scorer on the list was forty-two goals, but given his prolific record he would surely overwhelm that total within another couple of years. Joint second on the list above him, were Jermain Defoe and Robbie Keane, each with ninety-one goals. While top of the pile in the Premier League era proudly stood Teddy Sheringham, on ninety-eight goals.

But it had taken Teddy seven years to amass his haul, from 1992 to 1997. Jermain had needed ten years, and three spells at the club from 2004 to 2014, for his total while Robbie had completed his tally of goals in nine years, and two spells from 2002 to 2009. Clearly, given those time frames, none were as prolific, or as deadly, as Harry Kane. Further back in time, a couple of marksmen set records that Harry himself would be proud of, none more so than the great Jimmy Greaves. Greavsie notched a total of 220 in the league, and 266 in all competitions and Bobby Smith grabbed 176 league goals and 208 overall. Third on the club's all-time scorers' chart was England striker Martin Chivers, with 118 in the league and 174 in all tournaments. Then came Cliff Jones, on 135 league goals and 159 overall.

Bringing us into the modern era, Defoe came in at fifth, with his total of 143 goals overall, including those ninety-one in the league. And Sheringham lies ninth with 124 overall. Greavsie wins hands down even when you look at scoring records at Spurs in terms of goals per game ratio, with a goal every 1.42 matches, a quite incredible feat. In comparison, Sheringham's ratio is 2.23 and Defoe's 2.53.

But Kane is determined to shatter all records – and not just at the club. In March 2016, he told how he was gunning for Alan Shearer's all-time Premier League goals haul of 260 from 441 appearances. At the time, that put Shearer sixty-eight ahead of his next challenger, Manchester United's Wayne Rooney, while Kane had hit forty-five in just seventy-nine appearances. Harry told reporters he would give Shearer's record his best shot, saying, 'It's a lot of goals and I'm still a long way off but Shearer was an idol of mine growing up. I take it season by season. I don't like looking too far ahead because you never know what can happen. But is it good to aim for? Definitely. They're the goals you dream of.

'When you're a younger player, you watch them scoring goals week in and week out, so to be doing that now is a dream come true.'

Harry was on a high, speaking after grabbing a brace in Tottenham's 3–0 win over Bournemouth. It was his twenty-first goal of that season, equalling the previous campaign's tally and Harry, at twenty-two, had become just the fifth Englishman to score twenty goals in consecutive Premier League campaigns. He had added his name to those of Shearer, another Spurs hero Les Ferdinand, Andy Cole and Robbie Fowler.

Harry spoke about how he hoped his example would encourage fellow young English strikers to aim high. 'I think sometimes managers like to buy players because they're more experienced from abroad or when they've got players under their nose that will give everything to the club they've been brought up with,' he added. 'The more people get chances at a young age, I think you'll see more talent coming through as we have done this season.'

Certainly the fans, and not just Tottenham fans, admired and respected Kane for his ambition and humility. For a young man with the world at his feet, he was well grounded and nothing like the stereotyped spoilt modern-day footballer, who can appear cocooned and selfish to the extreme. As one fan, Chandler, said after Harry's statement of scoring intent: 'It's actually great to see people like Kane and see how humble he is. He's the complete opposite of modern-day English footballers. You can't help but like him, from a football point of view he's a breath of fresh air. Good on him – I hope this kid goes far, he deserves it.'

While another, John, added, 'If Kane avoids serious injury like the two cruciate ligament injuries which robbed Shearer of two years of his career, and diminished his effectiveness for the last seven or eight years of his career, then he might have a chance. When you take into account how much those injuries took out of Shearer it's incredible that his goal-scoring record is so far ahead of any other striker in Premier League history.' And Jay said, 'This guy Kane will be captain for club and country. If you look at his stats, they are pretty impressive. Seems to have his feet on the ground and wants to play for Spurs.'

Another fan, Seb, pointed out why Harry's target may have been a tad on the ambitious side, 'It's unlikely – but it's great to see an ambitious target being set. Shearer had an advantage of having forty-two league game seasons as opposed to the current thirty-eight-game format. But, to Kane's credit, he has already hit the twenties in both of his first two proper seasons in the Premier League.'

It was refreshing that Harry had publicly set himself such a daunting target as overhauling Shearer – and also refreshing to see how fans from around the country clearly had time for Kane. That he was universally well liked and respected in an industry that often arouses hatred among fans of differing clubs. Harry Kane was bucking the trend; he was a young man everyone everywhere seemed to like, and whom they would happily welcome into their club.

It's worthwhile taking a look at some of the modern-era Spurs goalscoring legends whose footsteps Harry was following in – and who, as a keen student of the game and centre-forward play in particular, he was hoping to join in the pantheon of White Hart Lane all-time heroes. Harry had once said Teddy Sheringham was his idol, the player he had learned most from and whom, consequently, he most admired. Harry made that clear when told before Euro 2016 that Teddy had tipped him to win England's star man at the tournament and that he should be first-choice striker.

Teddy had told the bookmakers, Paddy Power, 'It makes more sense to play Harry Kane with Wayne Rooney in behind and leave Jamie Vardy on the bench for England. That's not the Tottenham bias in me either – Kane has more to his game than Vardy. If you assess everything that Kane and Vardy can both do – they can both run the channels, they can both score from long distance, and they both get goals with their right foot.

'However, Kane is better on his left foot, Kane is better in the air, and Kane is better at receiving the ball. Vardy's pace is probably exceptional and that makes him different, but Kane has something more to his game and at international level you need that.'

Teddy insisted that Harry could challenge for the Golden Boot at Euro 2016 and pointed out that Harry had already won the Premier League's Golden Boot for his twenty-five goals for Spurs in 2016, one ahead of Vardy and Manchester City's Sergio Agüero, and that he was the first Englishman to do so since Kevin Phillips in the 1999/2000 campaign. And, as Teddy added no doubt with a smile on his face, he was the first Tottenham player to win that award since... Teddy Sheringham!

When told of Teddy's praise, Harry beamed and told *Mirror Sport*, 'It's amazing to hear things like that. Teddy was an idol of mine growing up through the way he played and the goals he scored. To hear him complimenting me like that only gives me more confidence. Going into the Euros, I need to believe that I can score goals. If I do, hopefully the rewards will be there.'

Back in 2014 Harry had told how Teddy was indeed his role model, and how he had felt in awe when he met him. Harry told reporters, 'He's a great finisher and was very good at getting in the box, scoring so many goals, especially for Spurs. As I grew up I tried to use him as a role model and if I can score as many goals as he did, it would not be bad. I met him once at a golf charity day and got to talking about Millwall [where Harry had been on loan] because he played for them as well.

'It was great to meet him. He told me just to score goals. As a striker you have got to score goals. It was only last year – we had a little chat about football. He's a great bloke and it was nice to meet him. I was a little bit star-struck, to be honest. When you meet your idol you don't really know what to say but he had great conversation.' The previous year Sheringham had told the *Daily Star* that he felt Kane, even at the then age of twenty-one, was a better player than he had ever been. Teddy said, 'He is an outstanding player. As for being like me, I think he's probably got a little bit more than me. He can do everything I could do but he has got a bit of pace as well. He can go a long way.'

Generous words from a man who won the Treble with Manchester United in 1999. But then Teddy was always a class act, both on and off the pitch and, as a role model, is an ideal pick by Harry, both for Tottenham and England. Teddy starred at three major international tournaments for his country, gaining fifty-one caps and scoring eleven goals.

He joined Tottenham in 1992 and spent five happy years at White Hart Lane before moving to Old Trafford. He would return to Spurs in 2001 after leaving United. Obviously, he had his greatest success in terms of medals at United, but he scored more goals in north London. In his four years at Old Trafford, he made 104 appearances and hit thirty-one goals. In his first five years at Spurs he scored seventy-six in 166 appearances, and twenty-two in his second coming in seventy games.

Never the speediest of strikers – which he himself would be the first to admit – he nonetheless was one of the deadliest. Like Harry, he instinctively knew where the goal was and, also like Harry, he had a footballing brain that meant he wasn't simply a goalscorer. Intelligent forwards are a gift that any top-flight manager will gladly embrace, for they can dictate play in and around the box as well as snapping up chances with relish. Sir Alex Ferguson would often say that Sheringham's first yard was in his head, and astute commentators watching England made the point that Kane could even play as a number 10 rather than simply an out-and-out centre-forward, such was his ability to play a divine pass or find a teammate in a dangerous position. Of course, if he did play as a 10, you would lose some of his goal instinct, which explains why he was usually chosen as an out-and-out striker for club and country.

Teddy's first season at Tottenham ended joyfully with him being the top scorer for the Premier League's inaugural campaign, with one goal from when he was still at Nottingham Forest and twenty-one after signing for Spurs from Forest. In the 1994–95 campaign Teddy partnered the brilliant German striker Jürgen Klinsmann at the Lane. Klinsmann would love working with Teddy and commented that he was 'the most intelligent footballer I have worked with'. Those words were like music to Teddy's ears, for he was just as appreciative of the work put in by his German co-star. Teddy told *Spurs TV* that Klinsmann had helped him develop his own game, saying, 'He was infectious, clinical… just awesome really. He won balls in the air, he would run in the channels, hit volleys that came at him neck-high, he would run and take players away to make space for you. He was unselfish, but at the end of the day, he was a goalscorer. If you gave him half a chance he'd hit the back of the net. That's the difference between good and fantastic players. I was very lucky to play with Jurgen at that time.'

The Spurs fans also loved Teddy and the class he brought to the team. But in June 1997 he shocked them by agreeing a £3.5 million move to Manchester United. However, many consoled themselves with the thought that at the age of thirty-one he was probably past his best and that they had enjoyed his finest years. Sir Alex Ferguson clearly thought differently and after chatting to Teddy about a potential move was convinced he had brought in a talisman capable of helping plug the gap of Eric Cantona's departure the very same month. I was told by sources that Fergie sensed Teddy still had a hunger to compete at the top and, even more importantly, a hunger to win some medals to complete his career.

The wily old Scot was proved right on both counts – with Sheringham in the team United finally won the European Cup, or the Champions League as it is now known, for the first time in thirty-one years. Teddy, famously, scored the equaliser against Bayern Munich in the 1999 final held at Barcelona's Camp Nou stadium, paving the way for Ole Gunnar Solskjær to score the injury-time winner a minute later.

In 2001, he returned to White Hart Lane and was given a generous welcome by fans who had been angered at his departure four years earlier. The supporters were more upset that he had chosen to criticise the club for what he saw as a lack of ambition than the fact he had decided to leave. But they gave him a chance to redeem himself when he finally returned. They saw his refusal to sign a new twelve-month deal at Old Trafford as a sign that he still retained a love for Spurs and the club.

Sheringham helped them to reach the League Cup final in 2002 but they lost 2–1 to Blackburn. He left the club a year later at the age of thirty-seven, after being made skipper by boss Glen Hoddle. Teddy was upset not to be offered a new contract by the club he had supported as a boy and said in a statement, 'I am disappointed not to have been offered a new contract at Tottenham Hotspur and will be considering offers made to me shortly.'

Hoddle paid tribute to Teddy, saying, 'Teddy has performed a great service for us, not just on the field but by setting such a superb example for our younger players. He has also just completed another marvellous season for the club and we wish him well in the future.'

And the club itself showed its appreciation of the striker in 2008, announcing he had been inducted in their Hall of Fame along with Clive Allen. The club announced: 'To complete our 125th Anniversary celebrations there will be another double induction into the Tottenham Hotspur Hall of Fame to follow the enormously successful inductions of Ossie Ardiles and Ricky Villa held in February. We are delighted to announce that Clive Allen and Teddy Sheringham will be the next Spurs Legends inducted into the Hall of Fame.

'Both of these great goalscorers have made significant contributions to our illustrious history. Clive Allen, currently Development Coach, joined the Club in 1984 and scored 84 goals in 135 appearances. In one season, 1986/87, he scored an incredible 49 goals. Teddy Sheringham had two stints with the Club, joining us in 1992 and re-joining in 2001 and scoring a total of 124 goals in 277 appearances.'

To celebrate the honour, Teddy spoke extensively to the club's website a couple of months later. He admitted he believed his first spell at the club was his best, saying, 'I was probably in my prime during my first spell at Spurs. I think I arrived at the age of twenty-six and left around thirty-one, which is the prime of any footballer. I also think I played some of the best football of my career during that time, but it was great coming back for a second time as well.'

And he now paid tribute to the brilliant Spurs fans who had taken to him when he first arrived and encouraged him to become the top-striker he became – just as they did with Harry years later, putting it like this: 'I scored on my home debut but didn't have the best of times during the first half of my first season because I hit a bit of a barren spell, although I ended up winning the Golden Boot at the end of it! My brother had a season ticket and he told me to start pulling my finger out because he'd heard a few rumblings, and I don't know whether that perked me up but it certainly did the trick. The end of that first season was fantastic.'

Just as they had taken to Teddy and Harry Kane, so the fans also loved another top goalscorer, the aforementioned Clive Allen. Like Harry, he was a striker who sniffed out chances and simply loved scoring. Like Harry, goals were his bread and butter. Unlike Harry and Teddy, he was not a striker who could drop deeper and pull the strings around him. Not that that is a fault or a criticism; it is simply a fact. No striker will be condemned if all he does is keep hitting the back of the net: that, after all, is the job of a centre-forward. And Clive Allen certainly did his job well.

Clive was the son of Les Allen, one of the stars of Tottenham's greatest team of all time, the 1961 double winners – the league and cup triumph. Clive's four-year spell at White Hart Lane in the mid-80s was a special one in which he bonded with the fans as he banged in goal after goal. He had provided an inkling of what he was capable of by grabbing a brace on his debut as Spurs walloped Everton 4–1 at Goodison Park on 25 August 1984. That season he finished with a commendable ten goals from eighteen appearances as the team finished third in the league.

His best campaign was the 1986–87 one as he hammered thirty-three league goals and a remarkable forty-nine in all competitions. Clive entered the history books with his haul, breaking the record set by Greavsie. It remains unbeaten and not just at Tottenham, but by any player at any top-flight club.

Clive also won the PFA and Football Writers' Footballer of the Year gongs for his feat that season. Inevitably, he also scored in the FA Cup final at Wembley – a second-minute header that was his forty-ninth goal – but it wasn't enough to stop Coventry winning 3–2. In a fans' special hosted by the *Daily Mail* in 2006, Clive was asked if he felt the Wembley defeat was the biggest disappointment of his career. He answered, 'Yes, I think it was one of, if not the biggest disappointment of my career. You don't get too many cracks at the FA Cup. If you are lucky you may get ten in your career and obviously once you are beaten, you are out and then you have to wait another year for another chance.

'We went into the game against Coventry as favourites and were expected to win. It was a boyhood dream to score in an FA Cup final, which I did to put us in front after two minutes, but we were ultimately on the losing team. Looking back I think it was destined to be Coventry's year. At the time you always feel you are in with a chance and you are playing to win the game, but it was never going to be our day.'

Clive moved to Bordeaux in 1988 but would return to White Hart Lane in coaching capacities. He remains one of Harry Kane's strongest supporters and was one of the first ex-players to make it clear he believed Harry would become an even better player, and more prolific scorer, after his Euro

2016 misery. Clive said, 'I thought Harry looked tired during the Euros. He just didn't look the same player as he did in the Premier League last season. Maybe he looked below par because this last summer was something like his third in succession when he didn't have a proper break. That has to have an effect. But I know Harry well. I knew him as a kid when he first came to Spurs and he has proved one thing beyond any doubt – that whenever he is faced with a challenge, he faces up to it, meets it and comes through it successfully. I am sure he will do the same again this coming season.'

It was a nice touch from one Spurs centre-forward legend coming to the rescue of the man who is a modern-day hero at the club – and who was being scapegoated unfairly by some commentators for England's Euro 2016 flop.

Another Spurs star of a former era much admired by Harry Kane is the great Jimmy Greaves. Harry hit that thirtieth goal of the season landmark in April 2015, when he scored in the 3–1 win at Newcastle. That made him the tenth player at the club to achieve the feat since Spurs joined the Football League in 1908/09. But the incomparable Greavsie scored thirty for Spurs on SIX occasions. No wonder Kane said he would love to be even considered in the same league as Jimmy.

And it was Jimmy who was among those praising Harry most for his rapid rise to stardom in 2015. In an interview, Greavsie told *Sky Sports*, 'Harry looks a good player. He's got to carry on, obviously, developing the way that he has, and that gets harder because it's difficult. He's come on the scene, and he's sort of caught people out a little bit with the way that he plays and obviously his goalscoring prowess.' Jimmy also warned Harry that he would have to keep improving so that defenders wouldn't suss him out. He added, 'Defenders learn very quickly, so you have to readjust. You have to keep thinking all the time: "How am I going to approach it?" You can't play the same way all the time.'

They were wise words of advice and, luckily, Harry was the type of down-to-earth lad who heeded any help from his peers. It was testament to his development that he DID readjust; he kept his goalscoring prowess but added the intelligent movement that had been a trait of his idol Sheringham. It meant he was a difficult target to pin down for any backline.

Greavsie arrived at Spurs in 1961 from AC Milan for a then massive fee of £99,999. The fee agreed by boss Bill Nicholson was deliberately £1 short of £100,000 so that Jimmy would not be burdened by being the first footballer sold and bought for that amount. Not that it would have worried him anyway: he was always confident of his ability to score goals and he did just that, more than repaying Bill Nicks's faith. Jimmy's goals fired the club to two FA Cups, the European Cup Winners' Cup and two FA Charity Shields. He also helped Spurs finish runners-up in the league in 1962–63.

He had settled in quickly under Nicholson and later admitted he was one of the managers he most enjoyed working under. Jimmy hit a hat-trick on his debut against Blackpool and formed a brilliant partnership upfront with Bobby Smith.

Jimmy hit the back of the net in their 1962 FA Cup final win over Burnley and also grabbed a brace in the 5–1 European Cup Winners' Cup triumph over Atletico Madrid the following year. He also enjoyed the sort of international career Harry is dreaming of, scoring forty-four goals which left him fourth in the all-time record book after Wayne Rooney, Bobby Charlton and Gary Lineker.

But he would later admit to his 'sadness' at missing out on the 1966 World Cup final after injury cost him his place to Geoff Hurst. He would reminisce, 'I danced around the pitch with everyone else but even in this moment of triumph and great happiness, deep down I felt my sadness. Throughout my years as a professional footballer I had dreamed of playing in a World Cup Final. I had missed out on the match of a lifetime and it hurt.'

It was a cruel twist of fate but in no way detracts from the goalscoring genius of the man. Greavsie suffered a debilitating stroke in May 2015 and was confined to a wheelchair. In 2016, he told the *Express* he feared he would never walk again, remarking that, 'I remain in a wheelchair and it's now likely I will stay this way for the rest of my life. The doctors have told me I won't walk again and that I will always need ongoing care. It was devastating to hear them say that but I will never stop trying to get better – and the main thing is that I'm still here fighting all the way.'

Indeed it was: a fighter and a legend who Tottenham fans, and Kane, will never forget.

Another England striker from the White Hart Lane annals is Martin Chivers, third on the club's all-time goalscorer list after Greaves and Smith, with 174. And Martin is also a confirmed member of the 'Harry Kane fan club' after Harry made history in March, 2016, by becoming the first Spurs player since him (in 1971–72 and 72–73) to score more than twenty top-flight goals in successive seasons.

Martin explained why he was glad Harry had finally matched his record – and why he admired him as a top-notch striker. He told Tottenham's official website, 'One of the main things about Harry in my view is that he can score with both feet. Not all great goalscorers can do that. Harry can also head the ball, so he's an all-round scorer of goals and that's a handy ability to have, especially when he gets into the positions he gets into.'

The following month Chivers, a Spurs match-day ambassador, told the *Daily Mail* how he zoomed in on Kane after one game while hosting a fans' meal. Martin said, 'I was hosting a table in one of the hospitality suites. Harry Kane had come in after the game and I got up from the table and trampled all over these kids and VIPs to get to him – pushed past them all. I run over and I'm holding out this paper for his autograph, "Please sign this". He looked up, "Hello, Chiv, how's it going?"'

Typically down-to-earth Harry, and Martin, too, for that matter. Given that characteristic, it is probably no surprise that many Spurs fans could see similarities in the way both men play the game. One said, 'Kane is so very like Chivers – he moves, heads, dribbles and shoots just like him and has a real eye for goal. Hopefully will score many goals for both Spurs and England too.' While another added, 'Harry is powerful like Chivers and I would rate him our best centre-forward since Chivers. Both are Spurs through and through and would die for the club.'

From the truly modern era, as in the last decade, only Jermain Defoe comes near to the goalscoring exploits Harry aims to emulate at White Hart Lane. Of course, both men are vastly different in style and size; Defoe the pocket rocket and speed king as opposed to the more traditional English number 9 encapsulated by Harry. Yet Defoe can boast that proud record of being in the top five (fifth) in Tottenham's all-time roll call of goalscorers, his 143 goals up to his final departure in 2013 being just sixteen behind Cliff Jones's tally.

When Defoe left he handed his Number 18 shirt to Harry with the accompanying comment, 'There are goals in that shirt!' Harry appreciated the gesture and was grateful to Jermain, before taking the club's legendary Number 10 shirt the following season. He was also glad of some advice Defoe gave him about the art of goalscoring, remembering, 'He told me once, "If I miss a chance then the odds are now in my favour to score the next one because the chances of missing two in a row are less than missing one". And that's what I try and take. If I miss, then the next one is more in my favour to score. It's about little things like that.'

Wise words, and Jermain remains one of Harry's biggest fans and is sure he will become an all-time legend at Tottenham. He told *Sky Sports*, 'Harry loves scoring goals, he loves the club, he's a local boy and I'm sure he and his family are delighted. It's not surprised me with the amount of goals he's scored, though. When I was at Tottenham I saw a young kid come through. I remember when he played in the reserves and I'd say to him "H, how many goals have you scored?" He always scored two or three goals in the reserves every game. If you've got a young kid scoring three or four goals every game in the reserves, at some point he's got to get a chance. Training with the first team, he was scoring goals easy. He's a natural goalscorer.'

And there you have it: when former Lane heroes have no doubt about what the boy Kane can achieve, the sky is the limit for the home-grown icon – as he was about to prove when he returned from that nagging ankle injury in November 2016, and then on into 2017.

CHAPTER FOURTEEN

HOPES AND DREAMS FOR 2017

After his return from injury on 6 November 2016, Harry had scored that vital goal to earn Spurs a much-needed point at Arsenal in the Premier League. As we have seen, the team had struggled badly without him. Goals were in short supply and Spurs had missed his leadership and commitment. So no one was more relieved than Mauricio Pochettino when Harry not only returned and scored in the Arsenal clash, but that he came through the match unscathed. It would have been a disaster for the boss if his main man had been injured again.

Tottenham looked a different team with Kane back in the saddle. His goal at Arsenal had lifted morale within the dressing room and provided a much-needed confidence booster among the players and around White Hart Lane. There was genuine belief that if Harry stayed fit they could have another good crack at winning the league. Pochettino spoke of his delight at Kane's return after the match, and stressed how important he was to the team and to morale. The Argentine said, 'I am happy with Harry Kane, it is tough after not playing for a few months. I am happy he is back, it is important for the team to feel one of our best players is available.'

Of course, you could argue it was dangerous to rely so much on one man. What if Kane got injured again? Who would score the goals? These were fair questions, as was the debate over whether Pochettino had made a mistake in believing Vincent Janssen could step in effortlessly and take over the goalscoring mantle when Harry was sidelined.

The Dutchman was talented but he was not as prolific or as deadly as Harry in front of goal. He had cost £17 million when he signed from AZ Alkmaar in July 2016 but had not set the world, or even the Lane, alight in his first season. Of course, that was looking at the scenario rather pessimistically. He was still only twenty-two and had years ahead of him. It was feasible that he would improve and hit the goal trail more often when he had fully adapted to the physicality of the English game – and he had four years to do so at Spurs, given the nature of the contract he had signed that summer in 2016. But by Christmas 2016, he had scored just two goals for Tottenham – a sign of how far he still had to go to impose himself on the team.

Again, on the positive side, he clearly knew where the goal was – he had hit twenty-seven for AZ in just thirty-four games. And Pochettino believed he WOULD come good. When Harry was out for eight weeks in the autumn of 2016, the manager said: 'This is a big opportunity for Vincent to show what he could do.' For all the fanfare, he scored just two goals in Harry's absence – in the 5–0 League Cup win over Gillingham and the 1–1 draw with Leicester, his first Premier League goal.

By comparison, Harry scored more goals than Vincent in his first two games back in the team – that one against Arsenal followed by a brace against West Ham United a fortnight later. That double against the Hammers helped Spurs to a 3–2 win, another vital victory as they aimed to get right back on track after Kane's absence. Harry was pleased with how his comeback after injury was panning out but refused to get carried away. Pochettino, however, had no such qualms, now admitting his man was one of the most deadly finishers around. He said, 'Harry Kane is always very important; he is our main striker. You miss that type of player when he does not play for ten or eleven games. He is one of the best strikers in the world.'

Three days later Harry was at it again, scoring for the third successive match after his return, this time in Monaco. But it would end in disappointment, as Spurs were beaten 2–1 and exited the Champions League at the first stage. After all the hard work in finishing third in the Premier League the previous season, and expectations of a good run in Europe, the club departed with a whimper. They did not deserve to win in the Principality and had not done enough in their group games overall to merit making it to the knockout stages.

Kane netted from the penalty spot seven minutes after the interval but it would not be enough. Spurs had won only one of their five group games and Harry and his teammates trooped off the field in Monaco down and out. Pochettino put the boot in further by suggesting his players had not shown the necessary battling mentality to advance. He added, 'We are out and we have time to assess and analyse. It is true we feel disappointed but today we missed opportunities. I think we made too many mistakes at home at Wembley. We don't deserve to go through to the next round because we didn't show enough quality. We will take many things from this defeat. You learn and improve every day. Now we are trying to reduce the gap on the teams above us in the Premier League.'

For sure, they had suffered without Kane during his injury spell and Pochettino was right about Wembley – the team had not settled at all at the national stadium during their home matches. The only positive, the manager told them in the dressing room, was that they could use their hurt next time they played in the tournament as inspiration. That hurt would spur them on if, as he expected, they qualified the following season.

Harry expressed his own disappointment to BT Sport afterwards, admitting he was 'gutted'. He said, 'It is disappointing. We got ourselves back in the game at 1–1 and it was schoolboy to concede straight after that. We had to try to grind out a win because we were not great – the second goal took the stuffing out of us. I just don't think on the day we were good enough. I'm gutted – we wanted to go far but it is something we will have to deal with. Losing two of our home games in this competition – yes, we played at Wembley this year but it has to be a fortress at home. We will look back and say it was the home games where we should've been better.'

It was probably the emotional hangover from the defeat, and the accompanying fatigue, that led to the 2–1 loss at Chelsea days later. There would be no Harry on the scoresheet on this occasion, although he was back in business at the start of December 2016. He grabbed yet another brace in the 5–0 league thrashing of visitors Swansea and followed that up with a goal in the 3–1 win over CSKA Moscow at Wembley. Yes, Spurs had finally come good in the Champions League – but it was too late. The consolation was that they had finished third in the group and so would now enter automatically into the Europa League. OK, it wasn't the premier European competition but Man United had also qualified for the round of thirty-two and the winners of the event now earned automatic qualification into the Champions League in September 2017. So it was certainly worth having a go at winning – as Harry told his teammates after the victory over Moscow. He, of course, wanted to win everything, even practice matches. But he was a realist and knew that getting into the Champions League by whatever means was essential.

By the Christmas of 2016 he had netted nine times in fifteen games for Spurs – a more than credible return given he had been out injured for two months. The team were fifth in the Premier League, a point behind Arsenal, who were fourth but ten off top-placed Chelsea. There was much to play for as 2017 loomed.

For Harry there was also the joy of knowing he and Kate's first child was due in the new year.

And he had signed off the old year by signing a new deal at the Lane – much to his delight and that of the fans, the management and everyone involved with the club. Tottenham had to break their pay structure to ensure their most valuable asset continued at the club until 2022. Insiders said he would earn around £100,000 a week which, at that time, was £20,000 more than club captain Hugo Lloris, although Harry's figure was bumped up with bonuses for hitting certain targets.

He could probably have earned double that at Man United or Man City, so it once again showed his commitment and loyalty to his boyhood club: the club he loved. As 2017 dawned, Harry Kane had once again proved that he was definitely one of Tottenham's own – and a striker worthy of comparison with the best. Including, as we will see in the next chapter, the former Spurs hero whose brilliant record of thirty goals in a season he equalled on 19 April 2015.

CHAPTER FIFTEEN
THE HARRY & GARY SHOW

On 19 April 2015, Harry Kane entered the record books by becoming the first player since Gary Lineker to score thirty goals in a season for Tottenham. It was a remarkable achievement, especially when you consider that Gary's record had stood since the 1991–92 campaign – twenty-three long years. Even the deadly striking boots of Sheringham, Klinsmann and Gareth Bale had proved incapable of matching that feat. Remarkably, it meant Harry had become the first ever home-grown player to hit thirty in a season for the club – as the fans sang loud that day, he was indeed 'one of their own'.

Naturally, he was delighted to have achieved the milestone and denied the prospect of doing so had made it even more difficult to achieve. He told BBC Sport: 'After I got to twenty goals, I set myself a target of thirty and it felt like I was on twenty-nine for ages. But now I've got here I'm delighted. Maybe I need to set myself another target from now to the end of the season. It was a special occasion and to get the win makes it even more special.'

Lineker is a decent chap and immediately tweeted his congratulations to Harry, saying, 'Well done @harrykane28 on being the first Spurs player to score 30 goals in yonks. Sheringham, Klinsmann, Defoe, Keane and Adebayor, where are you?'

Spurs boss Pochettino, while hugging Harry as he left the pitch, also made it clear he owed a debt to his teammates, saying, 'Congratulations to him because he deserves this moment. I think he needs to pay for a dinner this week for his teammates. The team work a lot and try to help him score.' The Argentine was smiling as he spoke; he knew that Harry was the one player in his squad who LEAST needed to have his feet keeping on the ground. As we have noted, it is simply not in his nature to let fame or glory go to his head; even when he had made the record books he remained, as ever, well grounded and always temperamentally sound.

We have already examined how Harry compares to great Spurs strikers including Sheringham, so it makes sense to take a look at him in relation to Lineker, given the two men share a page in the Spurs history books with those thirty goals apiece, and that Gary will, like Harry, always have a strong love-in with the Lane faithful after his exploits for the club.

Of course, there is no denying Gary was prolific in front of goal and fully earned his tag as an England legend. But I would argue that Harry is more of a rounded striker; he is not simply a six-yard box predator as Lineker was. As the website *backpagefootball.com* points out, Kane can score from a variety of positions and situations. They analysed his stats in July 2015, and found that, mainly, he scored with his right foot – but that he had also netted five times with his left foot and five times with his head. They added, 'The Spurs striker also managed to score in a variety of situations, including ten goals from open play and eight from set pieces. While 14 of his 21 goals were from inside the penalty area and Kane finished a further five from within the six-yard box.'

Like Harry, Gary was schooled for stardom from an early age. Born in Leicester in November, 1960, he was destined for the top when he signed schoolboy forms with City, his hometown club. He had grown up in the city, gone to local primary and high schools and played football with his older brother Wayne. His dad was a well-known greengrocer in Leicester, as the business had been around for decades.

Like Harry, Gary was also a talented cricketer at school and maybe could have made the grade there, too. He was the skipper of the Leicestershire Schools team and even thought at one stage that he could follow a career in cricket. And when he looked back on his life in March, 2010, he admitted he would also probably have tried harder in his school subjects if he had known that the competition to make the grade as a footballer would have been so tough.

Gary told *The Independent*, 'If I'd known how difficult it was to be a footballer, I would have worked harder at school. I did okay, but my mind was elsewhere. My last report said something along the lines of: "He concentrates far too much on football. He'll never make a living at that." These were wise words in many ways; a huge percentage of boys don't make a living at it.

'When you do well at one sport, you tend to do well at other sports. I was in both the football and cricket teams and got a lot of goals and runs. I was captain of the Leicestershire Schools cricket team from 11 to 16 and thought at the time I would probably have more chance afterwards in cricket than football.'

Harry too was a good cricketer at school but had no dreams of making it with the bat – football was and would remain his enduring love. But he did enjoy the same settled upbringing as Gary and was also encouraged by his parents to think that he could make the grade in big-time soccer.

Both men prospered after working their way up in local teams. Gary was spotted at the age of thirteen by the Leicester youth academy and at sixteen started to play full-time after leaving school. By the age of eighteen Gary was playing for the Foxes' first team and on the ladder that would rise to the heights of him becoming England's top all-time goalscorer (until Wayne Rooney surpassed his record).

Gary made his debut for Leicester on New Year's Day, 1979, in the 2–0 home victory over Oldham Athletic.

Harry would make his first Premier League start for Spurs at the age of twenty, in April 2014. Whereas Gary had always been tuned for the top at Filbert Street, Harry had had to learn the hard way with several loan moves. It made the boy even tougher and more determined that he would make the grade when he eventually returned to Tottenham. Ironically, of course, one of those loan moves would be to Gary's hometown club: Harry, then nineteen, would sit on the subs' bench with another unknown striker aiming for the stars. Yes, that was Jamie Vardy. The duo would rotate sub duties as Foxes persevered with David Nugent and Chris Wood in attack.

When he was finally given a chance at the Lane, Harry made an immediate impact. Similarly, at Leicester, Lineker was clearly destined for the top. His pace would prove a massive asset as an out-and-out striker. He was good on the wing but he was better as a predator in the six-yard area. Later in his career, at Barcelona, Gary would be played out of position on the wing by Johann Cruyff, a blunder by the Dutch legend. Was Cruyff trying to make the point that he was the boss now after Terry Venables had left the Camp Nou? If so, Lineker would suffer by association.

Back at Leicester, Lineker's most productive league season would come in the 1982–83 campaign when his goals helped the club win promotion to the First Division. He scored twenty-six in forty matches. But Gary was not as strong and powerful as Harry. His manager at the time, Gordon Milne, said that he 'used to fall over a lot' and his legs 'would get tangled up'. Harry had no such worries: after bulking up as a teenager and on his loan spells, he became a strong, powerful centre-forward who could hold his own against the most physical centre-backs.

It would be tough for Milne and Lineker as the Foxes struggled on their return to the big time but Gary's twenty-two league goals helped the club beat the drop as they finished the season in a respectable fifteenth position out of twenty-two clubs.

And the following season he netted his best ever overall total of twenty-nine goals in forty-nine games for the club. That total consisted of twenty-four in the league, three in the FA Cup and two in the League Cup. But that success brought distress for his hometown club as he now left for Everton, the then dominant force in English football. The Toffees splashed £800,000 for his services; they saw him as a direct and immediate replacement for Andy Gray.

It is certainly hard to foresee a day when Harry would leave the Lane. In my book, he is a one-man club and loves Tottenham so much he will stay for life if all goes to plan. In his first season at Everton, Lineker learned that the grass isn't always greener on the other side of the road. The fans did not take easily to him, even though he recorded a phenomenal strike-rate of thirty-eight goals on fifty-two games. They were still fuming that he had been brought in to replace their hero, Gray.

It seemed a problem solved for everyone, then, when Spanish giants Barcelona came in for Lineker at the end of his debut campaign – especially when Barça offered a more than enticing fee of more than £3 million. With revenue lost from no European competition (English clubs were banned from Europe over the Heysel Stadium disaster), the cash was a way to balance the books for Everton.

Gary told the football magazine *FourFourTwo* that he accepted the European ban probably curtailed his Everton career, saying, 'Everton would perhaps have been in a better position to keep me. It was very much Howard [Kendall's] decision to take the money. When your club tells you they've accepted a bid, you take that as a sign you're not wanted. The opportunity to join a club like Barcelona comes along once in a lifetime, so I had to take it.

'It was a shame because in an ideal world I'd be able to say, "Give me another couple of years at Everton, let me win a few things, and then I'll go."'

The league season ended bittersweet for Lineker as Everton finished runners-up – to local rivals Liverpool. And Liverpool defied them once again in the FA Cup final at Wembley, running out 3–1 winners with a brace from Ian Rush. Liverpool had secured the league seven days earlier and now notched the double. Gary's consolation was that he scored Everton's goal at Wembley in the twenty-seventh minute.

Gary then went to Barça and was applauded for his efforts. Finally, in July 1989 he he arrived back in England – and his love-in with Tottenham began.

Spurs boss Terry Venables persuaded Lineker to return home – and to opt for White Hart Lane rather than Old Trafford. Yes, Sir Alex Ferguson had wanted the Leicester-born striker to boost his firepower options at Man United but Lineker opted instead to work with 'El Tel', who paid £1.1 million for the striker's services. It would be money well spent: in three seasons Gary would hit the back of the net sixty-seven times in 105 league games. He would also end up club top scorer in those three seasons. His quality up front would also see the FA Cup won at Wembley.

Venables was delighted to acquire his services – and Gary was delighted to escape the clutches of Johan Cruyff. He said at the time, 'I am leaving Barcelona with mixed feelings of happiness and sadness, but I did not want to stay with a club whose coach I don't respect.' That was never likely to be the case with El Tel, who had, of course, coached Barça himself. He told Lineker his days isolated out on the wing were over; now he would play in his preferred, and best, position, up front as the number 1 striker.

Kane has been lucky in that the two managers who have overseen his development at Spurs both loved him and encouraged his development. Tim Sherwood was always his biggest fan, having worked with him in his younger days, and Pochettino soon stressed that Harry was his top boy after taking over from Tim. That is not to say that Harry had it all delivered on a plate – no, he still had to toil and graft for his place in the team. But it does help if the boss appreciates you for your best assets – at Barca, the legendary Cruyff clearly did not accept that Lineker could effectively lead his line.

The official Spurs website has no doubt how effective he was at the Lane, though, dubbing Gary, 'the greatest striker of his generation'. His work over those three seasons at the Lane would certainly substantiate that viewpoint. Top scorer every season and an influence that brought the FA Cup to the club – a trophy which was also his first major one in the game.

Kane would also love to end up top scorer every season. But sources told me he was aiming higher than the FA Cup. As the club moved into its new stadium, and with teammates and a manager who was just as ambitious, Harry wanted to win the Premier League with Tottenham – and, hopefully, the Champions League. The former was doable, especially when you consider Leicester's triumph in 2015–16, and the latter may yet land in Kane's lap if things go to plan. This is a club very much on an upward trend, with astute leadership at the top and players who would walk into most other teams – the likes of Harry, Dele Alli, Christian Eriksen, Hugo Lloris *et al.*

But when Gary helped Tottenham to that FA Cup win in 1991, he was feted as a hero, and rightly so. The 2–1 win over Nottingham Forest was their first major trophy triumph in nine years – since, in fact, they won the same cup in 1982. In 2001, Gary told BBC Sport just what the win meant to him, saying, 'Winning the FA Cup in 1991 was undoubtedly the highlight of my playing career. I was desperate to win it… I was coming to the end of my career and knew it could be my last chance to win the FA Cup.'

And his name was guaranteed legendary status with Spurs fans even if they had lost the final… after he helped them beat arch rivals Arsenal in the semis! Of course, Kane has his own Gunners story to shore up his legend at the Lane – how he ended up at Tottenham despite being in the Arsenal academy as a youngster. And how Arsène Wenger admitted he was unhappy that a player of Kane's potential had been allowed to leave the club.

Lineker grabbed a brace against Arsenal with Gazza scoring THAT wonderful free kick past David Seaman as Spurs won 3–1 to book their place in the final.

Kane and Lineker also have similar temperaments as footballers. Okay, Harry has double figures bookings for Spurs but he rarely loses it to a defender, or if he is struggling to make an impact. Paul Scholes told *The Independent* in 2015 how impressed he was with Harry's character, pointing out that Martin Škrtel had tried and failed to wind him up when Liverpool took on Spurs. Paul said, 'The more I watch him, the more I appreciate his temperament. Playing in attack is difficult. You are under scrutiny and you have to be able to deal with that. Kane seems to do it easily.

'Martin Škrtel is good at rattling the opposing centre-forward. He did it to a player as experienced as Diego Costa and got a reaction out of him. Yet Kane never reacted to Škrtel once, and never looked like doing so. Then, when the chance presented itself, he was ruthless.'

Gary was similarly renowned for not taking the bait. He was never booked, never mind sent off, in his glittering football career. He was Mr Cool on the pitch – a man who was hot when it came to scoring but who had ice in his veins with his admirable level of self-control. Who can forget the time he pointed to the bench in the World Cup semi-final of 1990 in Italy when Paul Gascoigne lost the plot after getting booked against Germany? The tears started to roll and Lineker beckoned to the England bench that the youngster was in trouble mentally, as he realised the booking would rule him out of the final if England won.

England manager Bobby Robson revealed to the press that he knew Gazza had 'gone' and how 'clever' Lineker had been to alert him of the situation. Robson said, 'I saw his face change, from being aggressive, fighting for the ball, to realising he'd committed an error, and he'd been booked, and he knew now the final was not for him. Tears began to well into his eyes. And Gary Lineker was very clever, he saw it immediately and came as close as he could to me and said, watch Gazza. Watch him. He thought now his mind might just go a bit berserk…'

Lineker had a clever, quick mind and a fine line in reasoning. He always knew what he wanted and was aware of the world around him. Even in his later career as a TV pundit he managed to continue working for BBC's *Match of the Day* show *and* earn a deal that would see him become presenter of BT's Champions League coverage. He was a top player in football and a top player in life; he knew how to look after himself and early on worked out that the best way to get what you want is to be conciliatory and amenable.

That is not to say that Lineker wasn't determined – I would contend he was (and remains) determined to succeed in all he does. It's the same with Harry, who will always work the hardest in training to ensure he has that bit extra in the tank. He is the first to say that the more you put in, the more you get out – just as Gary did in his playing days.

I can only think of one particular incident where Gary showed dissent and anger on the football field. That was in the summer of 1992 during England's disastrous campaign in the European championship finals in Sweden. In what would be England's final match of the campaign – and Lineker's final game for his country – he was subbed by then England boss Graham Taylor.

Clearly discontented at the way the team had played – and that he was seemingly the scapegoat as captain – he threw down the skipper's armband when Taylor substituted him. Taylor had appointed Lineker captain when he became boss two years earlier but the substitution with almost half an hour to go in the game against Sweden would sour their relationship. England failed to win a game and finished bottom of their group. It was a sad way to exit international football for Lineker, who had entertained hopes of surpassing Bobby Charlton's goals record for his country.

I can understand Gary's frustration at the time and I believe it was a general frustration that England were poor and he himself had not lived up to the top billing that would have allowed him to beat Sir Bobby's record that led to the armband controversy. Certainly I don't think for one minute that it was a lack of respect for the armband.

In 2004, Gary backed up the theory that he was dejected about the performances that led to that one rare outburst in his career. He told *The Telegraph*, 'I will always be remembered for throwing down the captain's armband when England manager Graham Taylor substituted me in my final game for my country against Sweden in 1992, but far more disappointing was the fact that I did not taste a single victory from two successive tournaments. In 1992 we were a poor side... we went out with a team that had no flair or uniformity. We proved that by drawing 0–0 against both Denmark and France before losing 2–1 to Sweden.'

Final word on 'the armband incident' to Stuart Pearce, who would replace Gary as skipper. In his autobiography, *Psycho*, he recalls that the mood before the Sweden match was optimistic and that the team were relaxed after going to see Bruce Springsteen in concert. That in itself surprises me, as Pearce is more renowned as an aficionado of punk rather than the blue-collar rock that Bruce performs, but even more surprising is that old Psycho seemed to back Taylor rather than Lineker over the incident. In the book, he adds, 'I am sure Graham would not have pulled Gary off unless he thought he could win the match by doing it… Gary was clearly annoyed and made it look bad by taking off his armband and throwing it on to the floor, in my direction, as I was taking over the captaincy.'

For all the fact that Gary NEVER got booked, let alone sent off, I cannot imagine Harry Kane throwing a similar strop. He is the ultimate team player, a striker who thrives on the goals he scores but who, nonetheless, knows it is more important that the team is successful.

Harry had made no secret of the fact that he wanted to become one of the first names on the England team sheet and that his mission is to become the first choice centre-forward. He has never taken it for granted: with the likes of Vardy, Sturridge and Marcus Rashford on his coat-tails that would be foolish. Harry simply works twice as hard and hopes that his efforts will pay off. Certainly, if he could enjoy anything like as prolific an England career as Lineker, he would be 'over the moon', pals say.

Gary wrote his name in history as one of the finest – and deadliest – strikers to play for his country. His star started to rise when he became one of the first names in the England squad for the 86 World Cup in Mexico. His England debut came when he faced 'auld enemy' Scotland on 26 May 1984, aged twenty-three. Gary came on as a sub after seventy-two minutes, replacing Tony Woodcock up front in a home international championship match at Hampden Park, Glasgow.

Harry's debut, as we have mentioned, would come in March 2015, when he came on a sub for Wayne Rooney in the home

Euro 2016 qualifier against Lithuania – and scored! It was the first of what he hoped – and we expect – to be many, many strikes as his career progresses. He was still only twenty-one and had netted ten times for the England U21 team.

It would be a disappointment when Gary was not chosen for that summer's tour of South America – that was when John Barnes truly came of age as an England player when he 'did a Brazil' by scoring against them by dribbling through their defence as if they were ghosts. But Gary would be back the following March and duly scored his first goal for his country – some time after his debut, unlike Harry, but still a goal he said at the time 'he would never forget' and that 'it meant the world' to him.

It came against the Republic of Ireland the following March. Starting with the number ten on his back and partnering Mark Hateley, Gary scored England's winner in a 2–1 victory in a friendly at Wembley. Gary was 'well chuffed' to have grabbed the goal that separated the two teams.

Lineker went on to score five hat-tricks for England and is currently their third highest top scorer after Rooney and Charlton. Harry has ambitions to have a go at that stat, but for now is focused on firming up his role in the England team and happy that he achieved 'his dream' of scoring that debut goal. And, as the *Daily Mail*, pointed out after the match, that debut goal put him ahead of many other garlanded footballers who also failed to match his feat, going on to say, 'Since 2000, there have been eight other players who have found the net right away for the national team. Yet Kane, in scoring on his debut, is already one-up on the likes of Gary Lineker, Sir

Geoff Hurst, John Barnes, David Beckham, Wayne Rooney, Michael Owen, Steven Gerrard and Frank Lampard – to name but a few who failed to score on debut.

'Others have had more luck – Sir Bobby Charlton, who remains for the moment England's all-time leading goalscorer with forty-nine, netted on debut in a 4–0 win over Scotland in the 1958 British Home Championship.'

For the record, Jimmy Greaves, another of Harry's former Tottenham heroes, also scored on his England debut. He hit the back of the net against Peru in 1959 – although at the time he was still a teenager and turning out in Chelsea's colours at club level. It was a momentous moment in the career of the man who would go on to become a legend at White Hart Lane – but the day ended in disappointment as England lost 4–1 in Lima.

And over three years before Harry netted, another former Spurs star achieved the feat. Andros Townsend scored on his international debut against Montenegro in October 2011. His goal helped England to a flying 4–1 win over Montenegro in a World Cup qualifier.

Another former big-name striker to whom Harry is often compared also scored on his debut for his country. Yes, big, bustling Alan Shearer added his name to the international 'debut goal club' with his strike against France in 1992. It would help England to a 2–0 win at Wembley.

Shearer remains one of Harry's biggest fans, calling him a top-class centre-forward and telling the Premier League's official website in March 2015 he was convinced the boy would enjoy a long career at the very top of the game, adding that, 'He seems to have that natural ability to get goals. He's also young, fresh and his attitude appears to be very, very good. What I like about him, is that he is willing to run in behind defenders, as well as go short. When he gets opportunities he invariably takes them. He wants to get his shot away very quickly, which is good to see. It looks as if he could have a very good future in the game.'

Alan has said he sees a lot of his own play in Harry and complimented him by adding that Harry has more to his game in that he can also play as a number 10, linking and setting up play, as well as the more traditional powerful centre-forward role that he himself carried off so well. In September 2015, Harry even celebrated scoring in the 6–0 win over San Marino by emulating Shearer's famous goal salute, right arm aloft in the air. The pair had previously met for a chat after Harry had suffered something of a goal drought. And in a TV interview Harry told Alan he would copy his goal celebration as a thank-you for the tips when he eventually broke the barren spell. So after his goal Kane tweeted the Newcastle and England legend, asking what he thought of his attempt at a Shearer salute, 'How did I do @alanshearer?? #EURO2016.'

Shearer joined in the fun, tweeting back, 'Love that for a first attempt @hkan28 Now look forward to it on a regular basis!! Congratulations #goalscorer.' Alan then took it a step further, adding in another tweet that he didn't want Harry to get so used to it that it meant he had overhauled his thirty goals in sixty-one games for England!

Lineker keeps a close eye on his Tottenham prodigy in his role as a TV commentator and as a football fan and admits he sees a lot of his fellow *Match of the Day* staffer Shearer in Harry. The *Match of the Day* host said, 'Without wishing to make any horrible comparisons with someone, Kane does remind me a little bit of Shearer. I like Kane and I know Shearer likes him a lot as well. He has a really strong all-round game. He's not lightning quick, but he's not slow. That's the only thing you would look at and say, "If he was a yard or two quicker" … well, I don't know what you'd be looking at. He scores poacher's goals, great goals, takes free kicks, takes penalties. He does the whole thing.'

Gary believes that the Tottenham central core of Kane, Dele Alli and Eric Dier is great news for both fans at the Lane and England supporters – that they can be a key influence and bring success for years to come. At twenty-three, Harry was being compared to Spurs legend Lineker and England legend Shearer. He was grounded enough to not let any of the praise go to his head and to continue to knuckle down in training and to deliver the goods on the pitch. And the real bonus for both club and country was that, injuries permitting, he had a good ten years ahead of him to become an even deadlier marksman. Little wonder footballing idols of earlier eras were bedazzled by and queuing up to praise Harry Kane, the young man from East London, who was fast becoming a worldwide phenomenon.

*

If 2016 had ended on a high for Harry Kane, so 2017 began on an even higher note as he became a father for the first time. Just eight days into the new year he took to Twitter to tell his followers that he and Kate were celebrating the birth of a baby girl – little Ivy Jane Kane – weighing in at 7lb 8oz. He declared himself 'so proud' and that he was ecstatic; indeed it was 'an amazing feeling'. Well-wishers, including my good self, sent him messages of congratulations - as did many of his team-mates, including Dele Alli, and even his England skipper Wayne Rooney, joined in, tweeting, 'Congrats to you both,' while adding, rather mischievously, 'Your [*sic*] next Dele... '

It was just the tonic Harry needed to get 2017 off to a good start. Joy and fun; certainly it banished the misery of his injury woes the previous year and that of exiting the Champions League at the first hurdle. Now, he had a new addition to his family to swoon over and the prospect of challenging Chelsea for the league title and Man United for the Europa League and the FA Cup. Plus there would be key World Cup qualifiers for England to fit into his busy schedule.

The birth of Ivy Jane meant he was excused duties for Tottenham's third round FA Cup clash with Aston Villa. Even in his absence, the boys had little problem in disposing of the Championship strugglers.

Before that, Harry had got his own footballing year off to a flier on New Year's Day with a brace in the 4–1 win at Watford; never an easy place to go in the Premier League. That emphatic win consolidated belief that Spurs could be the main challengers to runaway league leaders Chelsea. That if anyone could reel in the Blues, it would be Kane and Co. Three days later that belief gained still more credence as Spurs beat Chelsea 2–0 in the league at the Lane. Harry, for once, was not on the scoresheet but was delighted that he and his team-mates had got one over on Antonio Conte's men. This time a Dele Alli double would win the points, at the same time ending Chelsea's thirteen-match winning streak. It also meant Tottenham had won five straight league games – they were making a statement at exactly the right time as the second half of the campaign now started to hot up. Boss Pochettino summed up the importance of the victory, saying, 'It is a massive victory, a very important three points to reduce the gap at the top of the table. Chelsea is in a very good position, but we are fighting to get points and to reduce the gap above us.' Harry agreed entirely with those sentiments; beforehand he had told pals that it was 'vital that we win' to keep up the pressure at the top of the table. Defeat would have left Chelsea so far ahead that catching them might have become Mission: Impossible.

It would be almost six weeks into 2017 before Spurs would taste defeat in the league, when they slumped to a 2–0 loss at Liverpool towards the middle of February. That was a low point, no doubt about it, but they – and Harry – had put in some pretty impressive displays in the run-up. Indeed, directly after the triumph over Chelsea, Harry had notched a hat-trick in the 4–0 win home win over West Brom. He would follow that with another trio of goals as Spurs powered to a 3–0 victory at Fulham in the FA Cup on 19 February. As March loomed, the club were still in the hunt for three trophies: the Premier League, the FA Cup and the Europa League.

After his hat-trick at Craven Cottage, Kane had scored nineteen goals in all competitions for the season and was hitting top form as Tottenham prepared for an exciting run-in. The club had not lifted a trophy since the 2008 League Cup, but hopes were high that the barren run could soon be over. Harry Kane admitted that he and his teammates were 'buzzing' as 'winning games gives you confidence'. With his goals and perennial positivity and optimism, most commentators agreed that it was now surely only a matter of time before a new trophy arrived at the Lane. There was also talk that new England boss Gareth Southgate was contemplating making Harry Kane his captain when Rooney retired. Yes, the future was truly bright for the country's top striker – indeed, it was glowing. And he was still only twenty-three years old.

CHAPTER SIXTEEN

WORLD CUP GOLDEN BOY

At the end of the 2018 FIFA World Cup, England skipper Harry Kane would be presented with the Golden Boot, the honour given to the top marksman in the tournament, after finishing on six goals, two ahead of five rivals – Belgium's Romelu Lukaku, French duo Antoine Griezmann and Kylian Mbappé, Portugal's Cristiano Ronaldo and Russia's Denis Cheryshev. It was a just reward to the man who had led his country with distinction, aggression and no little determination to succeed in Russia. At the age of twenty-four, he had inspired a group largely made up of youngsters to a World Cup semi-final and, just as importantly, to a future that would surely bring more glory as the team matured. Little wonder he was being spoken of as a £200 million target for Real Madrid, who had allowed Cristiano Ronaldo to exit for Juventus shortly before England's semi-final clash with the talented, and vastly more experienced, Croatians. Not that Tottenham, or tough negotiating chairmen Daniel Levy, would even contemplate such a move. No, Harry Kane was one of Tottenham's own, as the chant went, and no transfer would be sanctioned.

Harry's personal odyssey in Russia in June and July, 2018, saw him light up the tournament with a rush of initial goals and key moments and then drop off a little as England reached the last eight and the semi-final. Gary Neville, in his role as an ITV pundit, mooted the idea that Harry may have been carrying a secret knock and that inhibited his play. That is an interesting comment and would make sense, although my sources insisted that there was no injury and that Harry had given his all as he normally does. It was a simple case of it not coming off for him in those two games – he couldn't hit the back of the net as he normally, instinctively, would. But he was still a threat and a menace, particularly in the match against Sweden.

My belief is that he suffered in the Croatia match after particularly heavy challenges – both body checks and fouls – from the likes of Dejan Lovren and may have suffered a knock DURING, rather than before, the game that affected him. For all their pretty passing in midfield, Croatia's backline knew how to hit the England skipper hard and he had little protection from the normally reliable Turkish ref, Cüneyt Çakır. Harry was frequently wincing at the tough treatment meted out to him and on one occasion appeared winded after an assault on his ribs.

Kane's World Cup actually began in earnest a couple of weeks before any action kicked off in Russia. On May 22, it was officially announced that he would be the captain of the squad. He had beat off the challenge of Liverpool's Jordan Henderson and fellow Spurs star, Eric Dier, to lead the nation at the World Cup. Harry said he was proud to have been selected, 'It is an amazing honour. You always dream of playing for England growing up and to be the captain is that little bit more. I'm so excited for the World Cup. I can't wait to be there and experience it. To be leading the lads out is going to be special. But for me, nothing changes. I'm still the person, the same player. It is just about the team. We will do what we can and go as far as we can.'

England boss Gareth Southgate was confident he had made the right decision in choosing Harry as his skipper. He said, 'Harry has some outstanding personal qualities. He is a meticulous professional and one of the most important things for a captain is that they set the standard every day. He has belief and high standards and it is a great message for the team to have a captain who has shown that it is possible to be one of the best in the world over a consistent period of time and that has been his drive. My feeling is that over the last eighteen months in the camps that he's been with us he has shown that he has got the desire to take that into a team environment and he recognises the importance of bringing others with him. Of course, Harry will need the support of the other good leaders that we have got around him. You don't become a top team by just having a good captain with good values because that has got to spread right throughout the group but I think he is the one who is ready to take that challenge on.'

The waiting would soon be over. Harry, Gareth and the squad arrived in Russia on June 12, exactly one week before they would open their campaign in the group stage by taking on Tunisia. They touched down at St Petersburg airport after a good flight by private jet from Birmingham and all appeared in good spirits. This would be the first World Cup for most of the players and it would become clear as the tournament progressed that Southgate had instilled an excellent group mentality among them; a true 'Club England' as the grey suits at the FA had envisaged (but never previously achieved) until now. And it was down to Southgate and Kane that the feel-good atmosphere continued right through to the third place playoff match on the final Saturday. Sure, this squad had arrived with the least trumpeting of expectation EVER for an England team at a World Cup finals, but full credit to Kane and Southgate for their part in keeping the group together, ensuring there were none of the club cliques that had blighted the so-called 'Golden Generation', and getting the absolute maximum from the players.

Many pundits and fans had feared that England would exit the World Cup at the group stage – no one I know predicted they would make it through to the semis.

After landing in St Petersburg, the camp had another hour's trek to their base at the ForRest Mix Club in Repino, an area of St Petersburg. The plan was that they would return there after matches to establish a sense of stability. Some pundits criticised the plan, as it meant the team, as well as staff, friends and loved ones, would have to fly thousands of miles to and from games. In the group games alone, they would have more than 3,000 miles to fly to complete the three matches against Tunisia, Panama and Belgium. Wouldn't it leave the squad exhausted?

It was perhaps significant in that while England were again travelling from St Petersburg to the Luzhniki Stadium in Moscow for the semi-final, Croatia were already in situ. They had quit their base at St Petersburg as their coach Zlatko Dalic believed they would be better rested if they did not have that long journey to make before the match. Maybe that helped the Croatians fend off fatigue during the game, which many expected them to suffer after two excursions into extra time and two penalty shootouts?

The defeat by the Croatians will be debated hard and long – and mostly long – but this is non negotiable: Harry, Gareth and the England team did the nation proud, going from rank outsiders to near-finalists in one incredible summer. It had echoes of Italia 90 as the whole country rallied behind the team, and will always remain strong in the memory of those who shared the joys and ultimate anguish.

The journey truly began when Harry led England out to play their opening group match against Tunisia in Volgograd on 19 June. Harry's job was simple but not easy: to score the goals and inspire the team to beat the Africans and put an end to England's four-match winless streak at the World Cup. Their last victory, remarkably, was a 1–0 win over Slovenia, achieved at the 2010 World Cup in Port Elizabeth, South Africa. It was perhaps telling that NONE of the men involved in that long-ago triumph were part of the 2018 squad. Eight years was clearly a long time in international football at its peak, and so was a shortage of English players surviving the exigencies of merciless Father Time.

Kane duly turned up and delivered to lead his troops to a

vital first win. Harry reacted swiftly to a rebound, slotting the ball home for his and his country's first goal of the competition on 11 minutes. England were in control and playing some nice, fluid football, far removed from the traditional hustle and bustle, long ball endeavours of previous years. But Tunisia fashioned an unlikely equaliser with a penalty ten minutes before half time. Kyle Walker was the guilty man with his elbow challenge on Fakhreddine Ben Youssef, and Ferjani Sassi made it 1–1 from the spot. England keeper Jordan Pickford, whom Kane would later agree was England's player of the tournament, made a valiant attempt to stop the shot, but just failed to get his hand to the ball.

England had dominated play in the first half and should have put the game to bed, but blew several chances. And this would be no one–off failing – it would be the case in every match they played in this World Cup. As Sven Göran Eriksson famously used to say of England under his tenure, 'Good first half, not so good second half.' It was as if the team blew themselves out with their exertions during the first forty-five minutes and then had little left to see them out. Luckily, this team had a talisman who refused to accept a draw, and it was down to skipper Kane to boost morale with the injury–time winner. His late header from a Harry Maguire flick-on sent them back to St Petersburg believing they COULD achieve something. Previous England teams had drawn or lost their first group games and never recovered. That would not be the case this time, thanks to their master predator.

Inevitably, Harry was voted the Budweiser Man of the Match by the fans, with FIFA commenting, 'Harry Kane scored a brace in his debut match at the World Cup, twice popping up in the right place at the right time and delivering a long-awaited victory for his country at the tournament.' Afterwards, Kane told reporters, 'It's always in the back of your mind, that it's going to be one of those days. But that's what the character is about. We work hard to go into 90-plus minutes and we're thankful that we got one in the end. In the first half it felt good out there. We could've scored two or three goals in the first half and put the game to bed early. But in the World Cup against any team they're always going to fight and keep going and we had to deal with that. I'm really pleased with how we played.'

Another fact worth noting was that Harry had become the first England player to grab a brace in a World Cup match since Gary Lineker in Italia 90 – knowledge that the *Match of the Day* host was keen to impart in his role as a BBC World Cup TV pundit. Lineker also took time out to describe Kane as 'Harry the hero' after his two goals while former England captain Alan Shearer said, 'That's why Gareth Southgate named him skipper, to give him a bit of inspiration and hope and belief – and Harry has given him all of that tonight.' Another former England skipper, Frank Lampard, added: 'Harry is a superstar, and that is why we talk about these superstars, because they turn up at the right moment and score goals.'

Perhaps the most surprising compliments came from Germany, where two of the nation's biggest papers drooled over Kane. *Bild* said, 'We wish we had Kane! There's something different about England at this World Cup. They played like Germany should play, fast and direct.' And *Der Spiegel* offered a perspective that provides a tonic for fans still finding it hard to come to terms with England's subsequent semi-final loss, 'Even if they aren't good enough to win the title this year, in two years' time, when they have a bit more experience and a few more young talents have come up, England will be ready to win the European Championship.'

That was some prediction from England's traditionally biggest arch-rivals. For now, Kane and Co. had enough on their plates simply getting out of Group G. After the Tunisia win, they relaxed for a couple of days, bonding and speaking to their loved ones. Harry said the players would spend their spare time playing table tennis or the computer game *Fortnite*, while some would even partake in more 'intellectual' activities, such as reading a book! Harry said, 'We have a great bond together, we are similar ages and all get on.' It was difficult for Harry in that his fiancée, Kate Goodland, had not made the trip to Russia, and would not, because she was pregnant with their second child. Of course, they kept in regular touch on the phone and on FaceTime but he still missed her and their 18-month old daughter, Ivy. Kate in turn uploaded a photo onto her Instagram page of Ivy in a red Number 9 England shirt with the word 'Daddy' on the back.

It was hardly surprising he missed Kate. They had known each other since school and had been a couple for a long time. It was testament to his commitment to the England squad, and his role as captain, that he never let his feelings be known to the other players, although he knew he could confide in Gareth Southgate. The role of captain was often a lonely one, but Harry was just grateful to be England's number 1. He was a man who had had to work for everything in the game, and being England skipper, especially leading his country at a World Cup, was the pinnacle.

During the tournament he would give a TV interview in which it was brought up that he had been forced to fight every inch of the way to become a top professional. The common put-downs he had to face were, 'Too slow, not good enough, a one–season wonder', and he just laughed when reminded of it. How Harry Kane had proved the doubters wrong. He had gone from playing for Leyton Orient away at Rochdale, to leading England to their first World Cup win in the space of eight years.

Southgate stepped up the training schedule as the second match loomed. Panama were a fairly unknown quantity, although they eliminated the United States by finishing above them in CONCACAF (the North, Central American and Caribbean World Cup qualification group) to make it to Russia. In the event, the Panamanians proved to be one of the worst teams in the competition and Harry had a ball, grabbing a hat-trick and inspiring England to a 6–1 win in the Nizhny Novgorod stadium on Sunday, 24 June. Two of Harry's goals came from penalties while the third was a fluke, clipping his heel and flying into the net from a shot by Ruben Loftus-Cheek. But they all count, and Harry was more than happy to claim this one. It meant he had joined Geoff Hurst (1966) and Gary Lineker (1986) as the only Englishmen to score a hat-trick in a World Cup. It was also England's biggest ever win in a tournament match. Panama were so poor that even centre-back John Stones scored twice, with the other goal being a cracker of a long–range shot from

Jesse Lingard. Thirty-seven-year-old Felipe Baloy hit Panama's one consolation.

This was also only the third time that England had triumphed in their opening two World Cup games (the others being in 1982 and 2006) and, most importantly, it meant that they had qualified for the tournament's knockout stage with one game to spare. The final group match against Belgium would now only be relevant in that it would decide who won Group G and who would be runners-up. At this stage, England were top, courtesy of having one less yellow card than Belgium, with both teams on six points and both having scored eight goals and conceded two. Harry was delighted that the team had won in such emphatic style and more so that they had progressed to the knockout stage. He said, 'I'm extremely proud. We're proud of each other, the way we played, the discipline, the hard work. And we had fun out there as well, which is important. It could have been a tough game. We started well, we've been working hard on set pieces and they came together as well. We've got to enjoy this. It's not every year that we go through after two games. We knew it would be an aggressive game, they'd do everything they could to stop us. I thought the discipline was really good from us, we didn't get involved in anything silly, we made sure the ref was aware of holding and pulling. And we got what we deserved. I'm very proud of the lads for that.'

Southgate, meanwhile, was also delighted that his boys had reached the next stage – and admitted he owed a debt to Kane and his incredible goal-scoring talent, 'We wouldn't swap him for anyone at the tournament in terms of Number 9s. We know that when he gets opportunities he's going to bury them, you sit there very confident in his ability to take chances.' Finally, Harry was asked by reporters if he was focussed on winning the Golden Boot. His answer showed that, although he was now undoubtedly one of the world's top five marksmen, he remained first and foremost a team player and a man who put the success of colleagues before his own personal ambition. He said, 'There's going to be a lot of talk about it but there's a long way to go. We've got some of the best players in the world scoring goals, doing well. For me, it's about the wins. And we've got another big game on Thursday to try and finish top. Hopefully I can score more goals and help my team.'

It didn't happen on either score against Belgium in Kaliningrad. In what was effectively England reserves against Belgium reserves, the opposition won 1–0 to top the group. Harry remained on the bench for the whole ninety minutes as Southgate put his trust in his squad players. Only Jordan Pickford and John Stones of England's 'first eleven' started the match. Belgium reserve Adnan Januzaj scored the decisive goal and England would now meet Colombia in the last 16, while Belgium had the easier initial task, on paper at least, of Japan. Of course, in hindsight the Belgians drew the short straw as they would have to face Brazil in the quarter–finals while England got Sweden. So much for the advantages of topping a World Cup group!

Stats–wise, Belgium's victory also ended their 82–year winless run against England. That previous win came in a friendly played in Brussels in 1936, with England losing 3–2. There were suggestions that Harry had been disappointed not to have started, or at least come off the bench, to try to increase his goals tally. But he said, firmly, 'Not true.' He was happy to do as the manager suggested, to use the free time to rest and prepare physically and mentally for the more important task in hand, the knockout round of 16. After the Belgium game, he tweeted his feelings, simply saying, 'Qualified from the group games. Into the knockouts. Full focus on Tuesday.'

He and Southgate would have several one–to–one discussions over the next few days as they plotted how to overcome the dangerous Colombians in that match in Spartak Moscow's stadium on July 3. They both knew the initial tournament brief had been achieved already after the FA had told Gareth they would be happy if he got England out of the group. But he and Harry were determined to exceed that initial demand: they hadn't come all this way to merely bow out meekly now. Harry's whole career was littered with instances of how he had proved the doubters wrong and now he wanted to see off the challenge of the brilliant, if volatile South Americans. Let me say here that Gareth was also ably assisted throughout the tournament by assistant manager Steve Holland, the man whose influence and tactical genius was often underplayed. Holland, the former assistant manager at Chelsea, deserved immense credit for helping Gareth devise the 3–3–2–2 tactical system that enabled England to progress to the semis of the 2018 World Cup. Holland told the Guardian's Daniel Taylor how it evolved, saying, 'I spent a year with Antonio [Conte] when Chelsea won the league with a 3–4–3, with [César] Azpilicueta, a full–back, in a back three, Gary Cahill on the left and David Luiz, as it was then, in the middle. The first time we'd tried it [3–4–3] with England, in the friendly against Germany [in March 2017], we lost the game, but it was a more than reasonable performance. So the next stage was how to get the midfield balance right. We had good forwards and if we played [3–3–2–2] we could get two on the pitch, rather than one. The only criterion, after that, was: "Do we have the wing–backs?" And the wing–backs are the least of our problems: we have all sorts of different types of wing–backs. So it made sense.'

Indeed it did, not only sense – given England's shortage of quality central midfielders – but also made for success, as exemplified as they overcame the Colombians. England received an early boost when the South Americans' star player, James Rodriguez, was ruled out with injury. He was the playmaker and the man most likely to torment England with his magic. His loss was a big blow to them; a big bonus to Harry and Co. Kane was on target yet again, claiming his sixth goal of the tournament with yet another penalty. After being brought down in the box twelve minutes in the second half, he smashed the ball home after what seemed an indeterminate period of complaining by the Colombians, who were intent on trying to put Kane off. Little chance of that. They even scuffed up the penalty spot in a blatant act of cheating that wasn't spotted by the referee.

When they concentrated on playing rather than cheating, the Colombians proved a real handful and had England rocking with a series of inventive attacking forays powered by Juventus winger Juan Cuadrado. Their last–minute equaliser was probably deserved on the second half run of play, the massive Barcelona centre back Yerry Mina scoring with a powerful header. It would be deadlock after extra–time so England would face yet another agonising penalty shootout to determine their fate in a top tournament, but this time they would prevail thanks to the brilliance of gritty goalkeeper Pickford and the remarkably cool head of Eric Dier, the taker of the decisive penalty. England won 4–3 on penalties, finally banishing the demons and heartache of those semi-final defeats at Italia 90 and Euro 96. England had also won a penalty shootout for only the second time, the other occasion being when they beat Spain in Euro 96.

Kane, inevitably, had taken the opening penalty to send his team on their way. And he was breaking all sorts of records during the match. He became the first player to score in six consecutive England appearances since Tommy Lawton in 1939. Harry had overtaken Geoff Hurst (five) to become England's second–highest World Cup goalscorer behind Gary Lineker (ten). Kane was now also the second Englishman after Lineker to score six times at a single World Cup. Those six goals by Kane in his first three World Cup appearances for England earned him a further accolade. Just three players had scored more in the same time frame – Hungary's Sandor Kocsis (nine), Germany's Gerd Muller (seven) and Argentina's Guillermo Stabile (seven).

Afterwards, Harry said, 'I'm so proud. We played well and controlled the game. We were so unlucky to concede in the last minute. It shows our togetherness and character. These are the moments when you really see it. It's a big night for everyone. Obviously we knew that England's history with penalties hasn't been great. It was nice to get that one off our back. We're a young squad but we learnt a lot out there today and we would have grown up a lot too. We're in a great position and that could be a big moment going forward in the tournament. We stepped up when it mattered. We've just got to settle down and go again on the weekend.'

Now it was back to Repino for a day of ice baths and relaxation, then the realisation and preparation that Kane and his team–mates were in the World Cup quarter-finals. Not bad for a squad that had been written off pre-tournament as no–hopers. The Sweden match would present an altogether different test than the one posed by Colombia. The Swedes were a more honest, workmanlike team who were unlikely to batter England with fouls as did the Colombians. They also were not as dynamic when attacking, indeed there was something in the assertion that they were 'old England' playing 'new England'. Sweden liked to play long balls into their target men and relied on a traditional 4–4–2 line–up while England now preferred a much more measured, nay technical approach, with players fluid and moving between the lines. Or at least that was how it was supposed to work out.

In the event, England's 2–0 win in the quarter–final in Samara on July 7 owed as much to brute strength and traditional blood and thunder as any discernible technical largesse. Harry 'Slabhead' Maguire leapt high to reach Ashley Young's corner to put England in front with a powerful header and Dele Alli clinched victory with another header, this time from a cross by Lingard. So much for the anticipated wizardry and skilful dribbling; it was old-fashioned headers from crosses that took England to their first World Cup semi-final since 1990. No matter, it was the win that mattered, how it was achieved less so. Kane was not on the scoresheet but he put in a shift, battling against the big Swedish centre-backs and taking knocks that earned dangerous free kicks and left the Swedish defence rocking at times. He wasn't as effective as he had been in the group games and this probably was a result of the battering he took against the Colombians. They had left him bruised and struggling for full fitness. The Swedes provided another physical test and Harry was glad to rest up and have a massage to ease the aches.

Kane had looked exhausted and physically drained at the end of the ninety minutes. He hadn't been England's star man, or even their goal hero. No, those honours went to Jordan Pickford, Maguire and Dele. But Harry was still happy to talk to reporters, saying, 'So much preparation went into it and I thought we were fantastic today. It was a difficult game, Sweden made it tough – long balls, different to what we have faced so far. We were brilliant at set-pieces, crosses into the box and we are buzzing. We know there's still a big game ahead: the semi-final. But we're feeling good, we're feeling confident. We just have to go again. I know the fans here, and the fans back home – we'll see some videos later – are enjoying it. We just want to make the country proud.'

Well, Harry and the boys had already achieved that – everyone back home in England was proud of them. They had reached the World Cup semi-final and it was fever pitch in London and the rest of the country; the belief was growing that football really was coming home after all those years of hurt. Now just the

Croatians would stand in the way of England and a first World Cup final since 1966. Surely, the time had come for England to rise right back to the very top of the international game after fifty-two years of toil and struggle?

The venue was the Luzhniki Stadium in Moscow, where the final itself would be held and, like all the stadia in Russia for the World Cup, was an impressive piece of engineering. It was hi–tech, totally modern and put what we would dub the top stadia in England to shame. Only the new Wembley, the Emirates and the new Tottenham ground stand comparison; even Old Trafford is looking slightly worn and weary, suffering from a lack of updating investment by the Glazers for many years. If the England players could not feel inspired playing in a venue like this, it was hard to imagine what would give them a lift. And, to be fair, they came flying out of the blocks with a breath–taking speed and momentum that left the Croatians rocking. It was no surprise when England took the lead on eleven minutes, with Kieran Trippier cementing his place in his nation's history books with a splendid free kick that gave the Croatian backline, and keeper, no chance. The only problem was that after such an inspired start and, indeed, an inspired first half, England did not build on that lead. If they had gone in at the interval two or three goals ahead, it would surely have been a knockout blow for Croatia. In the event, England – and Harry – spurned chances they would normally have buried. I am thinking in particular of Harry's shot from a couple of yards to the side of the goal that he could not finish. Once again, he looked out of sorts; slightly sluggish and not 100 per cent fit, although he would again dismiss suggestions that he was not quite right or was carrying a knock. No matter, it wasn't to be his day and England paid the price for their first half profligacy in front of goal as Croatia grew stronger and started to overwhelm them. With the world-class duo of Ivan Rakitic and Luka Modric in midfield and the rampant Ivan Perisic on the wing, England simply could not cope. The equaliser was coming and it did – from Perisic in the sixty-eighth minute – and England now looked beaten. With twenty-odd minutes to go, they were on the ropes and it was only sheer spirit that took them into extra time.

There was still hope – maybe another penalty shootout victory with Kane at the fore, or maybe Harry could find some personal strength and crash the ball home from a pass or a corner? Instead, it was Juventus striker Mario Mandzukic who ended the contest – and England's fine run in the tournament, lashing the winner past a hapless Jordan Pickford in the 109th minute. Harry and his boys' dream, and the dreams of a nation, were over: they would not be in a World Cup final, or the final of any tournament for that matter, for the first time since 1966. It was a heartbreaking way to end a month that had seen England's Three Lions regain their pride under Kane and Southgate, and the nation fall in love with the national team after growing hostility.

England looked dead on their feet but Harry rallied his troops and they stumbled over to applaud the 10,000 fans who had made the journey to Russia for this semi-final. Afterwards, Harry showed what a trooper he is by carrying out all his media duties, even though he was hurting like mad.

'It is tough, we are gutted, we worked so hard and the fans

were amazing,' he told ITV. 'It was a tough game, a 50–50 game. I'm sure we will look back and there is stuff we could've done better. We created some good chances being 1–0 up. It is small margins and it went their way today. It hurts, it hurts a lot, but we can hold our heads up high – we have gone further than a lot of people thought we would. Obviously it has been great to get this stage and we know we have done everyone proud but we wanted to win. It hurts, it just hurts. It shows we can be up here, that we can win knockout games, can get to semi-finals and the next step is to go one step further. This is a great foundation we have built with the gaffer. We are proud of what we have achieved but we wanted more and are sad we couldn't give our fans a final.'

He and his team-mates now had to make the long trip back to their Repino base. It was a journey notable for its silence as the players and the backroom staff all continued to suffer and it would be a couple of days before they could all even contemplate Saturday's third place playoff against the Belgians. Just as inevitably, that match would prove a match too far and, with key personnel missing injured or emotionally and physically exhausted, England lost out to Belgium 2–0 for the bronze medal. The Belgians had put out a virtual first eleven and England found it tough going, particularly against Eden Hazard and Kevin de Bruyne. Harry, disappointingly, was also unable to really get into his stride and could not add to his goal tally. No matter, his six goals earlier in the tournament would prove to be enough to earn him the Golden Boot the following day.

Afterwards, he said, 'This game showed there is still room

for improvement. We're not the finished article, we're still improving and will only get better. We don't want to wait another twenty years to get into the semi-finals and the big matches. We need to improve, we need to get better but that will come. We have made huge strides. Now it is about resting up and getting ready for the next season. The lads couldn't have given any more. Belgium are obviously a good team. I can't fault the lads, we gave everything. We wanted to finish on a high. We're disappointed not to have won the game but it shows we can still learn and hold our head up high.'

And of his prospects of winning the Golden Boot, he added, 'It shows we had a good group stage, scored a lot of goals. Obviously I'm disappointed I couldn't get a goal in the last few games. Sometimes it goes for you, sometimes it doesn't. But if I win it, it'll be something I'll be very proud of.'

To use a phrase from England's wonderful 1990 World Cup efforts in Italy, he was 'all cried out'. Exhausted and ready to return home to see his family and have a good rest. He had earned it but one thing was for sure. This wasn't the end of Harry Kane, the international goal king. No, it was surely just the beginning of a bigger story that will hopefully end with him lifting a trophy with this exciting new England.